A Baseball Book of Days

ALSO BY PHIL COFFIN
AND FROM MCFARLAND

When Baseball Was Still Topps: Portraits of the Game in 1959, Card by Card (2024)

A Baseball Book of Days

Thirty-One Moments That Transformed the Game

Phil Coffin

McFarland & Company, Inc., Publishers
Jefferson, North Carolina

LIBRARY OF CONGRESS CATALOGING-IN-PUBLICATION DATA

Names: Coffin, Phil, 1953– author.
Title: A baseball book of days : thirty-one moments that transformed the game / Phil Coffin.
Description: Jefferson, North Carolina : McFarland & Company, Inc., Publishers, 2025 | Includes bibliographical references and index.
Identifiers: LCCN 2024062145 | ISBN 9781476695976 (paperback : acid free paper) ∞ ISBN 9781476654751 (ebook)
Subjects: LCSH: Baseball—United States—History. | Baseball players—United States—History. | Baseball—United States—Social aspects. | Baseball—United States—Miscellanea.
Classification: LCC GV863.A1 C57 2025 | DDC 796.357—dc23/eng/20250107
LC record available at https://lccn.loc.gov/2024062145

ISBN (print) 978-1-4766-9597-6
ISBN (ebook) 978-1-4766-5475-1

© 2025 Phil Coffin. All rights reserved

No part of this book may be reproduced or transmitted in any form or by any means, electronic or mechanical, including photocopying or recording, or by any information storage and retrieval system, without permission in writing from the publisher.

Front cover images iStock/Shutterstock

Printed in the United States of America

McFarland & Company, Inc., Publishers
 Box 611, Jefferson, North Carolina 28640
  www.mcfarlandpub.com

To Laura, who understands that a diamond
is a boy's best friend.

Table of Contents

Acknowledgments ix
Introduction: Moments of the Game 1
Glossary 5

One. January 1: Role Players Without a Role — 7
Two. January 5: In the Best Interests of Baseball — 13
Three. February 9: The Day They Banned the Wet One — 18
Four. March 16: Spring Training Comes to Indiana — 23
Five. March 18: Go West, Old Teams: The Migration Begins — 31
Six. March 21: The Uniqueness of Spring — 41
Seven. April 1: Parades, Presidents and Opening Day — 43
Eight. April 15: Jackie Robinson Opens the Door. Quietly — 49
Nine. April 15: Deep in the Heart of Dixies — 60
Ten. April 19: Boston's Trinity: Patriots' Day, the Red Sox and the Marathon — 65
Eleven. May 24: The Night the Lights Went On in Major League Baseball — 68
Twelve. May 25: Babe Ruth's Last Hurrah — 78
Thirteen. June 2: The Day Lou Gehrig Died — 85
Fourteen. June 15: Why Is There a Trade Deadline? Blame New York — 88

Fifteen. June 21: The Boys of Summer, and the Summers Boys ... 91

Sixteen. June 29: The Moonlight Grahams of the Majors ... 97

Seventeen. June 30: The First Modern No-Hitter (Maybe) ... 121

Eighteen. July 4: Born to Diamond Glory ... 125

Nineteen. July 6: An All-Star Game Is Born ... 130

Twenty. July 17: Stopping Joe DiMaggio ... 142

Twenty-One. July 21: The Last to Integrate ... 146

Twenty-Two. August 4: Birds Versus Baseballs ... 161

Twenty-Three. August 19: The Day in the Life of Eddie Gaedel ... 165

Twenty-Four. September 4: Gill's Boner ... 171

Twenty-Five. September 23: The Dominican Pipeline Begins, in New York ... 177

Twenty-Six. October 1: Fall Classics, From the Beginning ... 187

Twenty-Seven. October 1: That Close to Batting .400 ... 196

Twenty-Eight. October 2: A Day Off ... 199

Twenty-Nine. November 1: Here Comes Mr. November ... 204

Thirty. December 12: Veeck Does (Funny) Business at the Winter Meetings ... 211

Thirty-One. December 21: The Seldom-Seen Winter of Baseball ... 217

Bibliography ... 221
Index ... 225

Acknowledgments

When I joined the Society for American Baseball Research in 1994, I had only a hazy notion of what the group was. I had become loosely familiar with it in the early 1980s through reading analytical works by Bill James. He coined the term *sabermetrics* as a nod to SABR, which had been formed in 1971 but gained little traction in the mainstream world of baseball. (The first mention of SABR in *The New York Times* came in 1973, when the Pulitzer Prize–winning sports columnist Arthur Daley made a reference to "the Society for American Baseball Research, whatever that is.")

In 1994 SABR was still far from the mainstream, although it had become sufficiently accepted that a column in *The Times* used SABR research as support for Gil Hodges's candidacy for the Baseball Hall of Fame. Despite its regular publications, SABR did not become a vital part of my baseball world until I came across its *Baseball Biography Project*, which began in the early 2000s. By now it has more than 6,000 biographies, mostly of Major League ballplayers. It is a remarkable reservoir of information about players (and off-the-field luminaries), whether monumental or marginal, for both readers and researchers. Like me. This book is indebted to the foundational work of the *Bio Project*, whether as a direct source or as a starting point for further research. The growing SABR-Rucker of photos was also quite helpful.

The Society for American Baseball Research itself was still an abstraction, however, until I decided to join in the pandemic-inspired monthly Zoom meetings of my Northern New Jersey group, the Elysian Fields chapter. There I encountered a group of well-informed baseball researchers, authors and fans, led by the chapter president, David Krell, who have been an unanticipated but unquestionably reliable resource during the research and writing of my first two baseball books. Many thanks for their insights and support ... and I'll see you folks on Zoom.

One further invaluable research tool was *Baseball Reference*, whose statistics of all sorts are used throughout the book. Once upon a time, I thought *The Baseball Encyclopedia* was indispensable; now I believe

Baseball Reference is. (A bonus: Its player pages have links to their SABR bios!) Newspapers.com is also a tremendous tool, unlocking newspaper archives big and small going back more than a century. It is a treasure trove of colorful detail and noteworthy accounts.

Support for a book comes from many directions. Sean Alfano, a *Times* colleague and baseball buddy who performed yeoman work in copy editing my first book, *When Baseball Was Still Topps*, stepped up to the plate a second time, saving me again from many errors of commission and omission. Frank Coffin and Bob Taylor shared insights from their lifelong love of baseball as we enjoyed games in minor league ballparks. Rick Bozich, who suffers from being the world's biggest White Sox fan, has been a similar sounding board for decades. Running buddies Ron Wolfson, Craig Van Doren and the Thursday night Pizza Boys were gracious, even enthusiastic listeners to baseball tales over many miles together; I'll try to learn different topics, fellas.

Gary Mitchem, who signed up McFarland & Company for both of my books, shepherded them through the publishing process and helped shape the topics and approach of *A Baseball Book of Days*. He and the support team at McFarland are All-Stars.

The National Baseball Hall of Fame, a superlative research institution, was a trusted source for images, with diligent efforts by John Horne. Likewise, images were unearthed in the SABR-Rucker Archive and the Indiana University Archives, where Bradley Cook was a great help. Ellie Harrison at the Indiana Historical Society performed some nifty sleuthing to locate a tract about spring training in Indiana.

Writing a book can be consuming, which is not a blessing for those around the author. My wife, Laura Messina, without whose encouragement I might never have published any book in the first place, was patient and understanding even as I went through the process a second time. She has now heard some of the same baseball stories more times than is reasonable, and hasn't complained. I can never thank her enough.

Introduction
Moments of the Game

The first baseball book I ever read was *The Real Book About Baseball,* part of a series with dozens of books for young readers published in the 1950s. It was a hand-me-down from my older brothers, along with *The Real Book of American Tall Tales, The Real Book About Daniel Boone, The Real Book About Spies* and others long forgotten. *The Real Book About Baseball* was an unusual baseball primer, a mix of how to play the game (complete with illustrations), history, player profiles, anecdotes, and exhortations for good sportsmanship and love of the sport. In sum, it was perfect for a reader like me, who wanted to know a little about everything and concluded that accumulating background on many disparate parts could give me a good picture of the whole.

I never outgrew that, even as I became a more educated and focused baseball fan than I was at the age of eight. I liked the numbers (why else would I have spent so much time looking at the backs of baseball cards?), but I also liked the history and the stories and the insights into how the game had developed into the one I knew. *The Bill James Historical Baseball Abstract,* and its subsequent revisions, was ideal for the young fan tucked inside my adult brain, a mosaic approach to baseball knowledge that resulted in a comprehensive image of the game. *The Baseball 100* by Joe Posnanski made story-telling about players a way to tell the story of the game.

Not that my bookshelf isn't crammed with dedicated histories and biographies. But works by Roger Angell or Thomas Boswell—independent chapters that, within their books, added up to much more—and novel-at-the-time books like *Nine Innings* by Daniel Okrent, which analyzed two teams through the inning-by-inning lens of a single game, were also essential to my understanding and appreciation of the game.

Trust me, I'm not comparing *A Baseball Book of Days* to those books, though like them it scrutinizes slices of the game to provide insight into baseball's distinctive history. The moments are memorable in isolation—Jackie Robinson's first game, the first night game, the origins of the World Series, Babe Ruth's last hurrah, the final Major League team to integrate, the banning of the spitter—but packaged together, they tell a richer, more complex and more compelling story.

There are many ways to tell the stories of baseball history. Think of *A Baseball Book of Days* as an Advent calendar approach: Open this date on the calendar and consider how a latter-day application of the Best Interests of Baseball Clause might have prevented Babe Ruth's sale to the Yankees. Open another date and relive what was (maybe) the first no-hitter in modern baseball. Over on this date, a look at how a soggy field weeks earlier played a role in the end of Joe DiMaggio's 56-game hitting streak. And here: Who invented the knuckleball?

Even the moments that are well known have overlooked elements. For example, Robinson's ascent to the Major Leagues was a sociological breakthrough as well as a major baseball event, but many other ballplayers shared that day with him. Here we look at the players we *don't* remember for that day in 1947. And there is a counterpoint: Robinson's reluctant teammate Dixie Walker, an outfielder from Alabama, was far from the only Dixie in baseball. Here we look at the other Dixies who also made Major League Baseball what it is. Robinson also had pioneering successors of lesser renown: Pumpsie Green in Boston with the Red Sox, the Dominican Ozzie Virgil with the New York Giants.

There are also others just outside the spotlight who have some of that glare reflected on them. Eddie Gaedel was a 3-foot-7-inch pinch-hitter, but for other principals in that 1951 stunt, his appearance is in their obituaries as well. Jim Delsing may have played in the Major Leagues for 10 years, not one game like Gaedel, but the newspapers' obituaries of him all included references to his pinch-running for Gaedel. Delsing, a good sport, never seemed to mind that he could not outrun Gaedel in the public mind.

Sometimes our memories are hazy or just incorrect. The spitball was not banned because Ray Chapman died after being hit by a pitch from Carl Mays in 1920; the ban had already been set in place. And Babe Ruth did not hit three home runs in his final game; he played five more games and never had another hit. These were impressions—myths, maybe—that had taken hold when I grew up on baseball. Now I know better.

Some myths are unshakeable. Take Archibald Graham. He was a New York Giants outfielder for one game in 1905, with nothing, it would seem, to make him memorable other than the nickname Moonlight. He never even came to bat. But the author W.P. (Bill) Kinsella stumbled across Graham's line full of zeroes in the *Baseball Encyclopedia* and was entranced, so he inserted Moonlight Graham in his novel *Shoeless Joe*. Which was turned into the movie *Field of Dreams*. Which made Moonlight Graham a famous name after all. As it turns out, there were dozens of Moonlight Grahams—position players with one game and no time at bat—some with stories that outshine Moonlight's.

Baseball's history is so long that it is easy to overlook some remarkable nonfiction aspects of it. Because of World War II, spring training moved north, even to the chilly climes of Indiana, where nine of the 16 Major League teams prepared for the season beginning in 1943. You know the Grapefruit League and the Cactus League; here you can become acquainted with the Limestone League. The attraction for baseball-starved youngsters in Indiana was such that a couple of young brothers offered to chip in their savings—they had a dollar—to help get big leaguers to set up camp in their Hoosier town.

Go back further in time and you can find that the first modern World Series, in 1903 between the Boston team from the American League and the Pittsburgh squad from the National League (don't rush to call them Red Sox and Pirates), was played under circumstances that might befuddle us now. Labor issues? Sounds familiar. But open discussion of player gambling? Unfathomable.

There are player feats that are unfathomable, too. No player in the 20th century had ever caught in every one of his team's games in a season ... until two did it in 1944. (And another did so in 1945.) Another player, Don Padgett, lost his .400 season in 1939 when a hit was taken away by an umpire's call in his final time at bat that year. He's a .399 hitter forever.

Reputations can last forever, too. Fred Merkle's name became synonymous with "bonehead play" when he made a costly base-running mistake in the heat of a pennant race in 1908; it was reflected in the headline of his obituary nearly half a century later. But Doc Gill made the same mistake in the heat of the same pennant race, and no one remembers his name. His obituary made no mention of it, but did talk about his dentistry career. Merkle's obit merited 18 paragraphs in *The New York Times*. Gill's? One paragraph in *The Long Beach (California) Independent*.

Eddie Gaedel's name lives on, too, for his one moment in baseball. The shortest man ever to play in a Major League game, he was only seven inches taller than Babe Ruth's bat was long. It's hard to outlive that sort of renown. Not even the man who orchestrated Gaedel's appearance, Bill Veeck, could outlive the notoriety of that game. Veeck wrote that he knew his obituary would refer prominently to Gaedel (and it did, in the first paragraph in *The New York Times*). But Veeck—a baseball oddity himself, with a wooden leg, a hand in the planting of the Wrigley Field ivy and the ownership of three Major League franchises—made his name over and over. He was a part of the machinations for baseball's tumultuous franchise shifting in the 1950s (he failed; the Boston Braves and the St. Louis Browns team Veeck wound up selling did not). And he became still more renowned after a PR stunt at the 1975 winter meetings as owner of the Chicago White Sox, one of the final touches on a career full of winter-meetings escapades.

These moments are not, for the most part, related, but woven together, they help make up the tapestry of baseball. Enjoy the moments, enjoy the game.

Glossary

Baseball Reference: An online source for baseball statistics of all kinds and the game's history. An invaluable resource for any fan that is the modern-day equivalent of the *Baseball Encyclopedia*—only more complete and updated daily.

ERA+: A pitcher's earned run average normalized across the entire league (and accounting for other factors like ballparks). The league average is 100, so a pitcher with an ERA+ of 125 is 25 percent above league average; one at 88 is 12 percent below average. One of my favorite ways to compare pitchers, including across eras.

OPS: The sum of a player's on-base percentage and slugging percentage. It is a good way to look at the two prime elements of batting success, getting on base and power.

OPS+: A batter's OPS, normalized across the entire league (and accounting for factors like ballparks). The league average is 100, so a player with an OPS+ of 135 is 35 percent above league average; one at 80 is 20 percent below average. One of my favorite ways to compare hitters, especially across eras.

SABR (Society for American Baseball Research): An organization dedicated to research of the history of the game, often with a reliance on statistics.

SABR *Bio Project*: SABR's effort to write comprehensive biographies of all Major League players, plus profiles of managers, front office executives and others. The bios are well-researched and rich with detail.

Slash line: Batting average/on-base percentage/slugging percentage. For example: .280/.330/485.

WAR (Wins Above Replacement): A figure that includes multiple phases of the game to determine how many wins a player is worth compared with a replacement-level player at his position. A handy if not precise way to compare players' all-around value, including across eras. There are two versions: bWAR (from *Baseball Reference*) and fWAR (*from Fangraphs*); bWAR is used here.

WHIP: Walks and hits per inning. How efficient a pitcher is in allowing base runners.

ONE

January 1

Role Players Without a Role

Baseball changes every season, sometimes incrementally (mandatory batting helmets) and sometimes monumentally (lowered pitching mound, the DH, the banning of defensive shifts). Some changes occur relatively quickly (the end of the Deadball Era and the introduction of the power game); some over time (the expansion of pitching staffs, the demise of the complete game, the increasingly heavy use of relievers). But the game is a bit different every year. And so are the roles for various players.

For many seasons, the game featured slugging, often one-dimensional first basemen, light-hitting middle infielders and third-string catchers. And for many seasons in the era before the DH, numerous teams in the middle of the last century carried at least one player who was effectively a designated pinch-hitter.

On 25-man rosters that included nine or 10 pitchers, there was plenty of room for pinch-hitters, and they got

Herb Washington was the archetype for Charlie Finley's designated runners: 105 games, no times at bat, 31 stolen bases (and 17 times caught stealing) (National Baseball Hall of Fame, Cooperstown, NY).

plenty of use even though fewer pitchers were used per game than in the 21st century. Gates Brown had 500 career plate appearances as a pinch-hitter in the 1960s and '70s, with 16 home runs and 70 walks. (The man was immense, built sort of like Cecil Fielder, but he had five pinch-hit triples!) Elmer Valo played more than 120 games in a season only once, but he forged a 20-year career from 1940 to 1961 because he could pinch-hit; he amassed 469 plate appearances as a pinch-hitter, nearly a full season's worth coming off the bench. Dave Philley played 16 seasons from 1941 to 1962, in large part because he could hit off the bench—in 337 appearances as a pinch-hitter, he batted .300/.353/.388, with a 109 OPS+. Smoky Burgess was a chunky but regular catcher before putting on even more weight and transitioning to full-time pinch-hitter. (Playing from 1949 to 1967, he set the career record for pinch hits.) These were the best of their breed in the 1950s and, for Brown and Burgess, the '60s, but there were plenty of lesser lights who hit well enough off the bench to extend their careers. Heck, a guy named Bob Hale had 278 plate appearances as a pinch-hitter and only 392 as a position player over seven seasons. Talk about a specialist.

Professional pinch-hitters gave way to designated hitters, and even before the DH was extended to both leagues, expanding pitching staffs made it less practical to keep a player around to pinch-hit. But back in the 1970s, the realization of the DH led to talk of a DR—a designated runner.

Unlike the designated hitter, the designated runner never became an actual position. (Although the independent Atlantic League experimented with it in 2023 at Major League Baseball's behest.) But, perhaps inevitably, Charlie Finley made the designated runner a de facto position in Oakland. Finley, the Athletics' maverick owner from 1960 to 1981, wanted to innovate in baseball. He proposed many ideas that, while initially belittled by baseball traditionalists, became a standard in the game: colorful uniforms, night postseason baseball, interleague play. He pushed for geographic realignment (sort of on the model of the National Football League), which has made some inroads (the Astros and the Brewers changed leagues) and may well become more encompassing. He was an early and ardent proponent of the designated hitter.

And to accompany the DH, Finley wanted to establish the designated runner. Even though baseball never accommodated his wish, Finley created the role for the Athletics anyway, to the disdain of his managers and players. For a dozen years, from 1967 to 1978, Oakland employed, effectively, a designated runner—a player who pinch-ran frequently but rarely, if ever, played in the field or came to bat. The most famous was a world-class track sprinter named Herb Washington—he *never* batted or played the field in 105 games over the 1974 and '75 seasons—but he was hardly the first or the last.

One. January 1

The first was Allan Lewis, a minor league outfielder known as the Panamanian Express who was a terror on the bases (he stole 116 bases one season) but could not hit above Class AA. Finley brought him to the Majors, against Manager Al Dark's wishes, and over parts of six seasons, Lewis averaged five plate appearances and 23 pinch-running appearances. He was not an immediate success; in his first game as a pinch-runner, Lewis was picked off first base. Nor was he a long-term success; three years later, he was picked off twice during a September call-up, prompting Ron Bergman to write in *The Oakland Tribune*, "The Panamanian Express is a local that stops between first and second." He ran in two World Series, in 1972 and '73, but he did not impress one of his managers, Dick Williams, who said: "He's a switch-hitter. He batted .300 last year, .150 left-handed and .150 right-handed."

Lewis's run with the A's ended after the 1973 season, but Finley still wanted a designated runner. He aimed high: Washington, a world-record holder in the 50- and 60-yard sprints indoors. But Washington also had designs on a pro football career—he played football, not baseball, in college at Michigan State—and asked for a no-cut contract. Washington played 92 games for Oakland in 1974, all as a pinch-runner. He scored 29 runs and stole 29 bases, but he was also thrown out stealing 16 times. And his postseason was a nightmare: Washington was caught stealing twice in the American League Championship Series and then was famously picked off first in the World Series by the Los Angeles Dodgers' Mike Marshall, moments after the announcer Vin Scully said on NBC, "Marshall, for a right-hander, is *very* quick in coming over to first base." Washington's appearance on the roster was not embraced by managers or teammates. Second baseman Dick Green said he told Washington, "If you break a leg, we'll have to shoot you," according to *Charlie Finley: The Outrageous Story of Baseball's Super Showman*.

Still, Washington, was brought back for the 1975 season—his Topps card listed his position as Pinch Run—but Finley additionally brought up a minor league speedster, Don Hopkins, who could also play the outfield a bit (but also could not hit). Washington pinch-ran 13 times before being released on May 5 ("I'd feel sorry for him if he were a player," Sal Bando, the A's third baseman, said when Washington was cut, according to *Charlie Finley*). That move came a week after Oakland had traded for Matt Alexander, a swift, light-hitting utility man. Remarkably, Al Dark maneuvered both Alexander and Hopkins into games to run. Hopkins pinch-ran 74 times in his 82 games. He went to bat merely eight times and was 21 for 30 stealing. Alexander was a pinch-runner in 51 of his 63 games, batting only 11 times and going 17 for 27 stealing. (Combined, their success rate was a measly 67 percent.)

Oakland's sequence of World Series contention was over, but Finley's efforts to make a runner a fixture on his roster were not. Although Hopkins played only three games for the A's in 1976—all as a pinch-runner—Alexander was kept aboard. He managed 30 plate appearances, but mostly he pinch-ran, 45 times. Yet he shared the base paths with another designated runner, bantamweight infielder Larry Lintz, who pinch-ran 64 times and was 31 for 42 as a base stealer. Alexander pinch-ran 67 more times for Oakland in 1977 before being shuttled to Pittsburgh, where he kept running. Miguel Diloné picked up some pinch-running assignments in 1978, but Oakland's grand experiment with a designated runner was over.

Speed is a constant in the game, however. If speed *was* the game for designated runners like Herb Washington and those other A's, speed has merely defined the game for more accomplished players over the years: the blazing-fast guys who may not have hit much but ran wild on the bases. Billy Hamilton is the best example in the modern game, but if you look back at the 1970s and '80s, there were numerous Billy Hamiltons.

There is no better example than Otis Nixon. Nixon was a blade, listed at 6 feet 2 and 180 pounds, and he was fast from start to finish in his career, which lasted 17 seasons in the Major Leagues. There is not a lot to distinguish his numbers from many other speedsters other than his longevity, and his ability to become a regular in his 30s and hold the job for years.

He barely stole as a 20-year-old in rookie ball in 1979—five steals in eight attempts—but after that he was off and running. He swiped 67, 72, 107 and 94 bases in the next four minor league seasons. He hit pretty well and walked an inordinate amount—113, 110, 108 and 96 times in those four seasons. He had no power, never accumulating more than 20 extra-base hits.

Nixon had a cup of coffee with the New York Yankees, but he got his break when he was traded to the Cleveland Indians. He hardly settled into a productive role, however. For three seasons, he was a Major Leaguer, mostly a defensive replacement and pinch-runner (he pinch-ran 86 times from 1984 to 1986). He spent much of 1987 in the minors, was traded to Montreal and spent much of '88 in the minors as well. He ran everywhere he played; in 422 plate appearances before he was shipped to Montreal, Nixon stole 59 bases in 85 attempts. And, not counting errors, he was on base only 113 times. He just couldn't hit, and he didn't walk as much as he had in the minors.

Presumably his defense was good enough to go with his speed that he kept getting chances, though, and the Expos made him a half-time player. He still didn't hit—eight years into his big league career, his peak OPS+ was 88—but in 861 plate appearances over three seasons with the Expos, he was always running, stealing 136 bases in 174 attempts. (He did that under Buck Rodgers, who was pretty successful as a Major League catcher throwing out base stealers but whose teams as a manager ran. And ran. And ran.) For Nixon, that was a 76 percent success rate when everyone knew he would be running.

Then came his biggest break: He went, of all places, to the launching pad in Atlanta. At age 32, Nixon became a regular, going to bat 460 times as the Braves went from worst to first in their division. His defense must have been a comfort to the team's young pitching staff (Tom Glavine was 25, John Smoltz 24 and Steve Avery 21, and they combined for 105 starts). Nixon had what was then a career-high on-base percentage of .371 and stole 72 bases. He managed his career-high OPS+, 94.

The next year Nixon batted 502 times and hit .294/.348/.346 with an OPS+ of 93. He stole much less frequently and less successfully—he went 41 for 59, so perhaps he played with injuries—but he stayed on the field. In one more season in Atlanta, his offense sagged but he still stole 47 bases.

And yet at age 35 he began playing more than ever, an itinerant speedster who still couldn't hit—his OPS+ never came close to 90 again—but never stopped running. Over the next four very full seasons—with the Boston Red Sox, the Texas Rangers, the Toronto Blue Jays and the Dodgers—he averaged more than 50 steals a year while going to bat 461 times (in a strike-shortened year) and 656, 575 and 655 times. At age 39 he had 500 plate appearances for the Minnesota Twins while going 37 for 44 on the bases. At 40, back in Atlanta, his offense finally became unplayable—an OPS+ of 41—but he stole 27 bases in 33 attempts in 175 plate appearances. A speedster to the end.

He also made some notable highlight-reel defensive plays—I recall one from July 1992 on which he jabbed his spikes into the padding on the fence in center field and pushed off, skying high and stealing a home run from the Pirates' Andy Van Slyke. It's a move not unseen now, but it was then. His defensive WAR doesn't reflect it, but Nixon was on the field in large part because his teams thought he was a defensive asset.

Like most speedsters, he never hit; speed kept him in the game. His slash line was .270/.343/.314 with an OPS+ of 77. He had no power—11 home runs and only 180 extra-base hits in 5,800 plate appearances. But he stole 620 bases in 806 attempts, which works out to a steal attempt about 40 percent of the time he was on base.

As mentioned above, he was not particularly distinctive for his type of player, which was prevalent from the '70s into the '90s. Omar Moreno of the Pirates was very similar to Nixon as a hitter, with worse on-base skills (a career OBP of .306 while batting in front of those Pirates' big bats) and a little more power. In one three-year stretch he stole 71, 77 and 96 bases. The San Diego Padres had their own set of this kind of outfielder: Gene

Richards and Jerry Mumphrey. (Tony Gwynn stole a fair number of bases when he came up, but, well, he *could* hit.) Gary Pettis hit very much like Nixon and was considered perhaps the best center fielder in the game, and he stole 332 bases over an eight-year stretch. Vince Coleman developed the biggest reputation, even though he, too, was an offensive cipher: career OPS+ of 83. He led the National League in steals his first six years in the league: 110, 107, 109, 81, 65, 77. (Then he went from the St. Louis Cardinals to the New York Mets and his career began unraveling.)

There were infield equivalents of Nixon as well. Ozzie Smith was on this track in San Diego, without quite the same speed, until he learned to hit and walk well enough in St. Louis to hold his own offensively. Another Padre, Alan Wiggins, had 66 and 70 steals in his two full Major League seasons, but subterranean offense (OPS+ of 80), nondescript defense and a cocaine habit did him in. Another Pirate, Frank Taveras, joined Moreno as an offensive black hole—his OPS+ was worse than Nixon's, at 72—but he stole 58, 70, 46 and 44 bases in consecutive seasons. Julio Cruz averaged about 50 steals a year over six seasons, mostly with the Seattle Mariners, even though he, too, did not hit. (They were descendants of earlier middle-infield speedsters with weak bats, like Luis Aparicio and Maury Wills. Aparicio, who shook up the American League with his speed, made it to the Hall of Fame with a .311 on-base percentage and OPS+ of 82 because of otherworldly defense and game-altering base stealing. Wills was a little better hitter who stole bases in larger volume but got a late start in the Majors and was a very good defender, though not a paradigmatic defender like Aparicio.)

The game in the '60s and '70s was unlike the one we have seen in the 2010s and '20s. Managers, even those not handcuffed to Finley's scheme of a designated runner, employed different strategies (not always wise ones), attempting to steal at rates unseen since the Deadball Era of the early 20th century. More and more ballparks had artificial turf, which encouraged an emphasis on speed, and those circular stadiums of the era were not great home run parks, on the whole, and had more outfield space than many of the cozy or idiosyncratic stadiums of this era. Baseball had more African American players than it does now and was introducing more Latino players, many of whom had games predicated on speed, not power.

With all that action on the bases—even though stolen base success rates were generally worse than they are now—the game may have been more exciting. It definitely was different. And it allowed a different kind of player to thrive, the kind you may rarely see again.

Two

January 5

In the Best Interests of Baseball

If Bowie Kuhn had somehow been the commissioner of baseball in January 1920, the course of Major League history might have been radically different.

- Babe Ruth might not have become a New York Yankee.
- The Yankees, thus, might not have 27 world championships.
- The original Yankee Stadium—the House That Ruth Built, with that inviting short porch in right field—might not have been constructed, with no Ruth to build around.
- The Boston Red Sox, who won the World Series four times between 1912 and 1918, might have remained a competitive team instead of an American League doormat for two decades.
- Connie Mack might have had to sell his financially struggling Philadelphia Athletics instead of holding onto it into the 1950s.
- Or, had 1970s Kuhn relied on precedent over dollar signs, Charlie O. Finley, maverick owner of the Oakland Athletics, might have simply been using a time-tested approach to rebuilding a team.

Of course, Kuhn was *not* commissioner in 1920; he wasn't born until 1926. And baseball didn't even have a commissioner in January 1920. It had the remnants of a three-member National Commission running the game until baseball's nabobs hired Kenesaw Mountain Landis as the first commissioner 10 months later and handed him a Best Interests of Baseball Clause.

The Jenga version of baseball history above is built on a stack of what-ifs, but they show that the events of early 1920, and the results in ensuing years, were not preordained. Several are bound up with Ruth's big-bucks purchase by the Yankees.

A sale of Ruth by the Red Sox to the Yankees had been brewing for weeks and was formally announced on January 5, 1920. Ruth was not yet

Babe Ruth, but he was an undeniable star, one who was undergoing the unlikely transition from top-flight pitcher to unprecedented slugger. He was also a handful for the Red Sox organization, which had tired of his antics and salary demands, as Robert Creamer outlines in *Babe: The Legend Comes to Life.* The Red Sox had slipped from World Series champions in 1918 to a sixth-place finish in 1919, even though Ruth had hit a record 29 home runs while also going 13–7 with a 2.22 earned run average as a half-time pitcher.

He was a full-time pain. "Ruth had become simply impossible and the Boston club could no longer put up with his eccentricities," Harry Frazee, the Boston owner and Broadway impresario, said after the sale, *The New York Times* reported. "I think the Yankees are taking a gamble. While Ruth is undoubtedly the greatest hitter the game has ever seen, he is likewise one of the most selfish and inconsiderate men ever to put on a baseball uniform."

The sale was for $100,000, including three $25,000 promissory notes at 6 percent interest. That interest made the total sale price paid by the Yankees nearly $110,000. Plus the Yankees' co-owner Jacob Ruppert agreed to a $300,000 loan to Frazee, with Fenway Park as collateral. So the deal amounted to about $410,000 in 1920. That was a lot of money in 1920, but how much? Inflation calculators say that $410,000 then would be about $6.3 million in 2024 dollars, for one ballplayer.

That's a figure that would have interested Charlie Finley. In 1976, free agency had just been forced on Major League owners after an arbitrator's decision, and the tight-fisted Finley, whose Athletics teams had won the World Series from 1972 to 1974 and lost in the American League Championship Series in 1975, had a roster full of excellent players who didn't like him and especially didn't like their salaries. Their agents—figures new to the game—suggested salaries that Finley said he could not afford. So he, like Frazee more than half a century earlier (and like Mack of the Philadelphia Athletics in the teens and again in the 1930s), decided to sell off his stars. His plan, like Mack's, was to use the cash to sign new players and rebuild.

Finley had traded away potential free agents Reggie Jackson and Ken Holtzman before the '76 season started, but on June 16, at the trading deadline, Finley made headline-grabbing sales: closer Rollie Fingers and outfielder Joe Rudi to the Red Sox for $1 million each ($5.4 million in 2024 dollars) and pitcher Vida Blue to the Yankees for $1.5 million (the equivalent of $8.1 million in 2024). "I can't afford to pay these astronomical salaries they are all demanding, when we're drawing so poorly in Oakland," Finley said, as reported in *Charlie Finley: The Outrageous Story of Baseball's Super Showman.* He told *Sports Illustrated* he wanted to use the $3.5

million from the sales of the three players "to purchase a lot of players at the end of the season."

And now we come to Bowie Kuhn. Two days after Finley consummated the sales, with some of the players already with their new teams (but not yet on the field), Kuhn said no. Finley could not make the sales, and the players had to remain with their original teams, he said, invoking the Major Leagues' Best Interests of Baseball Clause. Kuhn's statement the next day said, in part, that the sales would be "devastating to baseball's reputation for integrity and to public confidence in the game." As the National Baseball Hall of Fame put it, Kuhn relied on Article 1, Section 4 of the Major League Agreement, written in 1921—just months after Landis took charge—which said the commissioner was allowed to take "steps as he may deem necessary and proper in the interest in the morale of the game." Finley was incensed, telling Kuhn: "You can't stop me from selling players. Guys have been selling players forever, and no commissioner has ever stopped them," according to *Charlie Finley*. The A's owner was right that owners had long sold players for big sums of cash, and the franchise had the history of Mack's own fire sales to prove it. But he was also wrong: Kuhn did stop him.

Kuhn addressed the issue in his autobiography, *Hardball: The Education of a Baseball Commissioner,* saying: "If such transactions now and in the future were permitted, the door would be opened wide to the buying of success by the more affluent clubs, public suspicion would be aroused, traditional and sound methods of player development and acquisition would be undermined and our efforts to preserve the competitive balance would be greatly impaired." It was not necessarily the sales of the players—those happened all the time—but the amount of the sales that ruffled Kuhn.

And it wasn't just in 1976. At the winter meetings in December 1977, Finley agreed to send Blue to the Cincinnati Reds for a top prospect, first baseman Dave Revering, and $1 million. Again, Kuhn killed the deal, citing the amount of cash. Three months later, Finley moved Blue across the Bay to the San Francisco Giants for seven players (cumulative career Wins Above Replacement of 19.9; Blue totaled 18.0 on his own the rest of his career) and $300,000. Apparently, $300,000 wasn't too much for Kuhn.

You look at the money and you look at the players involved in Finley's initial sales, and you can see that a commissioner thinking like Kuhn in 1920 might very well have concluded that the rich owners of the New York Yankees would take advantage of such sales and upset the competitive balance of the game. A 1920s version of Kuhn might well have prevented Frazee's sale of Ruth to the Yankees—and with no free agency in those days, Ruth would have been forced to remain with the Red Sox.

And Frazee would have been short of cash, which he sorely needed.

He had already made deals in 1918 and 1919 with the Yankees for players and cash (for $15,000 and $40,000), according to *Baseball Reference*. In subsequent years before selling the Red Sox in 1923, Frazee also made deals with the Yankees that included cash coming from New York in amounts of $100,000, $50,000 and $50,000, plus another deal with an unspecified amount of cash. Counting the Ruth deal, that is more than $665,000 in cash that Frazee might not have received had a Kuhn clone been in charge.

The Red Sox acquired 21 players, none of whom amounted to much, from the Yankees on Frazee's watch, plus the money. The Yankees, meanwhile, snagged such stars as Carl Mays, Waite Hoyt, Wally Schang, Bullet Joe Bush, Sad Sam Jones, Everett Scott and Joe Dugan. And Babe Ruth. Without the financial grease, all those deals might not have materialized, and the beginnings of the Yankees' monumental run of championships might not have either. In their first 17 seasons, from 1903 to 1919, the Yankees (and their predecessors, the Highlanders) never won a pennant and had an overall losing record. Not much championship pedigree without Ruth or the other Red Sox refugees.

And in a nice irony, it was believed at the time that a sale of Ruth to the Yankees *was* in the best interests of baseball. Mack, the Philadelphia Athletics' owner and manager, told *The New York Times*, "The sale of Ruth to the Yankees is a good thing for baseball all around." Creamer wrote that many others believed the same thing, that New York City needed a strong American League franchise, as the Major Leagues were still recovering from the effects of the bruising fight with the Federal League in 1914 and 1915 and World War I on its heels. It is a notion Kuhn did not endorse in 1976 when the Yankees, who had not won a pennant since 1964, and the Red Sox, who had not won a World Series since 1918, wanted to buy Fingers, Rudi and Blue.

The post–Ruth Red Sox most likely would not have become what the Yankees did in the 1920s without all their wheeling and dealing, but surely they would have been better than the team that had one winning season between 1919 and 1936. And by then, the big bucks of a new owner, Tom Yawkey, began to kick in.

Connie Mack was not worried about financing Broadway shows, as Frazee was, but he was worried about money. He built two great teams: The Athletics averaged 97 wins a year from 1909 to 1914, with three World Series titles in those six years, before Mack began his first great sell-off to keep the franchise afloat. That 1914 team had what was called the "$100,000 infield," and within two years, Mack had sold three of the four infielders (two of them future Hall of Famers) for nearly that much: $95,500. A very lean decade ensued, but eventually, greatness returned: The Athletics won 104, 102 and 107 games (in a 154-game season, mind you) from 1929 to

1931, with two World Series championships. To survive the Great Depression, however, Mack began dealing away more future Hall of Famers: Al Simmons (1933, $100,000), Lefty Grove (1934, $125,000) and Jimmie Foxx (1936, $150,000). Put in 2024 terms, that's nearly $8.5 million, plus a few players. Mack's ownership survived, but his next rebuild did not arrive. Still pinched, he sold the team at last in 1954.

Baseball's commissioner has invoked the Best Interests Clause at various times over the decades, said Walter T. Champion in the 2021 *Marquette Sports Law Review*, in the article "The Commissioner Goes Too Far: The Best Interests of Baseball Clause and the Astros' 'High-Tech' Sign-Stealing Scandal." The clause was used, for example, to countermand Curt Flood's request to refuse a trade; to suspend the Atlanta Braves owner Ted Turner over what was called tampering with a player; to punish pitcher John Rocker for his comments in a December 1999 *Sports Illustrated* article; and to punish the Houston Astros for their sign-stealing operation.

But Commissioner Landis did not halt Mack's fire sale, even though two of the players (Grove and Foxx) were sold to the team of the richest owner in baseball, Tom Yawkey of the Red Sox. The clause was at hand—it was written *for* Landis, after all—but not used against those Athletics.

Success on the field and financial problems off it were, apparently, part of the Athletics' DNA. Finley bought the team and wound up moving it from Kansas City to Oakland, where *his* rebuild did work. He went through his own boom-and-bust cycle, and he believed his team's continued dominance would be undone by what was a new going rate for star players that he refused to pay ... and Kuhn's decision to invoke the best interests of baseball.

Three

February 9

The Day They Banned the Wet One

On September 20, 1934, Burleigh Grimes, a grizzled Pittsburgh Pirates veteran, threw the last legal spitball, striking out the Brooklyn Dodgers' Joe Stripp, who almost never struck out, to finish his 19-year Hall of Fame pitching career. Figures a spitballer's career would end with a strikeout.

Grimes was 41 years old and had been baseball's only spitballer for exactly a year, since 45-year-old Red Faber of the Chicago White Sox wrapped up his 20-year Hall of Fame career. Struck out the last batter he faced, too. Two and a half months earlier, 50-year-old Jack Quinn of the Cincinnati Reds threw his last Major League spitter; *The Associated Press* reported that "old Jack Quinn" had quelled a Boston Braves rally in relief. The year before, 1932, 40-year-old Clarence Mitchell, who was lucky enough to be a rookie when baseball began its spitball crackdown, hung up his wet one with the New York Giants, getting his last Major League out on a spitballer's other best friend: a groundout.

And they used to say the spitball wore out pitchers' arms. After the spitball was outlawed, Grimes pitched 3,489 innings with 236 wins and 270 complete games. Faber threw 2,909 1/3 innings while winning 172 games and completing 196. Quinn was the slacker—2,299 innings, 148 wins and 124 complete games—but he had pitched nearly a decade in the Majors before the ban went into effect.

Maybe the spitball wasn't so bad for arms, just for batters. Grimes, Faber and Quinn pitched for more than a decade with a weapon almost no one in baseball could use: the spitball. Baseball banned the spitter on February 9, 1920, but it created loopholes that Grimes, Faber, Quinn and a few others were able to take advantage of until their careers ended.

The spitball's origins in the 19th century are murky, but its heyday—for two decades, beginning with the start of the 20th century—coincided with some of the lowest-scoring years in baseball. The ball was mush—it *was* the Deadball Era—but the spitter was a factor, too. "In the teens you could hardly open an issue of *Baseball Magazine* without coming across an article like 'Why the Spit Ball Should Be Abolished,' or 'Who Needs the Spit Ball?' or 'Why Freak Deliveries Must Go,'" Rob Neyer wrote in *The Neyer/James Guide to Pitchers. Baseball Digest* also lobbied against the spitter. Barney Dreyfuss, owner of the Pirates, did too. Clark Griffith, a former pitcher (and an occasional spitball pitcher at that) who became the manager and an owner of the Washington Senators, came around to their view as well.

The spitter had been tossed around for decades—John Thorn and John Holway suggest in *The Pitcher* that it goes back at least to 1868, when Bobby Mathews saw an opposing pitcher wet his fingers and the ball and get hellacious movement, and Neyer concurs. Pitching was evolving in those years (the distance to home plate changed, for example, and a rubber replaced the pitcher's box), but the spitter did not become an established pitch. Eventually, however, it may have found its way from a minor leaguer named Frank Corridon to another minor leaguer, Elmer Stricklett (with, perhaps, a stop at an outfielder, George Hildebrand, in between). Stricklett, at least, used it seriously, if not particularly effectively, but more important, along the way he was a mentor to Jack Chesbro and Ed Walsh, who used it seriously *and* effectively. Chesbro broke out in 1901, and in 1904, he won 41 games for the New York Highlanders. Walsh was a rookie in 1904 who took off in 1906, and he won 40 games for the Chicago White Sox in 1908. The later myth about the spitter hurting a pitcher's arm to the contrary, Walsh threw 464 innings in his big season; Cheney, 454 2/3 in his. They became the only American League pitchers to win 40 games in a season.

Chesbro's star flamed out quickly, but Walsh's did not, and other pitchers noticed just how good a spitball made him. "With Walsh carving up American League hitters every season, the spitball got real popular," Neyer wrote. With the spitter and other trick pitches on which the ball was defaced—the shine ball, the emery ball, balls lathered with tobacco juice or slippery elm, there was a whole constellation of such pitches—added to a dead baseball, offenses floundered. In 1904, Chesbro's sensational season, Major League teams averaged fewer than four runs a game for the first time, and offenses stayed stuck in the threes for 13 of the 16 seasons through 1919—the last year the spitter would be available to every pitcher.

After the 1919 season, a committee of four—Dreyfuss and William Veeck, Sr., of the Chicago Cubs from the National League, Griffith and Connie Mack of the Philadelphia Athletics of the American League—devised a plan to ban the spitter. Several reasons were discussed for doing so. In *Spitballers: The Last Legal Hurlers of the Wet One,* Charles F. Faber and Richard B. Faber laid out six possible reasons: "1. It is unsanitary. 2. It is hard to control. 3. It is dangerous. 4. It is difficult to field. 5. It is hard on the pitcher's arm. 6. It depresses hitting." The Fabers artfully debunk reasons 1–5 and conclude: "Does the spitter depress hitting? Yes. At long last we come to the real reason the pitch was banned. It was difficult to hit a home run off a spitter." A properly thrown spitter "dives as it reaches home plate, and the batter is likely to top it, hitting an infield grounder."

The owners had seen too many years of grounders. Babe Ruth had come along late in the teens, and the fans' response to power and offense was undeniable. "The owners and other powers-that-be in baseball wanted to see more home runs, thus enticing more paying customers into the ball parks," the Fabers wrote. The lobbying against the spitter and other trick pitches from over the years met receptive ears, and the ban was announced on February 9, 2020.

Not just the spitball was banned. The new rule read: "At no time during the progress of the game shall the pitcher be allowed to: (1) Apply a foreign substance of any kind to the ball; (2) Expectorate either on the ball or his glove; (3) Rub the ball on his glove, person, or clothing; (4) or to deliver what is called the 'shine' ball, 'spit' ball, 'mud' ball, or 'emery' ball."

But baseball decided to make a concession to pitchers who were acknowledged to already throw a spitter (but not the other trick pitches, which also created devilish, unpredictable movement): Some could keep throwing it. In the American League, each team could designate two pitchers who could use the spitball. The National League decided against any limits for the 1920 season.

The spitballers—the best ones, anyway—took advantage. The World Series participants, the Cleveland Indians and the Brooklyn Robins, each had two spitballers: Stan Coveleski (24–14, 2.49 ERA) and Ray Caldwell (20–10, 3.86) for Cleveland, Burleigh Grimes (23–11, 2.22) and Clarence Mitchell (5–2, 3.09) for Brooklyn.

Not long after Coveleski won three games as Cleveland captured the World Series, six NL teams voted to recommend that only certain pitchers be allowed to use the spitter anymore. The AL agreed, and beginning with the 1921 season, only 17 pitchers could legally throw a spitball: nine in the AL, eight in the NL. Here are the lists:

American League	National League
Doc Ayers, 29, Detroit Tigers	Bill Doak, 29, St. Louis Cardinals
Ray Caldwell, 32, Cleveland Indians	Phil Douglas, 30, New York Giants
Stan Coveleski, 29, Cleveland Indians	Dana Fillingim, 26, Boston Braves
Red Faber, 31, Chicago White Sox	Ray Fisher, 30, Cincinnati Reds

American League	National League
Dutch Leonard, 28, Detroit Tigers	Marv Goodwin, 29, St. Louis Cardinals
Jack Quinn, 36, New York Yankees	Burleigh Grimes, 26, Brooklyn Dodgers
Allan Russell, 26, Boston Red Sox	Clarence Mitchell, 29, Brooklyn Dodgers
Urban Shocker, 29, St. Louis Browns	Dick Rudolph, 29, Boston Braves
Allen Sothoron, 27, St. Louis Browns	

Missing from the lists: any pitchers from Griffith's Senators, Mack's Athletics, Dreyfuss's Pirates and Veeck's Cubs—teams whose representatives voted for the ban in February 1920. Missing also were some young spitballers—Frank Shellenback, for example, had pitched some for the Chicago White Sox, but he could not be grandfathered in because he was in the American Association at the time of the ban. He spent the next 18 seasons in the Pacific Coast League, expectorating his way to another 296 minor league wins. Not a single inning in the Majors.

The ban was a bit of a curious approach, allowing some players to have an advantage that was illegal for almost every other player. What if, after the 1998 season, Major League Baseball had created a list of 17 hitters who could use performance-enhancing drugs for the rest of their careers (as long as they agreed to be put on a public list), but no other players could? Would the baseball public—or the other baseball teams—have accepted an arrangement in which Mark McGwire or Sammy Sosa or Barry Bonds could use steroids forever without violating MLB rules? Seems unfathomable.

But the spitballers had their weapon, and some thrived (three Hall of Famers). At worst, most of them survived; 13 of the 17 pitchers grandfathered in pitched through at least the 1925 season.

As the legal spitballers faded from the game, you might think, given their success and longevity, that others would try the pitch illegally. That may have happened, but the evidence is scant. "Oddly, it's very difficult to find references to pitchers throwing the spitball between 1920 and 1940, aside from those who were still permitted to throw it," Neyer wrote. He didn't know why. But he noted that beginning in the early '40s, "a great number of pitchers are accused of throwing spitballs (and some of them would eventually admit it)." The trend did not subside in the 1950s and early '60s. Preacher Roe, Lew Burdette and Don Drysdale were all accused of throwing the spitter, and all admitted it—after their careers were over.

Actual spitballs were most likely replaced by other doctored deliveries. Although his autobiography was titled *Me and the Spitter*, Gaylord Perry most often used Vaseline or K-Y Jelly. Whitey Ford threw scuffed baseballs. Rick Honeycutt was caught with a tack taped to his glove hand. Joe Niekro had an emery board fly out of his hip pocket. Jay Howell had pine tar on his glove. More recently, the use of the sticky substance Spider Tack led to crackdowns by umpires. Ask Max Scherzer, who was booted from a game in 2023 and suspended because his hands were deemed too sticky.

Some people in baseball wanted the subterfuge to stop and called for the spitball ban to be lifted. In 1950, baseball voted on it, but the proposal lost, 7–1, the Fabers wrote. In 1955, Ford Frick, the commissioner of baseball, suggested it was time to bring back the spitball. "If I had my way, I'd legalize the old spitter," he told *The Milwaukee Journal*. "It was a great pitch and one of the easiest to throw." That proposal went nowhere, too. The respected columnist Red Smith lobbied for the spitter in 1957. Nothing happened.

Four years later, according to the Fabers, the White Sox's general manager, Ed Short, nudged the Official Playing Rules Committee to restore the spitter. Warren Giles, the National League president, was among the staunchest opponents, with a view that hadn't changed in four decades: Fans like home runs, spitters reduce home runs, fewer home runs means fewer fans. "It is my firm belief," Giles said, "that the long ball, particularly the home run, is what the fans want to see." The vote for the spitter lost, 8–1.

Four

March 16

Spring Training Comes to Indiana

It was January 1943, and the Pittsburgh Pirates were considering whether to conduct their spring training in Muncie, a Central Indiana city of 50,000, after holding it in California for 18 of the previous 19 years. (More on why in a bit.) Muncie was not the only possible new location, however. So two young baseball-loving brothers lobbied passionately for the move to Muncie and even offered to help finance it.

The Cincinnati Reds in the Indiana University Fieldhouse in March 1943. Indoor facilities—complete with a dirt floor—were a necessity because of inclement weather (courtesy Indiana University Archives).

Leo Ganter, 11, and his 10-year-old brother, Jimmy, wrote the Muncie newspaper, *The Star-Press,* offering up $1 to help bring the Pirates to town. "We have never seen a big game and if the Pirates don't come to Muncie we sure will be disappointed," their letter in the January 25, 1943, issue of *The Star-Press* said. They told the paper's editors, "We hope you can do something for all us baseball bugs."

The Ganter boys would be in luck. The Pirates did decide to train in Muncie, becoming one of six Major League teams that held spring training in Indiana in 1943—in Muncie, Bloomington (Reds), Lafayette (Indians), Evansville (Tigers) and tiny French Lick and West Baden (Cubs and White Sox)—along with several minor league teams. This was called the Limestone League, according to Steve Krah in a 1997 article for *The Baseball Research Journal,* and it was part of baseball's response to a federal suggestion that the game rein in non-essential travel as part of the World War II effort.

Less than a year after the attack on Pearl Harbor, Americans were being asked to make sacrifices, big and small. Baseball was no exception. In November 1942, Joseph Eastman, the head of the United States Office of Defense Transportation, suggested that Major League Baseball consider how it managed spring training in an effort to meet its travel needs "without waste in space or mileage." That meant railroads. While not having been given an order, Commissioner Kenesaw Mountain Landis enthusiastically agreed and told baseball owners to "abandon Florida and California, then followed up with a note telling them to forget about relocating anywhere in the Southeast," Richard Goldstein wrote in *Spartan Seasons: How Baseball Survived the Second World War.* So baseball instituted its version of the Mason-Dixon Line—the Landis-Eastman Line. Teams would have to conduct spring training north of the Ohio and Potomac Rivers and west of the Mississippi (with a tiny exception for the St. Louis Browns, who wound up on the western bank of the Mississippi in Cape Girardeau, Missouri).

No team other than the Cardinals, in 1911 (West Baden, Indiana) and 1919 (St. Louis), had held spring training north of the Mason-Dixon Line since the first few years of the 20th century, according to research by BaseballGuru.com. Teams trained in Alabama, Arkansas, California, Georgia, Louisiana, Mississippi, North Carolina, South Carolina, Texas, Virginia and—most frequently and eventually almost exclusively—Florida. Now, however, teams had to find someplace north to train, and quickly. They bumped into one another looking at sites at resorts, in college towns, anywhere that seemed suitable and near the home office. The Brooklyn Dodgers wound up at Bear Mountain in New York. The New York Yankees and Giants settled on the Jersey Shore. The Boston Braves landed at The Choate

School—it had been the prep school for John F. Kennedy—in Connecticut. And nine teams signed on to hold spring training in Indiana—the Limestone League. (Portions of south-central Indiana, centered on Bloomington and Bedford, sit on enormous deposits of excellent limestone, which has been used in numerous buildings, including the Lincoln Memorial, the Pentagon, the Empire State Building and the majority of state capitols.)

The competition for teams could be fierce. So could the competition for sites. The Cincinnati Reds forged an agreement to train in Bloomington at Indiana University, which had a suitable diamond and a huge fieldhouse with a dirt floor for indoor drills, while the Brooklyn Dodgers, the Cleveland Indians and the Pittsburgh Pirates were left out almost literally in the cold. With the Reds there and 2,500 young men taking wartime physical fitness instruction in Bloomington, there wasn't sufficient room for another Major League team, *United Press* reported.

The Pirates settled on another college town, Muncie, home of Ball State Teachers College (now Ball State University). Plans were for the team to train at the city's McCulloch Park, once home to minor league teams (including the Muncie Fruit Jars, named because of the prominence of the Ball canning jar company); the Ball State diamond; and the Muncie High School fieldhouse (with a capacity of 7,500 for basketball, it was the largest in the state then). To make McCulloch Park work, however, the Pirates requested changes to the park's lodge so it could be used as a clubhouse. They also wanted a tarp; it would be spring, and although the song *Little Green Apples* suggests it doesn't rain in Indiana in the summertime, it sure does in the springtime. The requests became an issue. *The Star-Press* said in an editorial that the city should not give in to the demands and cough up the money, but the mayor eventually said donations and loans of equipment would cover the needs. And the Pirates trained in Muncie for the rest of the war.

Spring training in these unaccustomed spots was not universally appreciated. Arthur Daley, sports columnist for *The New York Times*, wrote in 1944 that halfway through spring training in 1943, teams had become skeptical. "Northern training seemed needless and owners began doing some analyzing." One thing they realized: With ballplayers coming from all over the country for spring training to Indiana or Delaware or New Jersey or New York State, "In effect the saving in transportation was nil." And it's not as if no one was going to Florida; Daley wrote that so many people were vacationing and going to the races in Florida, the Office of Defense Transportation ran special trains to take the visitors back home. "On no count did the Northern training seem worth the sacrifice," he said.

Daley added that the Yankees, training in Asbury Park, New Jersey, "captured the undisputed championship for drawing the worst facilities of them all." He said that in the first 10 days of spring training in 1943—shortened to a month—the Yankees practiced outside only 45 minutes. Mostly they played basketball to get in shape. (Maybe more teams should have played hoops; the Yankees won 12 of their first 15 regular-season games and snagged both the American League pennant and the World Series title. But one spring in Asbury Park was enough for the Yankees; the next year they trained a bit farther south in Atlantic City.)

If the facilities in Indiana could be better, the weather often was not. "Several fields were of the makeshift variety and many workouts were forced inside because of Indiana's often-inclement March weather," Steve Krah wrote. "Long underwear was standard issue." Heavy rains flooded the diamond set up in French Lick in a couple of the war seasons, forcing the use of the French Lick Springs Hotel's golf course fairway as a baseball field. In 1943, White Sox Manager Jimmy Dykes was photographed in a rowboat on the flooded field.

The Yankees in New Jersey were not the only team that resorted to basketball. In Muncie, the Pirates wound up playing hoops in the Muncie High School fieldhouse. It did not always go well; a pitcher named Bill Brandt—a Hoosier native—injured his knee in one basketball workout. "I told him he was a fine example," Manager Frankie Frisch told *The Muncie Star-Press*. "The only Indiana boy on my ball club starts running around in a game that is supposed to be red hot in this state and what happens—why, he's the only one that winds up on his ear! 'A great advertisement for the Hoosier state you are,' I tell him!"

Asbury Park, on the Jersey Shore, may have had uninspiring facilities for training. But Lafayette was simply uninspiring, according to a *Cleveland News* columnist, Ed McAuley, who wrote about how boring the place was. After spotting pitcher Allie Reynolds napping in an armchair at the Indians' hotel, McAuley said: "Fortunate is the athlete who can sleep away the daylight hours in Lafayette. There isn't much else to do." A columnist in *The Lafayette Journal and Courier,* Gordon Graham, defended local honor, rebutting McAuley by quoting a no-doubt-partial Purdue University alum that the Indians had loved the quiet surroundings of Lafayette. But Reynolds had clear misgivings about training at Purdue. "Spring training at Purdue was tough," he told Harrington E. Crissey, Jr., in *Teenagers, Graybeards and 4-Fs*. "Working on the soft ground outside and hard ground inside gave me a beautiful case of shin splints."

There could be advantages to training on a college campus, however. Ted Kluszewski, a football star for Indiana University, picked up some extra money by helping prepare the baseball facilities for the Reds' spring training. He also managed a little baseball of his own. In 1945, his only

Four. March 16

season of college baseball, Kluszewski and the rest of the IU team would practice after the Reds did, and the Cincinnati groundskeeper noticed how far Kluszewski hit the ball. And how often he did so. Stories of 500-foot blasts made the rounds, *The Indianapolis Star* said. He earned an invitation to a tryout in Cincinnati and hit "five towering drives in the rightfield bleachers in approximately 30 swings," *The Cincinnati Enquirer* reported. The Reds signed him away from a half-dozen other teams for $15,000 (and the taxes on the signing bonus).

So spring training in Indiana could provide opportunities to look creatively for players at a time when the war had drained so much talent. Krah said that by Opening Day in 1944, about 340 Major Leaguers and more than 3,000 minor leaguers were serving in the military. United Press reported in December 1944 that 462 of the 530 Major Leaguers would have their draft status reviewed. That included 223 players classified 4-F (meaning more than 40 percent of players on the 1945 rosters were considered physically unfit for military duty).

Those hunts on campus for players had limited success, however. The Tigers, training in Evansville at the longtime minor league stadium Bosse Field, tested an unusually tall pitcher from suburban Detroit, Ralph Siewert. The Associated Press said he was 6 feet 11 inches, although later sources said he was, in 1946, the first 7-footer in professional basketball at 7-1. Detroit's Briggs Stadium was renowned for its high mound, and the prospect of employing the tallest player in the game on that mound must have been tantalizing. And at 6–11, or 7–1, he was too tall for the military. But that didn't help his career. "Normally Siewert would be sent for minor league experience," The Associated Press reported, "but the Tigers just couldn't imagine him folding his long legs under a bus seat. So the job of batting practice pitcher was revived for him."

Bosse Field was the best-developed location used for spring training, having been a minor league ballpark since 1915. (It is still in use for an independent league team. The only two older ballparks still in regular use are Fenway Park and Wrigley Field.) Bosse had been the home of a Boston Braves farm team in 1942. The universities had their own baseball facilities and fieldhouses for indoor drills. But the location that had the richest history of use by Major League teams was in a tiny pocket of Southern Indiana: the "twin cities" of French Lick and West Baden Springs.

French Lick, population 2,000, and adjacent West Baden, population 1,000, were in the Springs Valley, which was rich with mineral springs that became the basis for large resorts in the late 1800s. Spring training for baseball teams began in the 1870s, Charles Fountain wrote in *Under the March Sun: The Story of Spring Training,* but more as an opportunity to get players in better physical condition than to hone their skills in exhibition games. By the 1880s, Fountain said, spring training trips had become commonplace. It wasn't long—just before the turn of the 20th century—that Major League teams began stopping in West Baden and French Lick to play exhibition games on their way north from spring training locations farther south, Roger Sanders wrote in a 2021 history of local baseball.

West Baden and French Lick had some advantages in those early years. The resorts were plush and an enormous draw. "This place was Las Vegas before Las Vegas," a marketing manager for the French Lick Resort Hotel said years later. Not really an exaggeration: 14 illegal casinos were said to operate in the Springs Valley area. (Al Capone purportedly visited.) Because of the amenities, the hotels—the West Baden Springs Hotel and the French Lick Resort Hotel—could provide unexpectedly good athletic facilities. The West Baden Springs Hotel, for example, had a one-third of a mile wooden velodrome in the middle of which a baseball diamond was set up.

In addition, the mineral springs in West Baden and French Lick were said to be therapeutic and cleanse the system—West Baden had Sprudel Water, French Lick had Pluto Water. (The sulfur-tinged water was not universally loved; a local history said that Honus Wagner did not like the mineral water treatments on two stops in West Baden in the 1890s, but agreed to make a visit there, however reluctantly, with his Pittsburgh Pirates in 1912.) And there was good baseball being played in the twin cities. Each of the resorts fielded teams of its African American staff members; local newspapers said the resort teams even played a few scrimmages against Major League teams, long before baseball's integration.

The accommodations were spectacular. The West Baden Springs Hotel, for example, had a 200-foot dome above the atrium that was the largest in the world when it was built in 1902 and remained the largest in the United States until 1955. It also had a natatorium, a golf course and the double-decker velodrome, which was also used for horse racing.

The pennant-winning Chicago Cubs made stops in the Springs Valley in 1907 and 1908, but the only team that conducted its full spring training in the area was the 1911 St. Louis Cardinals, who had trained in Little Rock, Arkansas, the previous two springs. Those Cardinals had just been taken over by Helene Britton, who inherited the team from her uncle (much to Major League Baseball's dismay). By the next spring, the Cardinals held camp in Jackson, Mississippi.

Teams were arrayed across the South, Texas, and California, but Florida began to carve out a foothold. Some teams began training there in the 1880s, according to *Under the March Sun*, but it wasn't until the teens that teams began to train there regularly. It eventually became the spring hub, and in 1925, 14 of the 16 teams held spring training in Florida. Teams had stopped visiting West Baden and French Lick after the spring of 1922. West Palm Beach was a lot warmer than West Baden, and by then a lot more accessible as increased automobile use and better roads made Florida an easier destination. After the stock market crash of 1929 and the onset of the Great Depression, the twin cities' resorts slid into a steady decline; the demand for resort hotels, especially ones off the beaten path, cratered. The West Baden velodrome had already blown down in a 1925 storm, and, although the hotel was the site of the 1931 winter meetings, the owners closed the hotel in 1934 and donated it to the Society of Jesuits. Yes, the place went from hosting mobsters to men of the cloth.

The French Lick hotel, however, never closed. And when Commissioner Landis limited spring training to northern sites—remember, Washington, Cincinnati and St. Louis were the southernmost cities in the Major Leagues—French Lick appeared as a suitable location for a team. Or teams.

One day after the Boston Red Sox became the first team to relocate its spring training in 1943, both the Cubs and the White Sox said they would train in French Lick, *Spartan Seasons* said—280 miles south of Chicago, but more than 700 miles north of Florida.

The area still had some of the opulence of its heyday. "The French Lick Springs Hotel had the finest of everything; the wealthy people, businessmen, used to go there," Len Merullo, the Cubs' shortstop, remembered years later in *Spartan Seasons*. "The leading bands were still coming in, fellows like Glen Gray," a saxophonist and bandleader. Merullo said the players took advantage of the mineral springs and spring baths. "It was great; it was something we had never experienced before," he said. "The big fellas, especially, went down there to lose weight."

But accommodating baseball, not just baseball players, was something else. The White Sox and Cubs loosened up in what had been a stable, reads a passage in *Spartan Seasons*. The Cubs did calisthenics in a ballroom. White Sox pitchers warmed up one day in the hotel ballroom—a workaround necessitated by the flooding of the baseball diamonds set up on the hotel golf course (the Cubs) and a nearby semipro ballpark (the White Sox). In 1944, it snowed. Incessant rain became a factor in friction between the two clubs, who squabbled over who got to use the golf course, which had better drainage, as a diamond during flooding. The White Sox's manager, Jimmy Dykes, and a coach, the appropriately named Muddy Ruel, "scouted the countryside for a dry practice place," Steve Krah wrote. "They learned of several big barns in the community" that had the potential for use for batting practice "with some energetic use of pitchforks and rakes." The White Sox could do without such extra training and moved to Terre Haute, Indiana, in 1945. Good timing; the train to French Lick was taken out of service that spring.

But Terre Haute was not without its own peculiarities. The hotel was 26 blocks from the baseball field, Richard Goldstein wrote, and Dykes was grumpy about having to make the walk every day. A solution arose: The mayor had a Model T police wagon pick Dykes up ... only for it to break down.

But 26 blocks? That was nothing. Travel restrictions were tightened in 1945, and the Tigers, training in Evansville, faced the prospect of all of their exhibition games being canceled as a result. French Lick, the closest Limestone League site, was nearly 100 miles away; Terre Haute was 112. General Manager Jack Zeller had a brainstorm: His players, working their way into shape, could walk from Evansville to Terre Haute. Manager Steve O'Neill estimated it would take five or six days—but "if they walk, they'll have to go without the manager."

O'Neill did not have to take a hike, as the Tigers decided to use the railroad to get to Terre Haute, *Spartan Seasons* recounted, stuck around for a few practices and then took the train to St. Louis to open the season. They never did return to Evansville. With the war over, the Tigers trained the next spring in Lakeland, Florida. And have ever since. The Limestone League's days were over.

But there was one last spring training hurrah for the Springs Valley: In 1950, three teams from the All-American Girls Professional Baseball League—think *A League of Their Own*—the Racine Belles, the Kenosha Comets and the Grand Rapids Chicks, spent a week and a half there preparing for their season. New league, same obstacles: *The Kenosha News* reported that camp was cut short because of wet grounds. Even an exhibition game in Louisville, Kentucky, was rained out.

Five

March 18

Go West, Old Teams: The Migration Begins

World War II was over, and the boys were back. Including the ballplayers. The fans responded, and no one was happier than the owners of the ballpark at Commonwealth Avenue and Babcock Street in Boston. In 1946, the Boston Braves, like the rest of baseball, were experiencing an unprecedented attendance boom—an increase of nearly 160 percent over the final year of the war, to a record 969,673.

It wasn't just the end of the war that was helping the Braves at the box office; in addition, a team that had been among the dregs of the National League for three decades was finally winning. The Braves were 81–72 in 1946, after posting only five winning records in the 29 seasons from 1917 to 1945. The Braves never finished higher than fourth in that time, and their attendance matched that dismal record.

But things were changing. New ownership had taken over the team in 1941, and in early 1945, Lou Perini, the owner of a local construction company, became team president. He pushed hard for night baseball while the Red Sox disdained it, and he made radio broadcasts a priority. The team also brought in more talented players; in 1948, the Braves won the National League pennant, their first since the Miracle Braves of 1914.

It was quicksilver, however. Only four years later, in 1952, the Braves finished in seventh place and drew a mere 281,278 fans—3,701 a game. (How paltry was that? The Pacific Coast League's Los Angeles Angels averaged 3,991.) On March 18, 1953, only a month before the season began, the Boston Braves became the Milwaukee Braves, setting off a stampede of Major League teams from the cities that had been their hosts for half a century or more.

After the Braves had acquired the territorial rights to Milwaukee (they bought the minor league Brewers) and moved there, Walter O'Malley, the Brooklyn Dodgers' owner, told *The Associated Press*: "This can set up a chain reaction. You'll see more territory being drafted than you can shake a stick at."

O'Malley was correct. In 1954, the St. Louis Browns moved to Baltimore (a minor league city). In 1955, the Philadelphia Athletics moved to Kansas City (a minor league city). And in 1958, O'Malley's Dodgers headed to Los Angeles and the New York Giants ventured to San Francisco (both minor league cities). In the span of five years, nearly a third of the 16 Major League teams changed cities. And more changes were coming—more franchise shifts, and expansion after expansion, prompted in part initially by the threat of a competing league.

Although the National League and the American League had seemed uncommonly stable—after 1903, no team shifted cities until 1953—warning signs were visible. Five of the 10 Major League cities had at least two teams, and those two-team cities, while sustaining population declines, had also seen plenty of bad baseball in recent decades: the Braves, the Browns and the Athletics (and the Philadelphia Phillies, too, for that matter). Attendance was as dismal as the records (so were finances), and a city's ability to support two Major League teams was becoming increasingly suspect. In fact, the Braves, the Browns and the Athletics were all last in their league in the standings and in attendance the season before they moved. Cause, meet effect. But it was the Braves who set off the transformation of the Major League landscape. And returned baseball to the turmoil of its early years.

In the first three decades of professional baseball, Major Leagues came and went. (Hello and goodbye National Association, American Association, Union Association.) Teams came and went. (Remember the Troy Haymakers? The Fort Wayne Kekiongas?) The one league that endured was the National League—and it was hardly unchanging. In 1892, the NL, formed in 1876, expanded to 12 teams from eight by absorbing teams as the American Association disbanded. By 1899, it was clear the 12-team league wasn't working, and the next season, the NL shed four teams—and was back to the eight teams that, never moving, would make up the league for more than half a century. Gone were the Baltimore Orioles, the Washington Senators, the Louisville Colonels and the Cleveland Spiders.

Gone from the National League, anyway. By 1901, the American League had formed and declared itself a Major League, including teams from former National League cities Baltimore, Cleveland and Washington.

While the National League had settled into its seven cities—it had a quarter-century head start—the American League was more precarious. After one season, the AL's Milwaukee Brewers moved to St. Louis and became the Browns; in 1902, the Baltimore Orioles were taken over in midseason by new investors, who fielded the team the next year in New York as the Highlanders. And with that, the Major Leagues were cemented in place for 50 years. Or, at least that is the perspective from decades later.

Five. March 18

In reality, various forces would threaten the NL and AL stability without upending it.

Competitor leagues loomed quickly, if not for long. In 1912, something called the Columbian League came and went without playing a game, and another rival, the United States League (among its eight teams were the Chicago Green Sox), folded after five weeks, tried again the next year with fewer teams and folded within a week. In 1914, after one season as a minor league, the Federal League emerged as a competitor. It challenged the established leagues in four places (Brooklyn, Chicago, Pittsburgh and St. Louis); chose to forgo the reserve clause, which the NL and AL had used to bind players to their teams in perpetuity; raided the established teams' rosters for players; and pushed players' salaries far higher.

That off-season, the Federal League also brought an antitrust suit against the NL and AL; its legacy was that it went before Judge Kenesaw Mountain Landis, who pleased the NL and AL owners so much with his handling of the case (he deferred a decision for more than a year, by which point the Federal League had folded and he dismissed the case) that he was eventually named baseball commissioner. While that case was in limbo, the Federal League fell apart after the 1915 season. Half of the teams were bought out, one team went bankrupt, and two owners were allowed to buy teams in the established leagues (the Chicago Cubs and the St. Louis Browns).

The Federal League's Baltimore Terrapins were the outlier and refused to go quietly, hoping to move an established Major League franchise to Baltimore. When they failed, they sued, contending that the National and American Leagues had violated the Sherman Antitrust Act, according to Steven Gietschier in *Baseball: The Turbulent Midcentury Years*. The Terrapins' owners eventually lost before the Supreme Court, where Justice Oliver Wendell Holmes wrote in the unanimous 1922 decision that baseball was not involved in interstate commerce under the Sherman Antitrust Act, its teams in different states notwithstanding. That is: Baseball had an antitrust exemption, which the Supreme Court upheld in 1953 (the Toolson case) and 1972 (the Flood case). "With its 1922 antitrust exemption, baseball was effectively immune from competition from upstart leagues," Daniel Levitt wrote for the Society for American Baseball Research. "Since the demise of the Federals, no rival has ever emerged to challenge major league baseball on the field."

Other challenges, however, lurked from within. In 1930, Major League Baseball set an attendance record and records for offense like runs per game and batting average, as *Baseball Reference* notes. The Great Depression, however, devastated attendance, which by 1933 had cratered by 40 percent (not helped, perhaps, by a 19 percent decline in runs per game as the ball was changed). There were great and exciting teams (Yankees, Athletics, Cardinals), special World Series moments (the 1932 "Called Shot") and a surfeit of future Hall of Fame players. But numerous teams were hopeless, failures on the field and, not at all coincidentally, at the box office.

The St. Louis Browns were one of those teams, and more than a decade before the Braves moved, the Browns extensively examined the possibility of moving from St. Louis to Los Angeles. Michael E. Lomax, a former University of Iowa professor of sports history, recounted in a 2012 paper in *Northeast Popular Culture Association* that one of the Browns' three primary owners, Donald Barnes, met in midseason 1941 with officials in Los Angeles. Barnes said the ownership group would be willing to sell some of its stock in the team to raise the money to buy the Los Angeles Angels of the Pacific Coast League, the team that owned the territorial rights to the city. Barnes said he had lined up approval from American League owners to pursue transferring his team; had come to an agreement with Phil Wrigley, the Los Angeles team's owner, to buy the Angels and their ballpark; and worked out a deal with the Browns' tenant in St. Louis, Sam Breadon of the Cardinals, to buy out the Browns so they would leave. Los Angeles would become an AL territory, St. Louis an exclusive NL territory.

Barnes, Lomax wrote, went so far as to draw up a 1942 schedule with a Los Angeles team and met with executives of Trans World Airlines to work out travel plans. That meeting, however, was on December 6, 1941, and after the bombing of Pearl Harbor the next day, any plans for the Browns to move to Los Angeles were moot. On December 9, AL owners voted unanimously to reject the Browns' proposal to shift to Los Angeles.

The Browns' abortive effort did, however, show the steps teams would need to take to try to move to another city, Lomax said. It also revealed the potential costs. Edwin Pauley, who made his fortune in the oil business, wanted to buy the Browns in 1947 and move them to Los Angeles, but he backed away after calculating the real price tag. He said the cost of not only purchasing the team but also paying ancillary costs like buying out the minor league Angels and indemnifying the other PCL owners, totaling $8.75 million, were too great, according to Gietschier in *Baseball: The Turbulent Midcentury Years*.

But it would be the Browns once again who would try to move, only a few years later, although in a much-altered landscape. After enormous attendance gains right after World War II, Major League attendance suffered in the new decade: In 1950, attendance dropped sharply, then went from 17.2 million to 15 million in 1952. Considering this environment, Lomax said, baseball's owners at the 1952 winter meetings softened the requirements for moving a team, from a unanimous vote by the owners of both leagues to unanimous consent from the owners in that team's own league. "The other league could not block the move, if the invaded area was the property of a club in the same league," he wrote.

The location that became desirable was Milwaukee, one of the fast-growing cities amid changing U.S. demographics and a community that had already begun building a new ballpark. It was a city that Bill Veeck, now owner of the Browns, wanted. He knew the place well; Veeck had owned the minor league Brewers in the 1940s.

Milwaukee, through the Greater Milwaukee Committee, "made overtures to lure the most coveted franchise ripe for relocation—the St. Louis Browns," Lomax wrote. Discussions began with Veeck, who had decided his ability to compete in St. Louis had vanished after the Cardinals were purchased by the Busch Brewery Company. But there was a roadblock: The Braves and Lou Perini now owned the minor league Brewers and thus the rights to Milwaukee. The Greater Milwaukee Committee offered Perini $500,000 to move the Brewers to Toledo, Ohio, so Veeck could move the Browns to Milwaukee, Lomax said.

Perini saw opportunity and said no. Veeck began looking at Baltimore instead. And Perini began looking at Milwaukee for his Braves.

Concurrently, there was Congressional pressure (including from a Wisconsin Congressman) on Major League Baseball about its antitrust/monopoly status, enhancing its willingness to move franchises, Gietschier wrote. That angered city leaders in Milwaukee, but it gave Perini leverage to get approval from NL owners to move there. (He got a sweet deal: rent of $1,000 a month to play at County Stadium, and the city also got 5 percent of gate receipts and most of the concessions revenue, Lomax pointed out.) Perini announced the plan on March 14. Veeck sought approval to move to Baltimore, which the AL owners, who were always leery of Veeck, rejected on March 16. On March 18, NL owners approved the Braves' move to Milwaukee, and the minor league Brewers moved to Toledo, where the Mud Hens had left for Charleston, West Virginia. Perini said of the rationale for leaving Boston: "I don't think we can ever take the town away from the Red Sox. Boston justifiably belongs to the Red Sox."

It did. Despite being formed a quarter-century before the Red Sox, the Braves eventually suffered in their competition with their neighbors at Fenway. Soon after their World Series championship season of 1914, the Braves became uncompetitive—just as the Red Sox, with Babe Ruth, became champions themselves. Even though the Red Sox also turned uncompetitive from the time of Harry Frazee's dispersal of the star players all the way through the '20s, they acquired what the Braves never did: a well-heeled owner. Once Tom Yawkey bought the Red Sox in 1933 and began funneling money into the operation, his team began improving and was consistently a much bigger draw than the underfinanced Braves.

The Braves had been bought in 1923 by a New York lawyer named Emil Fuchs, widely known as Judge Fuchs (hey, the Yankees had Colonel Ruppert), but he could not stem the tide of losing teams that hemorrhaged money. It got so bad that in 1929, he made himself the manager. He saved money but could not salvage the team—he finished with a 56–98 record. (Must be something about Braves owners, as Ted Turner managed the hapless Atlanta Braves for a game in 1977. He lost, too.)

Fuchs investigated ways to improve the Braves' attendance and finances. He was interested in the possibility of night baseball, and he pursued having greyhound racing after games at Braves Field. The National League was not interested, a Society for American Baseball Research article by Bob Lemoine said. (Especially greyhound racing, with its taint of gambling. As Jimmy Powers wrote in *The New York Daily News*, "President William Benswanger of the Pirates raised his delicately chiseled snoot yesterday and cried: 'I will vote against this proposal. I am in favor of keeping baseball on a high plane.'" In a nice paradox, a generation later, a new Pirates owner, John W. Galbreath, owned and raced thoroughbred horses.) In another effort to goose the gate, Fuchs disastrously brought in the aging, cranky Babe Ruth in 1935, and Fuchs was out the door not long after Ruth was.

For the start of the 1936 season, the team had a new man in charge (Bob Quinn) and a new nickname (the Bees), but the same problems (not enough talent or fans). It got so bad that the manager, Bill McKechnie, resigned in 1937 so he could become the manager of the last-place Cincinnati Reds. That same year, the Red Sox, who under Yawkey had been loading up on high-priced players from other teams, signed a kid outfielder from San Diego: Ted Williams.

The Braves' fortunes did improve, though slowly. Perini and others bought into the team in 1941; in 1944, he and two others became the majority stockholders, and the next year, Perini was named team president. And in 1946, the Braves became a winning team, at 81–72, their second-best record in 30 years. As luck would have it, though, while the Braves finally became a winning team, the Red Sox were becoming a championship team, capturing the 1946 American League pennant and outdrawing the Braves by nearly half a million fans.

Talent on the field was only one obstacle; as Charlie Bevis points out in *Red Sox vs. Braves: The Battle for Fans' Hearts, 1901–1952*, demographics were also a problem. Boston was one of five Major League cities with more than one team, but by 1940 it was the smallest of those cities and was also the second-smallest city in the American League.

Still, Perini thought his team could survive in Boston. He pushed hard for night baseball in 1946. That was a major success, especially as the

Five. March 18

Red Sox held out against night games until 1947. With a veteran lineup and a pitching staff anchored by the stars Warren Spahn and Johnny Sain, the '47 Braves improved again, to 86–68. Attendance continued to leap up, by nearly 32 percent. And 1948 was even better. After a nondescript start to the season—the Braves were a .500 team on June 5—they got hot, and the rest of the National League did not. The Braves, aided by the trade acquisitions of shortstop Al Dark and second baseman Eddie Stanky, slipped into first place for good on June 13 and went on to capture their first NL pennant since the Miracle Braves of 1914. Fans responded; the team set another attendance record, 1,455,439.

The outcome was excellent; the timing was not. A mile away, the Red Sox, a sixth-place afterthought in 1947, chased Cleveland for the American League pennant, losing out only in a one-game playoff. In the Braves' best attendance year ever, they still drew 100,000 fewer fans than the Red Sox. And that was the high-water mark. The Braves had a losing record in 1949 while the Red Sox chased the AL pennant until the last game of the season, suffering an excruciating loss to the Yankees. Braves attendance plummeted by nearly 400,000; Red Sox attendance inched up.

Bevis wrote that more of the fan base of the Braves had moved to the suburbs than had Red Sox fans, and they found it challenging to get to the ballpark for night games (the Braves had more of them). He also theorized that Red Sox fans were *Red Sox* fans, while Braves tended to be *baseball* fans who periodically went to Braves games. The advent of a heavy television schedule affected the Braves' attendance more than the Red Sox's attendance, he said.

Perini saw the signs and began to consider following the fans to the suburbs with a new ballpark, but Bevis noted that it made the best sense if the Red Sox shared the stadium. Yawkey declined, and the land became an industrial park.

In 1950, the Braves signed their first Black player, the Negro leagues star Sam Jethroe, who, at the age of 33 became the National League Rookie of the Year. (The Red Sox would not promote a Black player to the Major Leagues until 1959.) Bevis cites speculation that some of the Braves' attendance losses were a result of backlash to their signing Jethroe, with fans who had lived near the ballpark constituting part of Boston's "white flight."

The Braves certainly made missteps. They poached the Red Sox's radio broadcaster, Jim Britt, but the Red Sox replaced him in the booth with a voice who turned out to be even more popular, Curt Gowdy. In 1951, the Braves decided to ban the sale of beer in the stands—ostensibly because of complaints that women and children could not see the games while vendors were working the stands and beers were being passed down the aisles, Bevis wrote. That was as popular as you might imagine. Perini added promotional events that did not work but would become the sort of staples of ball games decades later. Televised baseball was not a problem, Bevis said; television was. He wrote that the Braves' drop in attendance at night games was in large part because fans were staying home to watch stars like Milton Berle and Arthur Godfrey on TV.

Attendance became disastrous. Opening Day at Braves Field in 1951 drew only 6,081 fans. But Perini talked publicly about baseball expanding, not his team moving. He suggested two 12-team leagues, adding four teams in California (from the Pacific Coast League, which was lobbying, not for the first or last time, to be regarded as a Major League). He also suggested Montreal and three teams from among a list of five: Baltimore, Houston, a third team in Chicago, a second team in Detroit ... and possibly in Milwaukee. That fall, the House Antitrust and Monopoly Subcommittee also raised the possibility of the Major Leagues expanding.

Opening Day 1952 was even worse—a "crowd" of 4,694—and the season got no better. The Braves drew only 281,278 fans and lost $459,000 according to a Congressional investigation, Lomax wrote. Yet Perini said he intended for the team to stay in Boston. That was what he said publicly. That October, Lomax wrote, Perini said at a staff meeting that the team would be moving to Milwaukee, but that it must be kept secret. It was.

Lomax wrote that Perini would have been viewed as a villain had he stopped a Major League team—the Browns—from moving to Milwaukee and saw an opportunity for himself and the Braves with a move there. But the Browns were certain they needed to move somewhere. They had been abysmal through almost all of their existence. They competed in only one pennant race over four decades, finishing second by a game in 1922, and by the end of the 1930s they averaged 105 losses a season over a three-year span. It's no wonder that the team considered a move to Los Angeles in 1941. When that fell through, the team's fortunes paradoxically improved in St. Louis during World War II—the Browns had three of their 12 winning seasons in St. Louis during the war, including their only pennant in 1944.

That success was a mirage, as was quickly made clear: The Browns skidded to seventh in 1946. Fans deserted, and the Browns were last in the American League in attendance every year from 1946 through 1953. The team signed Black players early on, in 1947 (but released them very quickly); sold off capable players to finance the operation; and brought in a new owner, the wheeler-dealer Bill Veeck, but nothing worked.

Veeck's promotional wizardry improved attendance in 1952 even as the team remained a steady loser. Veeck considered two possibilities for moving the Browns, according to an article for the Society for American Baseball Research by Dennis Pagot and Greg Erion—Milwaukee and Baltimore, both of which had stadiums suitable for a Major League team. Pagot and Erion wrote that Veeck talked with officials from the city of Baltimore in the summer of 1952 and the owner of the minor league Orioles that fall and thought he would be able to get league approval to move to Baltimore. (Veeck was also talking with Milwaukee during this time, ultimately being cut off by Lou Perini's maneuvering.) As Veeck wrote in *Veeck as in Wreck*, he was woefully naïve—what he at first thought would be a 6–2 vote in his favor for approval to move to Baltimore became a 6–2 vote against him.

Shut out of Milwaukee and prevented from moving to Baltimore for the 1953 season, Veeck tried again—and was once more rejected by the AL owners. He acknowledged that he was near bankruptcy. Pagot and Erion wrote that Baltimore investors, determined to get a team, came up with the money to buy out Veeck. The Browns ended the season on September 27 with, predictably, a loss—their 100th—and four days later, the American League approved the sale of the team to the Baltimore group. With that, a second Major League team was moving.

Soon there would be a third. *Veeck as in Wreck* reports that Roy Mack, son of the longtime Philadelphia Athletics owner/manager Connie Mack, told Veeck during his efforts to move to Baltimore: "I don't see why you want to leave St. Louis. We'd never leave Philadelphia." That was in early 1953. In November 1954, the Athletics, embroiled in family upheaval (Roy Mack was at odds with his father and brother Earle), were sold to Arnold Johnson, who moved the team to Kansas City. So much for "never."

That was the outcome, but the move almost did not happen, Robert D. Warrington wrote in SABR's Fall 2010 *Baseball Research Journal*. Roy Mack, with an option to buy Connie and Earle Mack's stock, had worked out a deal with Johnson, which AL owners approved in October 1953 in Chicago. Roy Mack then went back to Philadelphia and denied that he had an agreement with Johnson; he was still negotiating with investors who wanted to keep the team in Philadelphia, *The New York Times* reported. As Warrington wrote, "The Philadelphia syndicate fell apart quickly," having relied on the Macks to get league approval for their deal. *The New York Times*, in an Associated Press article, reported that the Philadelphia group made its own missteps. After Connie Mack, who was 91 and ailing, signed the final papers from his sickbed, his wife, Katherine Mack, told reporters from their apartment: "We said whoever got here first would be the buyer. Mr. Johnson got here at 9 o'clock, the Philadelphia group came at 10 a.m. The Philadelphia group dilly-dallied." Johnson and Kansas City, then, was the only realistic option for the Macks. The Athletics were, in fact, headed to Kansas City.

Just as with the Braves' and Browns' moves, others were putting their thumbs on the scale for the Athletics' shift. Both Veeck and Warrington wrote that the New York Yankees were pulling strings in the background to assure that Johnson acquired the team. Johnson and the Yankees were already in business together—he owned Yankee Stadium and Blues Stadium in Kansas City, where a Yankees farm team played. With the Yankees' quiet help to land the Athletics, Johnson became a willing, if unequal partner of the New York powerhouse. Between 1955 and 1960—Johnson's reign—Kansas City and New York made 16 trades involving 58 players, Warrington said, noting, "In most cases, the trades brought the Yankees prized prospects while leaving the Athletics with over-the-hill stars." As Jeff Zimmerman calculated it for *Baseball Almanac,* those trades provided 64 Wins Above Replacement for the Yankees, 36 for the Athletics.

That made the Athletics just another example of a team with fewer resources, less success and a drastic option: to move. The Braves, the Browns and the Athletics all had spotty histories of success and lackluster, at best, attendance. Given the dynamics of post–World War II baseball—a surge in attendance, followed by withering support—and opportunity that had not been possible in earlier decades, the Braves, the Browns and the Athletics felt shifting to a new city was not only a reasonable alternative, but the only reasonable alternative. In the three seasons before they left Boston, the Braves were seventh, eighth and eighth in the National League in attendance (they led the NL their first six seasons in Milwaukee). In their final eight seasons in St. Louis, the Browns were last in the American League in attendance (they were fifth in their first season in Baltimore, with the franchise's first season attendance of more than a million). The Athletics were last in the AL in attendance in their final year in Philadelphia—the Browns had become the Orioles—and were next to last the previous four seasons (they were second their first year in Kansas City).

The moves of the Dodgers and the Giants to California after the 1957 season have been well chronicled, but surely attendance was some factor. In 1957, the Dodgers, fresh from two consecutive pennants, were only fifth in the NL in attendance; after winning the pennant in 1954, the Giants were sixth, eighth and eighth as their fortunes on the field flagged.

Major League franchises have not been nearly as unsettled since. After five (of 16) teams changed cities from 1953 to 1958, only six moved in the following 66 years—although the Athletics, once again, have vowed to move, this time to Las Vegas.

Six

March 21

The Uniqueness of Spring

Baseball and spring are so intertwined that teams go to spring training even though most of it is actually in winter. The regular season starts in spring, when hope, yes, does spring eternal. Yet in the more than 150 years of professional baseball, there has been only one Spring in the Majors: Jack Spring.

Jack Russell Spring—his nickname should have been Terrier, right?—was a reliever in parts of eight seasons in the 1950s and '60s. He played for mostly mediocre teams and had a nondescript career: 155 games pitched (and only five starts), a 12–5 record and a 4.26 earned run average (92 ERA+) in 186 innings. He was an early situational reliever, a lefty of course, one of the first pitchers to finish a season pitching more games than innings.

Spring has a teeny claim to fame, however: He was part of the famous (or infamous if you are a Chicago Cubs fan) trade that sent Lou Brock to the St. Louis Cardinals in 1964. Brock, Spring and Paul Toth, a little-used (on merit) right-hander, were traded for two former 20-game winners (Ernie Broglio and Bobby Shantz) and a journeyman outfielder (Doug Clemens, who had almost as many games as a pinch-hitter, 209, as he did in the field, 266). Few people remember any of those involved except Brock and Broglio, but Spring would forever be linked to a Hall of Famer.

He was linked to all manner of well-known baseball figures. He played high school ball with Ed Bouchee, who became a pretty good first baseman in the National League, but was best known for pleading guilty to exposing himself to two very young girls. A minor league teammate in Miami in 1956 was Satchel Paige, who was closing in on 50 years old (and still went 11–4, 1.86 in 111 innings in Class AAA). After apparently finishing up his career in the minors, Spring was persuaded to pitch one more season by the manager of the Dodgers' Class AAA Spokane team: Tommy Lasorda. Spring later was a minor league manager, and one of his players

41

in Walla Walla was Kurt Russell, who played three minor league seasons and got only 17 plate appearances above short-season ball before becoming an actor. And in 2005, Spring was inducted into the Northwest Sports Hall of Fame with the longtime N.B.A. star John Stockton.

He kept some interesting company. And, appropriately for the only Major Leaguer named Spring, he was born in March. Not actually spring (March 11), but close enough for baseball. While Jack is the only Spring in Major League Baseball history, there have been one Springs (Jeffrey) and six Springers (George, Russ, Dennis, Steve, Brad and Ed), according to *Baseball Reference*. Not a single March or April to be found, but a bunch of guys named May.

SEVEN

April 1

Parades, Presidents and Opening Day

Opening Day in Cincinnati is special. Has been for close to a century and a half. Former Reds Manager Sparky Anderson once said: "It's a holiday—a baseball holiday! Ain't no other place in America got that." Anderson was renowned for hyperbole, but in this instance he was correct. Cincinnatians *have* treated Opening Day like a holiday, even if an unofficial one. In many ways it is Cincinnati's version of Patriots' Day for the Boston Red Sox, only with a parade instead of a marathon. And Boston has never had elephants show up for its special day. Cincinnati has.

Opening Day is part of the civic DNA in Cincinnati, something that just *is*. The Reds have had their opener scheduled for Cincinnati every year but one since the team was a charter member of the National League in 1876. (There have been a few years when Cincinnati did open on the road, however, because of rainouts and labor issues.) Intermittently in the 1950s and '60s and then through the 1970s and into the '80s, Cincinnati actually hosted Major League Baseball's Opening Day, being given a day's head start on the other teams. Cincinnati has lost that special status, though; Major League Baseball has even opened in other countries nine times since 1999.

Thomas Boswell wrote *Why Time Begins on Opening Day* in 1984, but it might be just as true to say: Why Time Stands Still on Opening Day. It's a day of tradition, bunting in the stands, old players returning, proclamations and city celebrations, even a parade if you live in Cincinnati, which has embraced Opening Day and its history like no other city. Opening Day 2024 has plenty in common with Opening Day 1924.

Local newspapers suggested that Cincinnati's longstanding first-among-equals status for Opening Day was because Cincinnati had the first (openly) professional team, in 1869, but that really wasn't the case, according to Reds historian Greg Rhodes. Opening Day came to Cincinnati because of weather and money.

Cincinnati and St. Louis were the southernmost cities in the National League (Washington and St. Louis were in the American League). Southern tended to matter; it was generally warmer in Cincinnati and St. Louis than in the league's Eastern cities, Boston, New York, and Philadelphia. There was also less chance of early-spring snow. Seasons opened later in April then—and never in March, as they can now—but April weather could still be an issue. And better weather made bigger crowds more likely, an important factor because visiting teams got a cut of the gate.

Attendance was where the money was in the pre-broadcast days, and Rhodes noted that Northern teams "were happy to go on the road, and give up the opener for more comfortable conditions"—and more revenue. (Southern climes did not always matter, however; in 1931, for example, the Yankees opened in New York before a crowd of 70,000 on an unseasonably warm Tuesday, while the Browns opened that day in even warmer weather in St. Louis to a crowd of 7,000 "that was not a bad crowd for the Browns," Steven P. Gietschier wrote in *Baseball: The Turbulent Midcentury Years*.)

Cincinnati did prove to be a lucrative host. The 1890 opener on April 19, for example, drew about 20,000 fans, *The Cincinnati Enquirer* reported. Attendance data for that era are sketchy, but for the 20 other Reds games for which *Baseball Reference* has data, only one other date in Cincinnati that season drew more than 2,600 fans—a July 4 doubleheader. By comparison, when the Philadelphia Phillies opened their season at home three days after the Reds did, they drew just under 9,000 fans, *Baseball Reference* says. (The discrepancy wasn't because the Reds were a superior team; they finished the season a game and a half behind the third-place Phillies.)

Good attendance was a Cincinnati staple from the start. For the Reds' 1876 opener, *The Cincinnati Enquirer* reported a crowd of more than 2,000—a big number for a young team in a new league in a still-developing sport with a roster full of players imported almost all from the semipro ranks.

The Enquirer's account of the game is a reminder of how different the times were. The article mentions gambling pools on games and makes a point that "the whole of the grand stand is reserved for ladies and their escorts and holders of season tickets. It is so inclosed that a lady is as free from insult as at a theater; and special cars are reserved for their use in the train." (The big transportation problem: The railroad charged passengers 25 cents instead of the advertised 15 for round-trip fares. There were many unhappy riders.)

The sense of possibility on Opening Day was apparent in that *Enquirer* report, too. It said that the young, untested Reds had been "looked upon as the weak one in the League" and that *The New York Clipper*, known for its sports coverage, "even took occasion to ignore it as much as possible.

Other papers sucking the teat of the famous sporting paper did the same even in this city." (That 1876 Opening Day was noted in much less celebratory fashion in *The Cincinnati Daily Star*, which devoted a mere 81 words and a linescore, under the headline "The Victorious Reds," to the game. It was one of three accounts of National League games from the day before, running under an item about a court case in which the defendant was accused of "fraudulently removing liquors.")

As the years progressed, so did Opening Day attendance for many years. In 1883, Cincinnati's second in the new American Association, its season opener on May 1 drew more than 5,000 for the defending champion Reds, *The Sporting Life* reported. Of the other three American Association games that day, only the host Baltimore Orioles' 4–3 victory over the New York Metropolitans drew as many; Allegheny City (Pittsburgh) drew 2,500 fans, and Columbus, Ohio, attracted 1,500.

In 1890, the American Association had folded and the Reds were back in the National League. And pulling in fans on Opening Day. They saw more than a game, an inkling of what was to come on future Cincinnati Opening Days. *The Cincinnati Evening Post* reported that the 1st Regiment Band led the teams onto the field, and friends of the Reds' Lefty Marr made it a point to give him a gold watch and chain and a bouquet before the game. (The left-handed Marr played 63 games at third base and three at shortstop that season. He is second on the list for career games played by a left-handed third baseman, *Baseball Reference* says, to the barehanded Hick Carpenter.)

The NL in 1890 consisted of nine teams, but it grew to an even more unwieldy 12 by the end of the decade. It contracted in 1900 to the eight teams in the same cities that would make up the league for more than half a century. Poor-performing teams, weakly financed teams—they were gone. But despite encouraging crowds on Opening Day—Cincinnati drew 12,000 for its 13–10 loss to the Chicago Orphans—attendance in the contracted league was soon lackluster. *The Sporting Life* reported:

> Despite the anticipation of augmented popular interest the opening crowds were no larger than usual, there was no extraordinary enthusiasm manifested, and the attendance has not been above average since the opening. The outlook, therefore, is for only an ordinary season, despite the extraordinary, though misguided, efforts of the magnates to restore the League to former prestige. Evidently the alienated public and press are not to be won back in an instant.

The outlook was even dimmer the next year, when the American League began play as a Major League and competitor. The Reds drew only 3,000 for their opener, played in near-freezing temperatures after bad weather forced a day's delay, against the eventual champion Pittsburgh Pirates.

A parade had long been part of Cincinnati's Opening Day, but after the dismal 1901 season (the Reds finished last), the team canceled the parade. But fans, the historian Greg Rhodes wrote, resurrected the parade themselves, with rooter groups—bands of people from a business or neighborhood or social club—riding through downtown Cincinnati on horse-drawn wagons. Eventually, some groups hired streetcars; then came cars.

And then in 1920, a group from Findlay Market—a public market first opened in the 1850s—joined the parade, celebrating the Reds' 1919 World Series championship, "and soon became the biggest and best organized of all the groups," Rhodes wrote. By the 1930s, the pregame event had become known as the Findlay Market Parade. It still is. No one will confuse it with the Rose Bowl Parade, Rhodes said, but "it is grass-roots Cincinnati at its finest: a red convertible and pickup truck brigade, with a few modest floats, high school marching bands, and more politicians than roses." And even in his glory years, a Rose.

The Washington Senators opened their season at home almost as frequently as the Reds did (and sometimes got to open the Major League season by a day), and with their own level of pomp. In Cincinnati, an elephant once handed Sparky Anderson the ball to throw out as the ceremonial first pitch; in Washington, it was presidents who threw out the ball.

The Senators became interested in a presidential first pitch while they were still a struggling National League team in the 1890s. (As an NL team, the Senators never came close to a winning record in that decade.) In 1897, President William McKinley invited the Senators to the White House and offered to throw out a ceremonial pitch at their opener. The Senators' manager was Gus Schmelz, who had managed the minor league team in Columbus, Ohio, several years earlier when McKinley, as the Ohio governor, threw out the first pitch. As a promotional idea, McKinley's offer was a gift for the Senators, who had finished seventh in the 12-team NL in attendance the year before—by far their best showing at the gate. To accommodate McKinley, a presidential box, complete with flags and bunting, was built for the April 17 season opener against the Brooklyn Grooms. It was to be quite an event in Washington; more than 100 of the 357 congressmen showed up. But McKinley did not.

McKinley's successor, Theodore Roosevelt did not either. He liked boxing and lacrosse and football and polo, but he "detested baseball," wrote John Thorn, baseball's official historian. "Father and all of us regarded baseball as a mollycoddle game," Roosevelt's daughter, Alice Roosevelt Longworth, said, according to Thorn.

William Howard Taft had no such reservations. He was a 300-pounder in the White House, but he is said to have played second base when he was younger. His brother Charles was a co-owner of the Chicago Cubs and the Philadelphia Phillies (curiously, and contrary to league rules, at the same time). By now, the Senators, having been contracted out of the NL after the 1899 season, were in the American League, but they were no more successful on the field or at the gate. This was a team that Clark Griffith, its owner and manager, knew could use a boost at the box office. "Griffith hoped to permanently fix the presidential seal of approval on baseball as the national pastime once and for all," *Baseball Almanac* wrote in 2003. And on April 14 in 1910, Opening Day, Taft accommodated Griffith and threw out the first pitch, from his own specially constructed box before a crowd that was announced officially as 12,021 but that was more like 15,000, according to newspaper reports, with overflow fans being stashed on the outfield grass.

Plans for the ceremonial pitch went through several permutations. Taft was originally going to throw the ball from his box to Walter Johnson, the Senators' Opening Day pitcher. The unassuming Johnson declined the honor, so Taft was to throw the ball to catcher Gabby Street. Instead, he pivoted and made his pitch to Johnson, near the pitcher's box, after all. "Mr. Taft shot a nice, white shining sphere straight as a die into Walter Johnson's hands," *The Washington Herald* said. *The Washington Post* reported that Taft "opened the season with a true presidential flourish. He did it with his good, trusty right arm and the virgin sphere scudded across the diamond as true as a die to the pitcher's box, where Walter Johnson, also the possessor of a good trusty right arm, gathered it in and started winding up for one of his rifle shots across the plate."

The ball was taken to the White House by a friend of Johnson, *The Washington Evening Star* reported, and the next day, Johnson wrote the president asking if he would autograph it. Request granted. "I am pretty short of cash right now, as the club doesn't start paying salaries until the first of the month," Johnson said in *The Evening Star*, "but one hundred dollars wouldn't buy that ball from me." (Pause for a moment: The opener was on April 14, and the Senators would play 14 games that month—but the players weren't paid until May 1.)

The Washington Herald had a breath-taking succession of headlines on its account: THOUSANDS SEE OPENING GAME AND VICTORY/Demonstrations Unequaled in History of Fandom in Capital City/PRESIDENT TAFT TOSSES FIRST BALL/Grand Principle of the Equality of Men Demonstrated in the Mixture of Statesmen, Millionaires, and Social Favorites with the Humble Citizen and Ne'er-do-well

That overlooked the fact that Johnson nearly pitched a no-hitter in a 3–0 victory over the Philadelphia Athletics. The one hit was a fluke. In the seventh inning, the Athletics' Home Run Baker lofted a long fly to right field toward Doc Gessler. Gessler collided with a fan who was in the auxiliary seating on the field because of the overflow crowd. *The Herald* said Gessler "stumbled into a spectator sitting on the ground reading a newspaper. Gessler turned a half-somersault, and the ball landed within two feet of him, costing Johnson a chance to hang his picture in the Hall of Fame" (although the actual Hall of Fame did not exist until 1939). *The Post* said Gessler tracked it easily, but "stumbled over a boy sitting on the edge of the crowd." And *The Evening Star* said "Gessler made a valiant effort to capture a long, high fly off Baker's bat—and he would have succeeded, even though he was forced to rush through the wall of spectators in deep right field, if one of said onlookers had not scrambled directly into his path so that the two tumbled to earth together, and the ball fell safely." Well, Gessler ran into someone somehow and didn't make the catch.

But the presidential appearance on Opening Day had been a hit for everyone (especially for Griffith; it was the Senators' biggest crowd of the year, by far), and a tradition was born. Taft returned for Opening Day the next year, and the Senators drew, unofficially, a crowd of 20,000 that saw Taft toss "the hide-bound sphere into the diamond," *The Evening Star* said. Taft missed Opening Day in 1912—the *Titanic*, with a good friend aboard, had sunk only five days earlier, and Vice President James Sherman did the honors—but in 1913, it was back to presidential pitching: Woodrow Wilson made the Opening Day toss.

And so it went, through the Senators' years until they moved to Minnesota in 1961 and then for the 11 seasons of the second version of the Senators before they decamped to Texas in 1972. Presidents missed some years—official duties, war and all—but frequently attended Opening Day. Franklin D. Roosevelt threw out the ceremonial first pitch eight times before World War II intervened; Harry Truman and Dwight Eisenhower did so seven times. A few presidents wore a baseball glove; a few had terrible form.

Which was appropriate, as the Senators were generally bad. The original Senators had 41 losing records in their 60 seasons in Washington. The expansion Senators had one winning season out of 11. Since the Montreal Expos moved to Washington to become the Nationals, they have been better, if not consistently good: eight winning records in 19 seasons. And they are still opening the season at home.

Eight

April 15

Jackie Robinson Opens the Door. Quietly.

A total of 180 players saw action on April 15, 1947, as all 16 Major League teams opened the season. But the one we remember playing was a 28-year-old, one of 29 rookies who saw action on Opening Day, playing first base for the first time as a professional. Jackie Robinson, of course.

The 1947 Brooklyn Dodgers infield included, from left, Spider (Jorgensen), Pee Wee (Reese), The Brat (Eddie Stanky) and a rookie named Jackie (Robinson) (National Baseball Hall of Fame, Cooperstown, NY).

It was a big deal—the first African American player in a Major League game since the 1880s—but if you weren't paying close attention, you might not have known it. Robinson's Brooklyn Dodgers opened at home with a 5–3 victory over the Boston Braves at Ebbets Field, but the crowd was the second smallest of the eight Major League games that day; only the St. Louis Browns drew worse. *The Brooklyn Eagle* had two photos of Robinson with the game story on its first sports page, but Robinson was not mentioned until the story's ninth paragraph, and there was nothing in it to note the momentousness of the game. The *Eagle* columnist Tommy Holmes did make note, in the eighth paragraph of his April 16 column: "This was a historic occasion. For the first time ever, an acknowledged Negro played in a major league championship game." Holmes overlooked Fleet Walker's 42-game career back in 1884, but he did allude to the efforts to slide players past baseball's color barrier over the decades.

In *The New York Times,* the game story had a reference to Robinson's sacrifice bunt in the sixth paragraph. The historic moment? Nothing. *The Times*'s Pulitzer Prize–winning columnist, Arthur Daley, focused on Leo Durocher, the Dodgers manager who was suspended for the season. He got to Robinson about two-thirds of the way through his column and never specified what made Robinson's "quite uneventful" debut significant. Three-quarters of a century later, the language can be cringe-worthy, but it was a different time. "The muscular Negro minds his own business and shrewdly makes no effort to push himself," Daley wrote. "He speaks quietly and intelligently when spoken to and already has made a strong impression."

Daley did mine the clubhouse for thoughts on Robinson, quoting an unnamed "veteran Dodger": "Having Jackie on the team is still a little strange, just like anything else that's new. We just don't know how to act with him. But he'll be accepted in time. You can be sure of that. Other sports have had Negroes. Why not baseball? I'm for him, if he can win games. That's the only test I ask."

Oscar Fraley of *United Press* did make Robinson and the moment the lead of his game story, which ran nationwide. He called him "the first Negro to reach baseball's big top" in his second paragraph, again missing the mark a bit. (*The Associated Press* did correctly note in Joe Reichler's account that Robinson was the first Black player since 1884, although he had surveyed the debuts of four other rookies—Clint Hartung of the New York Giants, Sam Mele of the Boston Red Sox, Frank Baumholtz of the Cincinnati Reds, and Vic Wertz of the Detroit Tigers—before he came to Robinson.)

We remember that game because of Robinson, but 32 other players were involved (14 of them, including Robinson, were born in the South). Here's a look at the Braves and the Dodgers who played a small part in history. The players are in order of the day's lineup, with substitutes.

Boston Braves

Dick Culler, shortstop, 32, High Point, North Carolina. Culler was a prototypical good-field, no-hit shortstop whose career was mainly in World War II. He had no power—two home runs and 47 extra-base hits in 1,729 plate appearances—and finished with a .281 slugging percentage. As slick a fielder as he was, he was not even close to being the best shortstop from High Point. That was the Hall of Famer Luke Appling.

Tommy Holmes, pinch-hitter, 30, Brooklyn. Holmes could hit. In his five years in the minor leagues with the Yankees' organization, his worst batting average was .302. He was blocked by Joe DiMaggio and Charlie Keller in New York, but a trade to the Braves gave him an opportunity, and he made the most of it. He was one of the Braves' best hitters for almost a decade (including World War II; a sinus condition made him 4-F), and he had a 37-game hitting streak in 1945 that was the National League record until Pete Rose broke it. Still, Holmes, a left-handed, line-drive hitter, did not start this game because the Dodgers started a left-hander.

Sibby Sisti, shortstop, 27, Buffalo, New York. Sisti was called Sibby because his given name was Sebastian. Sibby played the infield at times with Nanny Fernandez (given name: Frolian) and Connie Ryan (Cornelius). Sibby, Nanny and Connie should be a song.

Johnny Hopp, center fielder, 30, Hastings, Nebraska. Hopp was sometimes called Cotney—his middle name—according to *Baseball Reference*. It was his brother Harry, who went on to play in the NFL, who was first nicknamed Hippity, although the papers later used that for Johnny, too. Hopp was a .296 hitter with some speed who lasted 14 seasons in part because he could pinch-hit: 221 plate appearances as a pinch-hitter, batting .262 with a .364 on-base percentage and more walks (29) than strikeouts (23).

Mike McCormick, right fielder, 29, Angel's Camp, California. Myron Winthrop McCormick—no wonder he wanted to be called Mike—came up hitting. He batted .300 and .287 in his first two seasons, 1940 and '41, and rarely struck out, although he walked even more rarely and hit for little power. He stopped hitting, though, and then lost two-plus years to the war. When he came back, he still wasn't hitting and was really a below-replacement-level player. In 1947, his bat came back to life, and McCormick had two pretty good seasons. It did not last, however, and he played for five teams in his final five seasons. He *was*, head-scratchingly, named to the Cincinnati Reds' Hall of Fame—a first baseman who hit six homers in 287 games for the Reds.

Bob Elliott, third baseman, 30, San Francisco. This Braves team had a lot of players who played through World War II, and Elliott was one of them. The best of them, in fact, although he spent those seasons with the Pirates. His career seems oddly shaped, but much of that is no doubt a result of his move from Forbes Field to Braves Field in 1947. His batting average remained the same (.292 as a Pirate, .295 as a Brave), but instead of hitting quite a few triples and very few home runs while spacious Forbes Field was his home, with Boston he quickly began hitting homers; Braves Field was only 355 feet to left-center field. Elliott hit as many as 10 homers only once in eight seasons with Pittsburgh, then hit 22, 23, 17, 24 and 15 in his five seasons with Boston. His on-base percentage went up 35 points and his slugging percentage 66 points. His career looks quite a bit like Paul O'Neill's (with a little less power), down to the changes that came with a move to a new, more favorable ballpark.

Danny Litwhiler, left fielder, 30, Ringtown, Pennsylvania. Litwhiler was always a good hitter, and he played 11 seasons in the Majors. But that was basically background noise for what he did in baseball. He was the coach for 19 years at Michigan State University, where he coached Steve Garvey and Kirk Gibson. He is credited with around 100 baseball inventions, including the radar gun, Diamond Grit (the absorbent stuff spread on infield dirt after it rains) and the bunting bat (a half-bat designed to force proper bunting technique), according to his SABR *Bio Project* profile. He had a hand in getting baseball into the Olympics. He was the hitting coach for the Reds, working with every Cincinnati hitter who started in the 1990 World Series. And he was the seventh son of a seventh son.

Bama Rowell, left fielder, 31, Citronelle, Alabama. Yes, Carvel William Rowell was born in Alabama. If you have seen *The Natural*, you actually know a little something about Rowell. On May 30, 1946, he hit a drive in Ebbets Field that smashed the Bulova clock in right field, sending shards of glass everywhere; an hour later, the clock stopped working. It's a scene Bernard Malamud apparently cribbed when he wrote *The Natural* and which Robert Redford sort of recreated in the movie (only he hit the lights). Bulova had promised a free timepiece to any player who hit the sign, but Rowell never got a watch. He also did not get a home run. The ball was still considered in play when it bounced back on the field, so all he got was a long double.

Earl Torgeson, first baseman, 23 Snohomish, Washington. Torgeson was a rookie in 1947, and what a player it looked as if he would be. A rangy, 6-foot-3 first baseman, he batted .281/.403/.481, with 20 doubles, 6 triples and 16 home runs in 487 plate appearances. He walked 82 times. He stole 11 bases. He played until 1961, but Torgeson matched that kind of season only once, in 1950. He became renowned for his willingness to scrap—with opponents, with teammates. He was the rare player who wore glasses on the field, and he figured out he should take his glasses off before getting into a fight during a game. He was from Snohomish, which was also the home of the Hall of Famer Earl Averill. The writers called both of them the Earl of Snohomish.

Phil Masi, catcher, 31, Chicago. Masi was involved in a controversial play in the 1948 World Series. He was leading off second base in Game 1 when the Cleveland Indians' Bob Feller picked him off. Pictures in the papers the next day clearly showed Masi was out. But the umpire called him safe, Tommy Holmes singled him in, and that was the only run as the Braves defeated Feller, 1–0. Feller never did win a World Series game.

Connie Ryan, second baseman, 27, New Orleans. What happened to Connie Ryan in 1951? Eight seasons into his Major League career, he had hit 23 home runs. By then he was playing for the Reds, and suddenly he hit 16 homers. The next year, after being traded to the Phillies, he hit 12 more. That was half of his career home runs in two seasons. He did have another home run connection, though: He was the Braves' third-base coach in 1974 and was the first person to shake Henry Aaron's hand after he hit his record-setting 715th home run, as Aaron rounded third.

Johnny Sain, pitcher, 29, Havana, Arkansas. Almost everyone who remembers Sain also remembers the poem about the Braves' 1948 pennant run: "It's Spahn and Sain, and pray for rain." What the sportswriter Gerald Hern actually wrote was: "First we'll use Spain / then we'll use Sain / then an off day / followed by rain / Back will come Spahn / followed by Sain / And followed we hope / by two days of rain." Which was poetic license, but not much; some early–September rainouts did allow Spahn and Sain to pitch more while the pennant was still in doubt. As it was, Sain started eight of the Braves' final 21 games and Spahn started seven of the last 22. At one point, they started four games in a row (that's where the rain postponements came in). Sain was spectacular, going 8–1. Spahn won his first four starts in the push to the pennant but lost his last three. Sain wound up pitching a career-high 314 2/3 innings. After going 24-15 with a 2.60 ERA (149 ERA+), it was four years before he had another good season, and by then he was a part-time starter with the New York Yankees. He was one of the best pitchers in baseball from 1946 to 1948, 65–41 with a 2.77 ERA—but then became generally average and was done at age 37.

Spahn pitched a more manageable 257 innings in '48 and shouldered a remarkably heavy workload, with great success, until he was 42. He didn't stop pitching till he was 44. Sain was a pitching coach at 41, and if you want to see just how successful—and iconoclastic—he was, re-read *Ball Four*.

Mort Cooper, pitcher, 34, Atherton, Missouri. Cooper wasn't even the best player in his household; his brother Walker was a standout catcher. But Mort was a pretty good pitcher who became a star during World War II.

He went 22–7, 1.78 ERA; 21–8, 2.30; and 22–7, 2.46 from 1942 to 1944 as the Cardinals won three consecutive pennants. Arm injuries, persistent drinking and loutish behavior caught up with him (his SABR *Bio Project* biography is sort of a horror show).

Tommy Neill, pinch-hitter, 27, Hartselle, Alabama. Neill managed only 61 plate appearances in the Majors over two seasons, and this game provided one of his 12 in 1947. He was hit by a pitch. He was back in the minors four weeks later. For good. He did play nearly 2,000 minor league games, with 2,163 hits. Sounds as if he was a Quad-A player of his era.

Walt Lanfranconi, pitcher, 30, Barre, Vermont. Only 38 players from Vermont have played in the Major Leagues, and only six of them have played since integration. The best? Carlton Fisk, of course. If you are familiar with the second best, you are a more knowledgeable fan than I am: Ray Collins, a pitcher who accumulated 25.6 WAR from 1909 to 1915 with the Boston Red Sox. Lanfranconi would rank, well, in the top 38 Vermonters. He threw only 70 Major League innings—six with the Cubs in 1941, then 64 with the Braves in 1947. He was 0 for 11 as a Major League hitter, but he had a remarkable 20 assists in his 64 innings for the Braves.

Brooklyn Dodgers

Eddie Stanky, second baseman, 31, Philadelphia. Stanky hit .243 as a high school senior. That's right, .243. Somehow he managed to find his way into professional baseball and then hacked out a productive 11-year Major League playing career. He never hit much in the Majors, either—a .268 average with 29 career homers (14 of them in one fluky season, in which he helped the Giants win the pennant, the Giants win the pennant, the Giants win the pennant). But he was continually drawing walks, leading the league three times, and played good defense and was so annoyingly scrappy they called him the Brat. Every decade after he quit playing, he would get a chance to manage, but it never ended well. No more so than his last job, with the Texas Rangers, where he got the position in midseason and quit after one game. (They won.) But he was a huge success as a coach at the University of South Alabama, sending 23 players to the Major Leagues.

Jackie Robinson, first baseman, 28, Cairo, Georgia. The Dodgers' infield was Spider, Pee Wee, the Brat … and Jackie. He had played first base only a few games that spring, as there were no openings for the positions he was familiar with. He was replaced for defensive purposes in the ninth inning by Howie Schultz (who, like Robinson, had an excellent basketball pedigree). Robinson went 0 for 3 with a sacrifice bunt—in his first at-bat—but bigger things were coming.

Howie Schultz, first baseman, 24, St. Paul, Minnesota. He was 6 feet 6 inches tall, so of course he was called Stretch. He nearly kept Robinson off the roster until the Dodgers decided to sign Jackie to a Major League contract shortly before the season began. After replacing Robinson on Opening Day, Schultz sat on the bench until May 9, when he pinch-hit and grounded into a double play. His Dodgers career was over, as Brooklyn sold him to the Phillies, whose manager, Ben Chapman, was perhaps the biggest antagonist Robinson faced on the field. "He was still fighting the Civil War," Schultz said. The next season, he hit .153 after missing spring training. "I couldn't hit a balloon," he said. His baseball career was done, but his career as a professional athlete was not; he played four seasons in the nascent NBA—with the Anderson Packers, the Fort Wayne Pistons and the Minneapolis Lakers.

Pete Reiser, center fielder, 28, St. Louis. Look at Reiser's first full season in the Majors, 1941, at age 22. He led the league in runs (117), doubles (39), triples (17), batting average (.343), slugging percentage (.558) and total bases (299), with above-average defense. He also slugged 14 home runs. Unfortunately, he began leading the league in concussions, as he kept running into unpadded outfield walls. (And yet even his own team was slow to pad the concrete wall.) He was not quite as superlative in 1942, but he was damn good—.310/.375/.463, with 33 doubles, 5 triples and 10 home runs while stealing 20 bases in 21 attempts. But his 125 games were the most he would play in a season the rest of his career. He lost three seasons to World War II and lots of playing time to injuries. In a parallel universe, he might have been a Hall of Famer.

Dixie Walker, right fielder, 36, Villa Rica, Georgia. Some fun facts about a teammate who made it clear to Dodgers management that he did not want to play alongside Robinson. He had almost the same number of runs scored (1,038) as driven in (1,023). He led the league in hitting at age 33 (.357) and RBIs at age 34 (124). He came up with the Yankees (pretty ironic, given how Southern he was) in 1931, but it was tough to break into an outfield with Babe Ruth, Earle Combs and Ben Chapman (a very good hitter before he showed he was a very bad man).

Tommy Tatum, pinch-runner/right fielder, 27, Decatur, Texas. Perhaps the most memorable exploit in the field of play in Tommy Tatum's 81-game Major League career was hitting a run-scoring double in his first at-bat. But his most memorable on a baseball diamond was memorialized in a newspaper photo. In the Dodgers' game against the Giants on April 18, 1947, Tatum was batting third in the lineup behind Robinson. When Robinson homered in the third inning, Tatum was at the plate to greet him. He reached out to shake Robinson's hand, and a photo of that moment was displayed the next day on the back page of *The New York Daily News*:

An image of a Black man and a white man from Texas shaking hands in public. Tatum acknowledged some initial hesitation about Robinson when they played the year before in Montreal, but he grew to admire Robinson's intellect. "He was a lot smarter than me," Tatum said in *Baseball's Great Experiment: Jackie Robinson and His Legacy*. "Hell, I had a high school education. He was a lot smarter than me as far as common sense and learning books." Coincidentally, exactly a year earlier a remarkably similar photo was taken when Robinson homered for the Montreal Royals and George Shuba shook his hand at the plate. Small moments for racial comity.

Arky Vaughan, pinch-hitter, 35, Clifty, Arkansas. Honus Wagner has the best career batting average for a shortstop, but who's second? Arky Vaughan (.318). Which shortstop has the best lifetime on-base percentage? Arky Vaughan (.406). In 1935, he led the National League in batting average (.385), OBP (.491), slugging percentage (.607), OPS (1.098) and OPS+ (190) and wins above replacement (9.8). When he wrote his *New Historical Baseball Abstract*, published in 2001, Bill James said that "was the best season ever by a Major League shortstop, other than Honus Wagner." James also rated Vaughan then as second overall only to Wagner, although the timing eliminates consideration of the great shortstops of the past two decades. His feud with Dodgers Manager Leo Durocher led Vaughan to leave the game for three-plus seasons, but Robinson had good things to say about him. Vaughan, he said, as told by Joe Posnanski in *The Baseball 100*, "was one of the fellows who went out of his way to be nice to me when I was a rookie. Believe me, I needed it."

Carl Furillo, right fielder, 25, Stony Creek Mills, Pennsylvania. Furillo and Rocky Colavito were slow, right-handed, hard-hitting right fielders of Italian descent who were renowned for their throwing arms. In the eighth inning of a game in 1951, Furillo fielded a sharp line drive by pitcher Mel Queen and threw him out at first base, preserving, for the moment, Ralph Branca's no-hitter. Colavito once threw a ball 440 feet at the minor league ballpark in San Diego as part of a publicity stunt, *The Washington Post* said. Furillo, who was 11 years older, grew up in Reading, Pennsylvania; Colavito played on a minor league team in Reading and retired there. Furillo was the one who hit for average (a single hit shy of a career .300 average), while Colavito hit for power (Furillo had 192 career home runs; Colavito had 193—at home).

Bruce Edwards, catcher, 23, Quincy, Illinois. Edwards had the best season of his life in '47. He played 130 games and hit .295/.364/.418. He drove in 80 runs. He was an All-Star and was fourth in the MVP voting for a pennant-winning team. And then Roy Campanella came along. Backup city.

Marv Rackley, pinch-runner, 25, Seneca, South Carolina. It's not the career you were hoping for when you pinch-hit in 48 games and pinch-run in 21 and you play only 105. In spring training in 1946, Manager Leo Durocher said of Rackley, "He looks like another Paul Waner." He was so fast, he once stole 65 bases in the minors and was called Rabbit. He was not another Waner, though, despite hitting .317 in his 519 plate appearances. He hit one homer. He was caught stealing on half of his 20 attempts. In an organization stacked with outfielders, he was in the wrong place at the wrong time. Wrong era, really; he might have flourished in the Deadball Era or been Matty Alou 20 years later.

Bobby Bragan, catcher, 29, Birmingham, Alabama. Bragan was one of five players who were vocal in their opposition to playing with Robinson, and he demanded a trade, as Jules Tygiel wrote in *Baseball's Great Experiment*. He was not dealing from a position of strength. Bragan had had ordinary success in his first four years in the bigs, playing his way into a part-time role, but then missed the 1945 and '46 seasons in the service. Branch Rickey refused to trade him, and Bragan remained in Brooklyn as a terrible-hitting backup (.188 in 48 at-bats over two seasons). Bragan later said his time playing with Robinson changed his outlook on African Americans. He managed three Major League teams and was not well liked. In his second job, with Cleveland, he was fired after three months; the general manager, Frank Lane, told him, "I don't know how we'll get along without you, Bobby, but starting tomorrow we're going to try." But he was credited with converting Maury Wills into a switch-hitter in Class AAA and persuading Phil Niekro to stick with his knuckleball.

Spider Jorgensen, third baseman, 27, Folsom, California. There was another rookie in the Dodgers' lineup this day: John Donald Jorgensen, nicknamed Spider by a teacher, according to his SABR *Bio Project* biography. (Jorgensen's shorts, black with an orange stripe, reminded the teacher of a black widow spider.) He went one for three with an RBI, but perhaps a more memorable game came two days later when he drove in six runs and homered. He had a capable rookie season—.274/.360/.410, 102 OPS+—as the Dodgers won the pennant. He actually hit better the next season, but he spent most of it in Class AAA, and his career was unraveling. In 261 plate appearances over three seasons, he batted .237 with three home runs.

Pee Wee Reese, shortstop, 28, Ekron, Kentucky. His numbers do not overwhelm you, but he was an All-Star nine years in a row and earned MVP votes 11 years in a row, including at age 37. He had surprising power (126 home runs) and could run—in one six-year stretch he stole 140 bases, at an 80 percent success rate. He had 25.6 defensive WAR. He really could play.

Joe Hatten, pitcher, 30, Bancroft, Iowa. By age 29, Hatten had not pitched much professionally, a result of the war and middling success in the minors. But he made the Dodgers in 1946, even with the veterans back, and went 14–11, 2.84. He earned the Jackie Robinson Day start and was relieved in the seventh, but he was a steady pitcher all season, finishing 17–8, 3.63. He had one more successful season (13–10, 3.85) before that success began to evaporate. But he never stopped pitching; Hatten finished up his career with nine seasons in Class AAA. He pitched until he was 43, in 1960. He was one of the last players in this game to still be playing professionally at that age.

Ed Stevens, pinch-hitter, 22, Galveston, Texas. Like Howie Schultz, Stevens found that being a backup to Jackie Robinson was not a path to success. He pinch-hit on Opening Day—he struck out—and played in only four more games for the Dodgers before being sent to Class AAA Montreal. There he crushed it, hitting .290/.404/.533 with 27 home runs in 133 games. All that earned him was a ticket to Pittsburgh, which in those years was similar to a Class AAA team. "I had no animosity towards Jackie; Branch Rickey was my object of anger," he wrote in his memoir, *"Big" Ed Stevens: The Other Side of the Jackie Robinson Story*, adding, "I'm proud of Jackie, but I still wish we could have truly competed for that spot." He later became a scout and was dead certain about a kid named Nolan Ryan—he was so skinny, Stevens told Jim Kreuz of SABR, that he would surely blow his arm out.

Hal Gregg, pitcher, 25, Anaheim, California. Gregg did not really play baseball until he was 18, but his brother persuaded him to attend a Dodgers baseball school in Long Beach, California. He was signed by a well-known scout, Ted McGrew. Gregg developed into a hard-throwing right-hander with little control—he led the National League in walks (137), hit batters (9) and wild pitches (10) in 1944 and the next year in walks again (120). He was 18–13, 3.47 in 1945, but his career fizzled afterward because of arm and back injuries. But he picked up the win in this game with two and a third innings of shutout relief.

Hugh Casey, pitcher, 34, Atlanta. Not many players are remembered most of all for one pitch. Maybe Tom Zachary for giving up Babe Ruth's 60th home run in 1927. Maybe Al Downing for allowing Henry Aaron's 715th homer in 1974. Maybe Bob Stanley for his wild pitch in the 1986 World Series. Then there is Hugh Casey, who is remembered for throwing a swinging third strike with a one-run lead and two out in the top of the ninth of a pivotal World Series game. And he lost the game. It was Game 4 of the 1941 Series, which Brooklyn trailed, two games to one, and the Dodgers had taken a 4–3 lead in the eighth.

Casey, a fearsome relief pitcher (and fearsome drinkin' man), got two strikes on Tommy Henrich with two out and no one on base. His next pitch fooled Henrich—he swung and missed badly—but it also fooled catcher

Mickey Owen, and Henrich made it safely to first base. It has long been speculated that Casey's pitch was a spitter (the same speculation exists around a famous wild pitch by Jack Chesbro in 1904), although Casey denied it. Whatever the pitch, the Yankees rallied: a single, two walks, two doubles, four runs. The Yankees won, 7–4, taking a three-games-to-one lead in the Series, which they went on to win the next day. It was the beginning of Dodger futility in the postseason against the Yankees; they lost again in 1947, 1949, 1952 and 1953 before breaking through in '55.

A more entertaining story involves a fight between Ernest Hemingway (the aggressor) and Casey in Havana in 1942, as the Dodgers announcer Red Barber recounted in *The New York Times* in 1976. The 1947 season was Casey's last good one—10–4, 18 saves—and his career ended, very unsatisfactorily and, with some irony, with the Yankees in 1950. His life was packed with turmoil after that. He was sued for child support and had tax liens placed on his bar. He threatened suicide, and, with a friend and his wife standing within 30 feet, killed himself with a shotgun, as detailed in *Hugh Casey: The Triumphs and Tragedies of a Brooklyn Dodger*. According to his wife, his final words, referring to the paternity suit, were "I am innocent of those charges."

NINE

April 15
Deep in the Heart of Dixies

April 15 is the anniversary of the first game Jackie Robinson played in the Major Leagues, an unforgettable milestone in baseball and racial dynamics in the United States. This chapter, however, is more about the opposite—a look at the 12 men called Dixie who played in the Majors.

Fred (Dixie) Walker, Villa Rica, Georgia, outfielder, 1931–49. Walker will forever be tied to Jackie Robinson in baseball history. He had had a lengthy but undistinguished career in the Major Leagues when he was sent to the Brooklyn Dodgers in 1939. The Dodgers acquired him on waivers from the Detroit Tigers, and he did not show that it was a particularly beneficial deal the rest of that season. But beginning in 1940, he became a real hitter with the Dodgers. His OPS+ over his years in Brooklyn was 111, 132, 126, 122, 172, 128, 137, 121. He won a batting title and led the league in RBIs once. Yes, this included the war years, but he hit even after the soldiers came home.

Including 1947, the year Robinson came to the Major Leagues. Walker was among several Dodgers who made it clear in spring training that they did not want to play with a Black teammate. Walker went so far as to write Branch Rickey, the general manager, a letter saying he wanted to be traded. He told Rickey that he thought his hardware store in Alabama would lose business if he were perceived as accommodating integration. Rickey demurred on a trade, not wanting to lose one of his best hitters and a player so popular in Brooklyn that the fans called him The People's Cherce. (Ah, Brooklynese.) So Walker and Robinson coexisted for the season. Afterward, however, Rickey did decide to move on from Walker; according to his SABR *Bio Project* biography, Walker was offered a chance to manage a Class AAA team of the Dodgers or be sent to the lowly Pittsburgh Pirates. He wanted to keep playing, so he went to Pittsburgh. Robinson had clearly won that battle, even if he had not yet won over all his teammates.

Walker played two seasons in Pittsburgh and then became the player-manager of the Atlanta Crackers. Yes, the Crackers. He stayed in the game for years as a minor league manager and Major League coach and was effectively rehabilitated by being named the Dodgers' hitting coach in 1969, a job he held until 1974. Walter O'Malley, the Dodgers' owner after forcing out Rickey, named Walker to his personal all-time Dodgers outfield. Robinson said in 1947, "No matter what you have heard, Dixie has been fine to me," according to *Dixie Walker: A Life in Baseball* by Lyle Spatz. For his part, Walker later called his opposition to playing with Robinson "the dumbest thing I did in all my life," Spatz wrote.

Ewart Gladstone (Dixie) Walker, Brownsville, Pennsylvania, pitcher, 1909–12. He was the father of the other Dixie Walker and Harry (the Hat) Walker, two Walkers who had strained relationships in their baseball careers. (Read about the Hat in *Ball Four*. His players really did not like him.) Curiously, the elder Walker—whose brother Ernie was also a big-leaguer—was not born in the South, but in Brownsville, Pennsylvania, in 1888. Still, his *Associated Press* obituary called him "one of the first Alabama players to make the majors," and Ewart did die in Leeds, Alabama (home of Charles Barkley). Walker was a teammate, and roommate, of Walter Johnson during his four seasons in the Majors, and he had a seven-year career in the minors. His Major League debut was promising—a complete-game victory with no earned runs—but he pitched his way out of the Majors by age 24.

Millard (Dixie) Howell, Harold, Kentucky, pitcher, 1940–58. Homer (Dixie) Howell, Louisville, Kentucky, catcher, 1947–56. Not only were there two Dixie Howells who played in the Major Leagues, but they were also both from Kentucky. And their careers essentially overlapped. One was a pitcher who was a better hitter than the Dixie Howell who was a catcher. They were even teammates briefly in 1949 with the Reds, and to confuse sportswriters and copy editors everywhere, Howell pitched to Howell in four games for Cincinnati. The potential for confusion eased when the New York Giants purchased pitcher Howell's contract in 1950.

Pitcher Howell slipped into three games for the Cleveland Indians in 1940 but returned to the minors and stayed there, year after year, until 1949. He then pitched for six more seasons in the minors before the White Sox called him up in midseason in 1955. He had three reasonably successful years in Chicago as a reliever, but he was back in Class AAA in 1958 and '59 except for a single game.

At that point he was 19–15, 3.78 (105 ERA+) in the Majors but had won 194 games in the minors. He was still pitching, in spring training with the Indianapolis Indians, when he died of a heart attack. He was 40. He had been a decent hitter, though, and was used as an outfielder some in the minors. He hit .243/.282/.500 in 79 plate appearances in the Majors, with five home runs (one per every 15.8 times at bat). Perhaps he should have been called Home Run Howell. As for his given name, he was named after the 13th president, Millard Fillmore.

Catcher Howell's given name was Homer, and it was a misnomer. He had no power. He hit 12 home runs in 1,013 Major League plate appearances (one for every 84.4 times at bat). He did not hit for average or get on base much either, finishing with a .246/.314/.337 line. Like pitcher Howell, he spent years in the minors, mostly Class AAA, including part of World War II—when, if you could play much at all, you were in the Majors. He wasn't. After five seasons as a backup on forgettable teams, he was acquired by the Dodgers, who, for the most part, kept him in the minors. In the final six seasons of his career, he accumulated only 62 plate appearances in the Majors.

There could have been a third Dixie Howell in the Major Leagues. Yet another Millard (Dixie) Howell played minor league ball from 1935 to 1942, but he was renowned for other athletic feats: He was an All-American halfback at Alabama, where he played with Bear Bryant on an undefeated Crimson Tide team.

Pitcher Howell was the only one of these Dixies about whom I could find any specific hint of why he was called Dixie (other than the implied—they were all from the South). Howell said that in his first season of pro ball, in Logan, West Virginia, Black fans liked him and would yell, "Come on, Dixie!" If they did, you have to think it's because the name Millard (Dixie) Howell was already so well known.

Frank Talmadge (Dixie) Davis, Wilson Mills, North Carolina, pitcher, 1912–26. Davis pitched mostly for the George Sisler St. Louis Browns, who were mostly mediocre before the team became mostly terrible. He was an above-average pitcher despite terrible walk rates (he led the American League in walks twice, in 1920 and '21). His most notable achievement was pitching a 19-inning complete game in which he allowed no hits over the final nine innings after giving up 13 in the first 10. The Browns won the game, 8–6. Different era, right?

Edward (Dixie) Parsons, Talladega, Alabama, catcher, 1939–43. Parsons was a big (6-foot-2-inch) catcher who hit well in the minors until he reached Class AAA, which hinted at what his brief Major League career would look like. He went 0 for 3 at the tail end of 1939 with the Tigers and resurfaced during World War II, when he hit .177 in 319 plate appearances. He hit .288 with 113 home runs over 10 years in the minors.

Gorham (Dixie) Leverett, Georgetown, Texas, pitcher, 1922–29. Some careers are a mystery. Leverett attended the University of Arkansas (*Baseball Reference*). Or Ouachita Baptist College (*Arkansas Baseball Encyclopedia*). He began his pro career at age 20 and spent three nondescript seasons in Southern minor leagues. Then his career falls into a five-year black hole, before he resurfaces at Fort Smith, Arkansas, in the

Class D Western Association, at age 27. He fashioned a 25–10 season with a 2.46 ERA in 336 1/3 innings, and in 1922 he leaped all the way to the Chicago White Sox, skidding through the fallout of the Black Sox scandal. He had two pretty good years in Chicago. As a rookie he went 13–10 with a 3.34 ERA—a 121 ERA+—and followed up by going 10–13, 4.06 (97 ERA+) the next year, 1923. After that he had sporadic stints in the Majors, with unsightly results: ERAs of 5.82 in 1924 and 6.00 in 1926 with the White Sox and 6.36 with the Boston Braves in 1929, when he was 35. Interestingly for a guy called Dixie, he came from a family, the Leveretts, who landed in the Massachusetts Bay Colony in 1633.

Douglas Wooley (Dixie) Parker, Forest Home, Alabama, catcher, 1923. Parker began his professional career in 1918 and ended it in 1941. In between he played in four Major League games—two as a defensive replacement, two as a pinch-hitter—and went 1 for 5 for the Phillies in 1923. In his few innings behind the plate, he gave up two stolen bases. What did his taste of the bigs earn him? Another 13 seasons in the minors, the low minors, almost all of those years in Class C and Class D. Muskogee, Oklahoma; Fieldale, Virginia; South Boston, Virginia; and Americus, Georgia, were a long way from Philadelphia.

Dorsey (Dixie) Carroll, Paducah, Kentucky, outfielder, 1919. For many years, the Pacific Coast League was nearly a Major League. It had long seasons because of the better weather, and players often earned as much or more in the PCL than they could in the Majors. Some would not move to the Majors because the Coast League was too lucrative. I wonder if Dixie Carroll was one of those players. His *Baseball Reference Bullpen* page says he hit about .303 in the minors with more than 2,600 hits over 20 seasons, including a pair of 200-hit seasons with the Los Angeles Angels in the PCL in 1921–22. He would have been 30 and 31 then. As a 28-year-old rookie with the Boston Braves, he played in 15 September games and acquitted himself fairly well—.265/.379/.367, with three doubles, a triple and five stolen bases in 59 plate appearances. The Braves were a bad team, with two older outfielders who hit considerably worse, but Carroll was not in Boston the next year. And was never back in the Major Leagues.

Oland (Dixie) McArthur, Vernon, Alabama, pitcher, 1914. Another mystery. McArthur was a college man, played at Bethel College in Tennessee, and in 1912 and 1913 he pitched for Hopkinsville, Kentucky, in the Kitty League. The next year, he moved up to Class C, where he played for Richmond—except for one game, one inning actually, that he pitched for the Pirates. He allowed a hit and struck out a batter in the scoreless ninth inning of Pittsburgh's 5–2 loss to the Philadelphia Phillies. That was on July 10, and he never pitched for the Pirates, or any other Major League team, again. He followed up that season by going 21–10, 2.26 and 22–10,

1.56 for Grand Rapids in Class B, but then his professional career was over. At age 24. Perhaps he put his studies to work.

R T (Dixie) Upright, Kannapolis, North Carolina, pinch-hitter, 1953. In 1953, Upright's career still had promise. He was 27, but in the previous four seasons in the minors he had hit .347, .302, .303 and .318, three of them at Class AA. For two seasons his on-base percentage was above .400, and in three of those seasons he hit between 17 and 20 home runs while playing first base and the outfield. He was traded by the White Sox to the Browns, who were abysmal (54–100 in 1953) and about to play their final season in St. Louis. He was good enough to make his first Opening Day roster, but while the Browns got off to a hot start at 5–1, Upright was rooted to the bench; he pinch-hit once (and struck out). The Browns began losing, as usual, but Upright couldn't find his way into the lineup, pinch-hitting eight more times over the next three weeks (he homered for his first Major League hit, singled once and walked once). But St. Louis, by then 11–13, sold him to the Cubs, and he never returned to the Majors. His name really was R T. He was originally signed in 1947 by the Pirates, who five years later signed another first baseman with initials only, R C Stevens.

Roy (Dixie) Walker, Lawrenceburg, Tennessee, pitcher, 1912–22. James Roy Walker was often called Roy in the papers, but sometimes he was called Jim. Then, after he began pitching for New Orleans in the Southern Association in 1913, he was called Dixie. He could have been called Trouble. After the 1912 season, in which he pitched in a couple of games for the Cleveland Naps, Walker was home in Nashville when he became involved in a fight, reputedly between members of the Eat 'Em Up Gang and the Chaw Gang, a Nashville paper, *The Tennessean,* reported. A fellow named Tom Northern was slashed on the stomach with a knife, and Walker was accused of attempted murder. (Yes, Dixie was accused of attacking a Northern boy.) He took off for Peoria, Illinois, and was arrested in Terre Haute, Indiana, and was returned to Nashville.

He professed his innocence to a *Tennessean* reporter, Robert L. Pigue, who bought it. "Roy Walker does not impress one as a criminal," Pigue wrote, "but on the other hand seems as inoffensive as a child." Still, Walker was convicted and sentenced to 10 years in prison. After a retrial, however, his sentence was reduced to 91 days, and in March 1913 he was in spring training. Trouble followed Walker, however, and that October he was accused of cutting a man severely, "the weapon passing almost through the bone and leaving the injured man's hand dangling," *The Nashville Banner* reported. *The Banner* noted that Walker "has figured in several affrays," but no charges were filed, and he pitched professionally until 1925. He later lived in a series of boarding houses in New Orleans, where he died at the age of 68 in Charity Hospital.

Ten

April 19

*Boston's Trinity: Patriots' Day,
the Red Sox and the Marathon*

On an April Monday for more than a century, three Boston traditions have converged downtown at Kenmore Square: American history, baseball and the marathon. It's Patriots' Day, a holiday that Massachusetts (and almost nowhere else) has been celebrating since 1894. The Red Sox play at Fenway Park, and the runners in the Boston Marathon come streaming through Kenmore Square after using the Citgo sign at Fenway—60 feet by 60 feet, and about 1,200 feet from home plate and more than 5,000 feet from the marathon finish—as a landmark for miles. All three traditions have lengthy histories.

Patriots' Day, celebrating battles at the start of the Revolutionary War on April 19, 1775, was formally proclaimed in 1894 by the Massachusetts governor, who set aside April 19 for the holiday. It honored the well-known battles at Lexington and Concord, which were memorialized by Ralph Waldo Emerson as the "shot heard round the world" in his poem *Concord Hymn*. The poem overlooked the bloodier Battle of Menotomy that day. Patriots' Day did not. It was all one big commemoration then, although few know of the Battle of Menotomy now. Or of Menotomy, which is now Arlington.

Three years later, in 1897, a battle among runners began on April 19: the Boston Marathon, the longest continuously run marathon in the world. The race called the marathon is named for the Battle of Marathon in Greece in 490 BC. Legend has it that a messenger named Pheidippides ran from Marathon to Athens (about 25 miles, after he was said to have run many previous miles over two days) to announce that the Greeks had defeated the Spartans. In a fashion that would seem appropriate to long-suffering Red Sox fans, he was said to have died at the finish. In 1896, Athens held the first modern Olympics, which included a 24.8-mile marathon, and, at the urging of an enthused Olympian from Boston, the city—the Athens of America, as the literary magazine *North American Review* called it in 1819—decided to have its own the next year.

In 1902, another athletic competition linked itself to Patriots' Day when Boston's two Major League baseball teams played on the holiday. The year-old Boston Americans, who had gotten permission from the American League to start their season early to take advantage of the holiday, according to the Fenway Fanatics website, defeated the Baltimore Orioles 7–6, at the Huntington Avenue Baseball Grounds; the Boston Beaneaters of the National League split a doubleheader with the Brooklyn Superbas at the South End Grounds. The teams drew larger-than-usual crowds, with the Americans reported to have lured 16,000. The marathon winner, Sammy Mellor, ran the course (which was then 24.5 miles, not the current 26.2) in 2 hours 43 minutes 12 seconds—longer than it took to play the ballgames.

And with that, the three traditions had come together. But they did not continue without hitches. In 1903, the Americans (eventually Red Sox) decided to get a head start on the Nationals (eventually the Braves) on Patriots' Day. Both teams played doubleheaders, but the Americans' first game was at 10 a.m. (with the game finishing about the time the race would start), while the Nationals employed a conventional afternoon start. The Americans vastly outdrew the Nationals, and the teams later came to an economic truce: Beginning in 1904, they would alternate years as a home team on Patriots' Day.

Eventually, the day's events began to almost literally overlap. Fenway Park was opened in 1912, but the ballpark was not the host for ballgames on Patriots' Day until 1913—and then with the Braves as the home team for a doubleheader (the Red Sox played out of town). The Red Sox finally got their chance on marathon day in 1914, although it was on Monday, April 20; the holiday was always pushed back when it fell on a Sunday. (Sunday baseball wasn't allowed in Boston anyway until 1929, as detailed in *Red Sox vs. Braves in Boston: The Battle for Fans' Heart, 1901–1952*.) Marathoners running past a ballgame was still dependent on which team played on the holiday, until the Braves moved to Milwaukee in 1953 and the Red Sox formally owned baseball in town. And the right to Patriots' Day games.

The Red Sox continued to play Patriots' Day doubleheaders only sporadically, and in 1967—the Impossible Dream year—the twin bills vanished for good. The convergence of the day's traditions was simplified in 1969, when Massachusetts began celebrating Patriots' Day on the third Monday of April. But the marathon has been more of a constant than the baseball games. Until 1959, the American League did not always schedule the Red Sox to play at home on Patriots' Day. Some years, the game was rained out (weather never stops the race). In 1995, a players' strike prevented the game. These days, the crowd at the ballgames just surpasses the number of marathoners (30,000 or so).

For years, the day's baseball began as early as 10 a.m., the marathon at midday. That meant that fans leaving the ballpark could see some of the fastest runners streaming by. The ballgame now starts just after 11, the top runners are faster, games are longer (the last year that the game took less time than the marathon winner was on a hot day in 1976), and the starting time for the first elite runners is around 9:30. That changes the dynamic outside Fenway, but with the last of the runners heading off from Hopkinton at 11:15, fans can still view the game *and* runners.

Patriots' Day has, overall, been good for the Red Sox—they are 71-55 on the holiday—just not against the Yankees. New York is 22-11 in Patriots' Day games at Fenway. "It's a given that on Patriots,' it's all about watching morning baseball before watching the marathon," Gordon Edes, the Red Sox team historian, said. "That's what makes this such a quirky holiday in New England."

Eleven

May 24

The Night the Lights Went On in Major League Baseball

Many a president has thrown out a ceremonial first pitch. On May 24, 1935, Franklin D. Roosevelt threw a ceremonial first switch. Roosevelt's action at 8:30 p.m. at the White House transmitted a signal by telegraph to Crosley Field in Cincinnati. There, the Reds' general manager, Larry MacPhail, threw the switch that actually turned on the lights in the ballpark—632 lamps of 1,500 watts each, on towers that were 115 feet tall—for the first night game in Major League Baseball.

The game had been scheduled for May 23, but it was rained out. On the 24th, the inaugural night game drew 20,422 fans despite chilly, threatening weather that may well have depressed the crowd. But it was a huge turnout for the Reds, who drew 2,000 fans the previous game and 2,085 the day after.

It was a milestone that nearly did not happen. At the 1934–35 winter meetings, National League owners had approved a limited number of night games, but Commissioner Kenesaw Mountain Landis told MacPhail, "Young man ... not in my lifetime or yours will you ever see a baseball game played at night in the Majors." He was wrong, of course, perhaps swayed by the economic realities of the Great Depression that were pressing on baseball. He soon allowed the Reds to play seven night games in 1935. And it was a gigantic boon; the Reds averaged 18,620 fans for their seven night games, 4,607 for their 69 day games at home.

That amounted to a lot of money. The Reds drew about 98,000 more fans to those night games than seven average day games would have. The top ticket cost $1.75. If you figure the average ticket was $1.25, that is $122,500 more revenue than from an equal number of day games. If concessions brought in another $100,000—roughly a dollar per customer— and you deduct the estimated $50,000 it cost to install the lights, that's a total of $172,000, or nearly $4 million in 2024 dollars. Take off a little more for the electric bill.

Other teams surely noticed, but none of them followed suit immediately, worried that night baseball would harm attendance at day baseball, according to Charlie Bevis's *Baseball Under the Lights: The Rise of the Night Game*. In 1936 and '37, the Reds remained the only Major League team to play home games under the lights, with continued attendance gains despite terrible teams. In 1936, the Reds averaged 18,188 for the seven night games, 6,759 for their day games; in 1937, it was 15,668 for the night games, 4,188 for the day games.

In 1938, another team finally leaped into night baseball—the Brooklyn Dodgers, who were then being run by ... MacPhail, who, though a nighttime pioneer, remained wary of a heavy night schedule. On June 15, Brooklyn turned on the lights for a game against the Reds that became historic; it was Johnny Vander Meer's second consecutive no-hitter. The Dodgers reaped even greater rewards than the Reds had, averaging 26,254 for eight night games compared with 6,970 for home day games.

Perhaps it was no coincidence, but the Reds and the Dodgers both flourished on the field a few years after they began raking in the money from playing night games. MacPhail invested in players in both cities, and the Reds won the pennant in 1939 and the World Series in 1940, and the Dodgers captured the pennant in 1941.

The Major Leagues' reluctance to play at night was generally over by then. In 1939, an American League team, the Philadelphia Athletics, another bottom feeder with poor attendance, added lights. By 1942, 11 of the 16 teams had lights. When World War II ended, only three teams did not have lights—the Boston Red Sox, the Detroit Tigers and the Chicago Cubs. Although the Cubs had bought the equipment to install lights for the 1942 season, they donated it to the war effort and remained a steadfast day-game team until 1988. (It may be merely a coincidence, but the conservative Red Sox and Tigers were the last two teams to integrate their Major League rosters. The Red Sox introduced lights in 1947, the Tigers in 1948. Boston integrated in 1959; Detroit, 1958.)

MacPhail's involvement in night baseball was no surprise. He owned the Columbus Red Birds, a St. Louis Cardinals farm team, in 1932 and, as was later the case in Cincinnati and Brooklyn, had a franchise with low attendance and financial problems. MacPhail arranged the team's first night game, but it was delayed by some unusual shenanigans, according to a history of Columbus baseball stadiums. Branch Rickey was the general manager of the Cardinals, and he wanted to acquire a shortstop from the minor league St. Paul Saints, Jimmie Reese. So he traded the rights to play in the first night game to the Saints—who would share in the gate receipts—for Reese. That meant the game could not be played until St. Paul came to town, which was two weeks later. Then, history.

As eventful as it was, MacPhail's introduction of night baseball in Columbus was not without precedent. According to the Baseball Hall of Fame, the first known game under the lights was between teams representing department stores in Hull, Massachusetts, on September 2, 1880. For a frame of reference, Thomas Edison had patented the incandescent light bulb only early that year. Another night game was played on June 2, 1883, in Fort Wayne, Indiana, against a team from Quincy, Illinois, and several minor league games were played at night before the 19th century ended, the Hall of Fame says.

Night baseball actually came to Cincinnati in 1909, between two Elks Clubs teams, played at the Reds' fabulously named ballpark, the Palace of the Fans. In 1910, two semipro teams played at night at Comiskey Park in Chicago—coincidentally, while the White Sox were in New York playing the Yankees in a game that ended in a tie when it was called because of darkness. The first night game in organized baseball was played on April 28, 1930, between the home Independence (Kansas) Producers and the Muskogee (Oklahoma) Chiefs of the Western Association, according to the Society for American Baseball Research. Other minor league teams followed that season.

Night ball really took off in the Negro leagues, however. The Kansas City Monarchs bought a lighting system that they hauled from town to town, an enormous boost for a team that played most of its games on the road and was highly dependent on gate receipts. Their first night game was played on April 28, 1930, in an exhibition against Phillips University, according to a history of night baseball in *The Ironton (Ohio) Tribune*. The game, in Enid, Oklahoma, drew about 3,000 people, the historian Phil S. Dixon told *The Enid News & Eagle* in 2015. The Monarchs also played numerous night games against another barnstorming team, the House of David, which employed its own traveling lighting system.

Dixon said that the Monarchs' co-owner J.L. Wilkinson believed that night games were baseball's future. "He said lights will be to baseball what talkies are to the movies," Dixon said. "The Major Leagues didn't believe it."

The Major Leagues' reluctance had varied reasons. Bevis wrote that owners feared the democratization of the fan base that night baseball was sure to bring—working stiffs actually had to work during the day— was at odds with what baseball thought its clientele should be. That was even though night games appeared to present a financial boon. Owners also feared that play would be subpar and that players would be at greater risk of injury. But the review of night ball at the Reds' first such game in 1935 was extremely positive. A reporter for *The Cincinnati Enquirer*, James Golden, wrote, "The great batteries of lights never seemed to bother the spectators or the boys in the field." Golden considered the game an aesthetic success:

> All that the fans cared about was that the visibility was plenty good from the stands and the bleachers, that the field showed up in a more uniform light green and tan than it does in daytime. It was as brilliant with the trim little white figures running about it, as a new baseball game board in the window of the corner drugstore. What clouds there were were so thin that the ball, when it flew high, shone through them like a bald head in a steam room. And when there was no mist, the sphere stood out against the sky like a pearl against dark velvet.

There were few pearls on the diamond, however. Only four of the 20 players who took the field ever made an All-Star team. None are in the Hall of Fame. The Reds wound up in sixth place at 68–85–1, the Phillies in seventh at 64–89. (Their saving grace: the 38–115 Boston Braves.) Now [ca. 2024], about two-thirds of Major League games are played at night.

Here's a look at the players who took the field that night in Cincinnati, a game the Reds won, 2–1, in only an hour and 35 minutes.

Philadelphia Phillies

Lou Chiozza, second baseman. Chiozza was sort of a good-field, no-hit infielder except he did not really field all that well (career defensive WAR of -0.8). He scored five runs in a home-field 18–7 victory over the Giants in 1935, an example of what playing in Philadelphia's Baker Bowl was like. As mediocre as Chiozza may have been, he was better than his brother Dino, who was a teammate in '35. Dino played in only two games, scored once as a pinch-runner, but never came to bat—he was on deck in the 10th inning when his final game ended. That game did feature a novelty, *Baseball Reference* notes—with Lou, Dino and reliever Pretzel Pezzullo in the game, it was the only time that three players with a double Z in their name were on the field at the same time.

Ethan Allen, center fielder. Allen was a .300 hitter in a 13-year career, but it was an era in which a .300 hitter was ordinary. (His career OPS+ was 93, as he rarely walked and had little power.) But Allen made his mark off the field. He was the coach at Yale when George H.W. Bush played first base there, and he invented a board game, All-Star Baseball, that had discs with real players' actual statistics and a spinner to determine the outcome of each at-bat. The game made its debut in 1941 and lasted for half a century, until the players' union required licensing fees for use of players' names and statistics. Now it's a collectible. Allen had one of the Phillies' six hits in this game, but he was also responsible for one of the Reds' four hits. In the fifth inning, he misplayed a fly ball. "Actually, it was scored as a hit, because it was a sort of low shot that went off my glove," he said, according to his SABR *Bio Project* profile. "The lights were so bright, it was almost like a day game, except you could see your shadow on all sides of you. I remember that very well, looking at those shadows."

Johnny Moore, right fielder. Johnny Moore and Jo-Jo Moore were contemporary National League outfielders. Johnny played from 1928 to 1937, with a few games as a pinch-hitter in 1945, with a line of .307/.352/.449 and an OPS+ of 111. Jo-Jo played from 1928 to 1941, with a line of .298/.344/.408 and an OPS+ of 104. Johnny had 73 home runs, Jo-Jo 79. Each walked more than he struck out. Their defensive WARs are similar, if not great (-5.3 to -5.9). But if you have heard of Johnny Moore at all—and I had not—it is because Babe Ruth's "Called Shot" home run in the 1932 World Series went over his glove in center field. Jo-Jo Moore was much better known, a six-time All-Star and three-time World Series participant owing to his good fortune to play for the New York Giants. Johnny Moore earned more renown as a scout for the Braves, signing Eddie Mathews and Del Crandall in the pre-draft days and pushing the Braves to trade for a minor league pitcher on the San Francisco Seals, Lew Burdette.

Dolph Camilli, first baseman. Camilli played five and a half seasons for the Dodgers, and he came to detest their archrivals, the Giants. When Brooklyn traded him to the Giants in July 1943, he refused to report and instead went home to his cattle ranch in California, his SABR biography says. The Giants needed a first baseman—theirs hit .230 with six homers that year—but Camilli was not about to move across town. "I hated the Giants," he said. "This was real serious; this was no put-on stuff. Their fans hated us, and our fans hated them. I said nuts to them, and I quit." He did play the next season for the Pacific Coast League Oakland Oaks.

Johnny Vergez, third baseman. Vergez (pronounced VEER-jess) was not really a power hitter—he hit 52 home runs in 2,540 career plate appearances—but he holds a home run record. He is the only player to hit his first 20 homers in the same ballpark; in fact, his first 27 were hit in the Polo Grounds. Interestingly, the next four players on this list also did it at the Polo Grounds: Burgess Whitehead (17), Bill Rigney (16), Freddie Fitzsimmons (14) and Andy Cohen (13). Ryan Theriot broke the mold in the 21st century; his first 12 came at Wrigley Field.

Al Todd, catcher. His obituary in *The Elmira (New York) Star-Gazette* gave Todd's account of his most famous moment in baseball: a 1931 fight with Dizzy Dean. Todd was a catcher for Dallas in the Texas League, Dean a pitcher for Houston. As Todd recalled, Dean knocked him down with three pitches, and after Todd yelled at him, Dean motioned him to come to the mound. Which Todd, who knew how to box, did. "Well, I walked to the mound, shot out one punch and Dean dropped in his tracks," Todd said. "He grabbed me around the knees, but I kept punching away until he had enough."

Dean remembered it succinctly in *The Gashouse Gang and a Couple of Other Guys*: "I can talk rings around that Todd any time, but I don't wanta fight him no more." Todd had one other memorable baseball fight, but he lost it. He and Zeke Bonura, another ex–Major Leaguer, were opposing managers in the Northern League when they got into it, and Bonura laid out Todd with a punch to the head, according to Todd's Elmira obituary. "Some smart reporter the next day, noting the sizes of Zeke and myself, headlined it 'the battle of the bulges.'"

George Watkins, left fielder. By the time he was 25, Watkins had served in the Navy, worked in Texas oil fields and moved on to a job at the Sinclair Oil refinery in Houston. There, he played in a top-flight amateur league that led to a chance to play against the local minor league team in an exhibition game. He played well enough that the team was interested in signing him, so Watkins did what many a ballplayer did: He lied about his age and said he was 23. Which, after a five-year apprenticeship in the minors, is how he came to be a 30-year-old rookie with the Cardinals in 1930. His wait was worth it: Watkins hit .373/.415/.621 with 17 homers in 424 plate appearances. It was the year the National League batting average was .303, but still, his OPS+ was 141. That was the peak of his career.

The nadir came in 1934, when he held out, was traded to the Giants, began the season 3 for 33 and was eventually blamed by Giants Manager Bill Terry for blowing the team's NL lead and losing the pennant to the Gashouse Gang Cardinals. "I lost the pennant when I traded [Kiddo] Davis for George Watkins," Terry said. "Watkins cost us five or six games that Davis would have won for us." The criticism was harsh and perhaps unfair. The Giants led by seven games with 21 to play but finished 8–13, coughing up a two-and-a-half-game lead by losing their final five. Watkins was on the bench for most of the slump, but he started the final six games and went 7 for 19 and played errorless ball in center field. Davis, by the way, lasted only 16 games with St. Louis and was dispatched to the hapless Phillies.

Mickey Haslin, shortstop. It is easy to overlook how much better fielding is now than it was decades ago. Better athletes, better equipment, better fields. In 1935, Haslin played 87 games at shortstop and made 34 errors. But five National League shortstops made even more errors: Lonny Frey (44), Billy Urbanski (40), Dick Bartell (37), Billy Myers (37) and Arky Vaughan (35). These were not chumps. Vaughan is in the Hall of Fame. Bartell received MVP votes in six seasons and played on three pennant-winning teams. Myers and Frey were both starters on pennant winners. Urbanski was among the league leaders in assists at shortstop from 1932 to 1934 and had a positive defensive WAR (2.9) for his career. Haslin did have the lowest fielding percentage among these shortstops. But he also couldn't hit.

Joe Bowman, pitcher. Curiously, all three runs in this game scored on groundouts. One of them was on a fifth-inning grounder to short by Bowman on which the Reds could not turn a double play. He then stole second but was stranded when Chiozza hit a fly ball to center. Bowman was not a bad hitter for a pitcher, with a .221 career average, and he was sensational in 1938 and 1939 for the Pirates: .342/.379/.444 in 130 plate appearances with an OPS+ of 123, eight doubles, two triples and 19 RBIs.

Jimmie Wilson, pinch-hitter. From 1928 to 1931, Wilson was perhaps the best defensive catcher in the National League with the Cardinals. He led the league in putouts three times (aided, no doubt, by catching those Dizzy Dean strikeouts), assists twice, double plays turned three times and base stealers thrown out twice. His greatest renown, however, came for his exploits as a 40-year-old emergency catcher for the Reds in their 1940 World Series championship run. Because of injuries in September to various Cincinnati catchers, including eventual Hall of Famer Ernie Lombardi, Wilson was activated for the stretch drive. In the Series, he started the final six games, batted .353 (7 for 19) and laid down a key sacrifice bunt in the winning rally in Game 7.

Jim Bivin, pitcher. Bivin pitched for a lot of years (17) and a lot of teams (13 different ones), but only one season came in the Majors: 1935. He pitched a 1–2–3 eighth inning in the first night game, but six days later he threw what was ultimately his most famous pitch. He retired Babe Ruth, on a weak ground ball to first base on which the Babe's swing spun him around, in Ruth's final Major-League at-bat.

Cincinnati Reds

Billy Myers, shortstop. The Great Depression crushed businesses. Between 1930 and 1933, 7,000 banks went under. Tens of thousands of other businesses went bust, too. Baseball was no exception. In 1932 alone, SABR reports, 12 minor leagues went under. Many independent teams and leagues also existed, but from 1932 to 1933, minor league teams affiliated with Major League teams shrank from 43 to 32, *Baseball Reference* says. Oddly, this contraction helped Myers, whose team in the Three-I league disbanded. Wanting to keep him in their system despite his lackluster hitting, the Cardinals promoted him to their top farm team in Rochester. He moved down a level in 1933, began to hit, advanced in 1934 and really began to hit—.313 with 37 doubles, 13 triples and 10 homers. Other teams were watching. The Giants purchased Myers's contract in the off-season and then traded him to the Reds. Cincinnati was so enamored that it made him the starting shortstop and, even though he was a rookie, the team captain.

Lew Riggs, third baseman. After spending nine years in the Major Leagues, mostly with the Reds, and three years in the service in World War II, Riggs returned with the Dodgers for Opening Day in 1946. He went 0 for 4 and never got the ball out of the infield. He was dispatched to Brooklyn's top farm team in Montreal, where he was a utility player and backup to Jackie Robinson, who was breaking the color barrier in organized baseball. At age 36, Riggs hit .303/.436/.556 with 15 homers in 375 plate appearances, while Robinson was hitting .349/.468/.462. The Royals won the Junior World Series, with both Riggs and Robinson playing vital roles.

Ival Goodman, right fielder. Goodman had a reputation as a pretty good defensive outfielder for the Reds, but one play he did not make in the 1939 World Series infuriated his pitcher that day, Paul Derringer. In the bottom of the ninth of a 1–1 game in Game 1 at Yankee Stadium, Charlie Keller whacked a fly to right-center field that Goodman, in right, and center fielder Harry Craft converged on. SABR's Goodman profile says that it looked as if either could have made the catch despite the Stadium's deep shadows, but that both backed off; a *Baseball Prospectus* account says they most likely feared colliding or running into the wall. Keller wound up with a triple and eventually scored the winning run. Goodman's SABR bio quotes his teammate Billy Werber saying that when Derringer spotted Goodman, he told him: "If you got no guts, get out of here. That was the most gutless effort I've ever seen."

Billy Sullivan, first baseman. It is not hard to come up with a list of catchers who moved to other positions as Major Leaguers. Craig Biggio. B.J. Surhoff. Joe Torre. Dale Murphy. Carlos Delgado. Todd Zeile. (Even Yogi Berra.) But few move the other way, from the infield or outfield to the backstop. Sullivan, the son of a Major League catcher by the same name, did. He was mostly a first baseman and third baseman when he came up, although he did catch in 14 of the 324 games he played in his first four seasons. But after Sullivan was sold to Cleveland in 1936, Manager Steve O'Neill—a catcher himself for 17 years in the Majors—concluded that Sullivan could become a useful catcher. He caught in 401 games and played elsewhere in 90 games over his final eight seasons. And he wasn't bad. Sullivan was around the league average in throwing out base runners, led American League catchers in fielding percentage one season and impressed Tigers ace Bobo Newsom sufficiently that he requested Sullivan as his personal catcher.

Harlin Pool, left fielder. There has never been another Major Leaguer named Harlin. Nor has there been another Major Leaguer named Pool. But plenty of guys could play like Harlin Pool, who lasted only one and a half seasons in the Majors. He *could* hit in the Pacific Coast League—a .334 average with doubles power over parts of eight seasons.

Gilly Campbell, catcher. Campbell was the definition of a backup catcher, never starting more than 65 games in his five seasons in the Majors. So perhaps it is appropriate that he was a bit-part actor, too, appearing (uncredited) in *The Pride of the Yankees* in 1942 and *Kill the Umpire* in 1950. A baseball signed by Babe Ruth, Campbell and numerous other ballplayers who had roles in *The Pride of the Yankees* was sold for $11,100 in 2020, according to Instagraphs (Memorabilia for People Who Have Everything). The star of *Kill the Umpire* was William Bendix, who also starred as the main man himself in *The Babe Ruth Story*, which was released three weeks before Ruth died in 1948.

Samuel Byrd, center fielder. Byrd was nicknamed "Babe Ruth's Legs" because he was often a late-inning defensive replacement or pinch-runner for the aging Ruth. Byrd fashioned an eight-year career in the Majors, but he was a much better golfer than ballplayer. When he was 28, he quit baseball rather than accept a demotion to the minors and took up golf professionally. He won six events on the PGA Tour and finished third in the Masters in 1941 and fourth in 1942. The sportswriter Gene Bleile wrote in *The Cape Gazette* that Ruth had taught Byrd a practice technique using a handkerchief tucked under the lead arm to hit the ball straight. Years later Byrd taught the same trick to a young pro who was struggling with a duck hook: Ben Hogan.

Alex Kampouris, second baseman. After the late 1990s and early 2000s, many fans came to look at a huge spike in a player's home run total as a sure sign of steroid use. Maybe yes, maybe no, but there were plenty of instances of abrupt increases in homers long before there were steroids. Take Kampouris, who never hit more than seven home runs in a season … except for 1937, when he homered 17 times in 526 plate appearances. That season, Kampouris homered once every 31 plate appearances; the rest of his career, once every 70 PA. It wasn't the ball, as homers in the NL increased only 3 percent in 1937. His teammate Ival Goodman had a similar spike in 1938, clouting 30 homers after a previous career high of 17; he never hit more than 12 again.

Paul Derringer, pitcher. Derringer was by far the best player on the field in the first night game, but he was far from the most likable. He drank and was not a happy drunk. His SABR *Bio Project* biography recounts a menu of incidents: He threw an inkwell at his general manager, Larry MacPhail. (He missed, a rarity for a pitcher with his control on the mound.) In a minor league game, he threw at Jackie Robinson in his first two at-bats to show his friend Clay Hopper, Robinson's manager, what Robinson was made of. (Robinson dusted himself off and got hits both times. "He will do," Derringer later told Hopper.) He fought with Dizzy Dean. He assaulted a guest at a fancy hotel in Philadelphia and wound up paying $8,000 to settle the case. Once, he knocked out a recovery room nurse when he came to after an operation.

It wasn't always his fault, he contended; in his divorce suit against his second wife, he said she threw a highball glass into his face in an argument over which of them made a better drink. But he knew the strike zone—he averaged only 1.88 walks per nine innings over 15 seasons—and he could pitch, even on bad teams. He was 7–27 in this third season, but with a 3.30 ERA, pitching mostly for the last-place Reds. When Cincinnati finally became good, Derringer was great. After finishing last in 1937, the Reds averaged 93 wins over the next three seasons and won the pennant in 1939 and '40 (when it also won the World Series).

Derringer was 66–33 with a 2.97 ERA (127 ERA+) over those three seasons. He teamed with Bucky Walters, who was acquired in the middle of the 1938 season and went 49–21, 2.38 (162 ERA+) through 1940; they formed the best 1-2 pitching combination in baseball. In the first night game, Derringer displayed his typical excellence: a complete-game six-hitter, allowing only one run and no walks while striking out three. At 38 years old, he helped the Cubs win the 1945 pennant by going 16–11 with a 3.45 ERA, yet Chicago did not want him back the next season. After he pitched one last season in the minors, baseball was done with him. Derringer died in poverty in Florida at the age of 81.

Twelve

May 25

Babe Ruth's Last Hurrah

May 25 had generally been a good day for Babe Ruth. By his final season, 1935, he had played 15 games on May 25 and batted .333 (13 for 39) with seven extra-base hits, three home runs and eight walks. But that last May 25 was one of his finest days in the Major Leagues.

Babe Ruth homered three times on May 25, 1935 ... and never got the ball out of the infield again (National Baseball Hall of Fame, Cooperstown, NY).

Ruth had landed with the Boston Braves, who would go on to win only 38 games, after his relationship with the Yankees had soured beyond repair and his production had skidded far below his mythic standards. He was old (40), overweight, prone to injuries, cranky and on the record, very publicly, as saying he would continue to play only if he could also manage. He asked the Yankees' management more than once about the status of Manager Joe McCarthy and was firmly told that McCarthy's job was secure. (With good reason: McCarthy, who had won the World Series with the Yankees in 1932, would go on to win six more.)

John Kieran of *The New York Times* wrote in June 1935: "He was pretty well washed up as a player, anyway. He knew it himself after he had been out there a few times." But the Yankees had boxed themselves in a bit, as Robert Creamer establishes in *Babe: The Legend Comes to Life,* when the owner, Jacob Ruppert, said the Yankees would not let another team have Ruth for nothing. What team wanted to part with anything for an old, overweight, cranky, slumping prima donna? But one team did want Ruth, though on the cheap: the Braves, a chronically undercapitalized franchise owned by Emil Fuchs. Creamer wrote that Fuchs, who was known as Judge Fuchs, concocted a complex plan that would get the Yankees off the hook, get Ruth to play in Boston (to hype the gate for a team that had averaged just under 4,000 fans a game in 1934) and not undermine his own manager, Bill McKechnie (Fuchs made Ruth an "assistant manager," with unspecified duties). According to *Judge Fuchs and the Boston Braves, 1923–35,* "the Judge liked to take on long-shot comeback players."

Ruth's stay in Boston worked about as well as you might expect. The Braves, who had finished 78–73 the year before, got off to a miserable start at 2–7. Ruth stopped hitting after the first week—he went 0 for 22 in one 10-game stretch and was infirm enough that he didn't finish any of those games. McKechnie, whom Bill James described in his *New Historical Baseball Abstract* as "the nicest of Hall of Fame managers," did feel undermined.

But in Pittsburgh in late May, with his batting average sinking toward .150, Ruth became *Babe Ruth* again. On May 23, he lost a hit when the Pirates' Paul Waner made a leaping grab at the right-field fence. On May 24, after a night of carousing, Ruth hit the ball well—he had only a single to show for it, but Creamer said reporters at Forbes Field agreed that two fly balls he hit would have been home runs anywhere else. Waner made another outstanding catch to rob him.

That brought Ruth to May 25 and Red Lucas, a journeyman right-hander whom he had never faced. With a runner on base in the top of the first inning, Ruth homered—*Baseball Reference*'s box score describes it as to deep right field—and Lucas didn't finish the inning. In the third, Ruth came up against Guy Bush, with whom he had a history going back to the "Called Shot" World Series game of 1932, and again he homered. Again to deep right. In the fifth, Ruth hit a run-scoring single off Bush. When Ruth strode to the plate again in the seventh, Bush was still pitching. Another big swing, another long fly ball, another home run: No. 714 of his career.

That third home run was memorable, even in the moment. *The Associated Press* that day called it "a prodigious clout that carried over the right-field grandstand, bounded into the street and rolled into Schenley Park. Baseball men said it was the longest drive ever made at Forbes Field."

Creamer said that the ball went completely over the double-decked stands, the first ball hit out of Forbes Field. He wrote that Gus Miller, the head usher, was sent to check out the home run and was told the ball hit the roof of one house, bounced off another and into a lot, where a boy ran off with it. Miller measured the distance from the first house to home plate as 600 feet. "His measurement may have been imprecise," Creamer wrote, "but it was still the longest home run ever hit in Pittsburgh."

Bush would very likely have agreed. "I never saw a ball hit so hard before or since," said Bush, who yielded 150 other homers in his 17-year Major-League career. "He was fat and old, but he still had that great swing. Even when he missed, you could hear the bat go swish. I can't remember anything about the first home run he hit off me that day. I guess it was just another homer. But I can't forget that last one. It's probably still going."

Duffy Lewis was an old Red Sox teammate of Ruth and was the Braves' traveling secretary, and Creamer says Lewis "told the Babe after the game that if he was going to quit, he ought to quit then, on top." If only there had been more May 25ths in store for Ruth. For his career on that date, he batted 17 for 43, a .395 average, with six home runs, two doubles and a triple for a 1.050 slugging percentage and eight walks for a .521 on-base percentage. On May 25, 1928, he homered twice in one game of a doubleheader, and he had four other multiple-hit games on May 25. But after May 25, 1935, Ruth played in only five more games and came to bat 13 times—without a single hit (although he did walk four times). In fact, Ruth never got the ball out of the infield again.

*　*　*

No one could compare to Ruth. Even a great player like his longtime teammate Lou Gehrig could not, and the other players in his final game on May 25, 1935, were hardly Gehrig. But there were others playing indelible parts in Ruth's dramatic finish, on and off the field. And on the movie screen.

Six months before the Broadway producer Harry Frazee sold the Red Sox in 1923, **Emil Fuchs** bought the Braves. Frazee sold Babe Ruth to the Yankees in 1920; Fuchs brought him back to Boston 15 years later, purchasing his contract for the Braves. Neither transaction worked out well for the Boston teams. In fact, little worked out well for Fuchs in Boston. The Braves were already unsuccessful on the field—they were 53–100–1 the season before Fuchs bought them—and remained so, managing only two winning seasons in Fuchs's 13 seasons of ownership. Unlike the wealthy Tom Yawkey across town, Fuchs, a lawyer and one-time magistrate in New York City, did not have vast reserves to sustain his team, especially as the Depression wore on. When the Braves finally did improve—their records were 77–77 and 83–71 in 1932 and '33—that did not move the needle on attendance, which remained in the middle of the pack in the National League.

Things would get worse: The Braves went 78–73–1 in 1934, but attendance plummeted by more than 40 percent, even as the country's gross domestic product increased by nearly 9 percent, according to the Bureau of Economic Analysis. Only 303,205 fans came to Braves Field, and Fuchs's financial problems only worsened. As Creamer lays out in *Babe: The Legend Comes to Life*, the judge's plan to sign Ruth as a box-office attraction was a spectacular failure, and by that August, Fuchs relinquished his majority interest in the team, which *The New York Times* said owed $200,000 to a Boston bank—almost $4.5 million 2024 dollars. The debts he incurred trying to salvage the Braves crippled him financially; as his SABR *Bio Project* profile notes, he declared bankruptcy in 1938, reporting $263,299 in liabilities and no assets. Fuchs could not make the Braves a winner or solvent, but he kept the team alive. When Fuchs died in 1961, *The Sporting News* wrote: "His career was not a bright one. There is this, though, to be said. With his own resources, he kept alive a franchise that would have collapsed."

The aging Babe Ruth was just the kind of player **Bill McKechnie** would not have wanted on his team. McKechnie prized defense above all else, and Ruth would not have been the plus defender McKechnie wanted at any point in his career, let alone in his final season. "Bill McKechnie was glove-crazy; he didn't care what a guy hit, if his glove was good enough," Bill James said in his *New Historical Baseball Abstract*. A short retrospective on his career at SB Nation, on the anniversary of his death, said: "McKechnie's greatest strength as a manager became his failing weakness. … He was so devoted to good defense that he lost sight of the offensive side of the game, which cost him his job in Cincinnati."

McKechnie also never valued home run hitters. In 25 seasons as a Major League manager, he had a 30-homer slugger only five times, despite managing in the 1920s and '30s. In some of those years, his team's home run leader was in single digits. While he was managing Reds teams in the 1940s whose offense continued to erode, he kept future MVP Hank Sauer, a plodding outfielder who could hit for average and power, in the minors. Yet McKechnie's focus on defense did pay off repeatedly. In Pittsburgh, he constructed an infield in which all four players had started out as shortstops, his SABR *Bio Project* biography says. That 1925 team won the pennant and the World Series. His 1928 St. Louis Cardinals squad won the pennant despite starting a shortstop and a third baseman who were considerably subpar hitters with no power, marginal on-base skills and an OPS+ of 87 and 68. Later, in Cincinnati, he put together another infield in which three of the regulars all started at shortstop at some point in their

Major League careers. What happened? The Reds won the pennant in 1939 and the pennant and World Series in 1940.

James wrote that McKechnie was widely considered an exceedingly nice guy, and he was a devout fellow often called Deacon. Yet he was treated with considerable disdain, especially for a manager who was so successful (four pennants, two Series titles). In the middle of the 1925 season in Pittsburgh, the owner, Barney Dreyfuss, brought in ex-manager and Pirates legend Fred Clarke, a vocal presence, as an assistant manager, McKechnie's SABR bio says. Pittsburgh won the World Series despite the mixed messages and players' animosity toward Clarke, but Clarke's presence undermined the following season. The players mutinied—they actually took a vote on whether Clarke should be removed—but it was McKechnie who paid the price with his job after the Pirates did not repeat.

It got worse in St. Louis. He won the pennant in 1928, his first season with the Cardinals, but they were swept in the World Series by the Yankees and the owner, Sam Breadon, pushed McKechnie out. John Kieran wrote in *The Times*, "The charge against McKechnie is that 'he is one of the finest fellows in the world, but—.'" Breadon didn't exactly fire McKechnie, he demoted him to manager of a Class AAA team. When the Cardinals scuffled under McKechnie's young successor, Billy Southworth, Breadon brought McKechnie back in midseason, but the manager announced before the end of the season that he was done. He wasn't, though, choosing job security (a four-year contract) over winning certainty (the cash-strapped Braves, with their owner, Fuchs, managing the team to save money, had finished 56–98 in 1929). McKechnie turned the penurious Braves into an above-.500 team, but in 1935, Fuchs made Ruth an assistant manager as well as a potential drawing card in the batter's box, again putting McKechnie's authority in some doubt. Eventually, he left Boston and took an offer from his longtime friend Warren Giles to manage the Reds, who had run through nine consecutive losing seasons. With an infusion of money, talent and McKechnie's roster construction, he had Cincinnati in the World Series in his second season.

Guy Bush lost two games to the Yankees in the 1932 World Series, but he is better remembered for his role in a game he didn't pitch: Ruth's "Called Shot" game. Charlie Root was the antagonist, the Cubs pitcher who gave up that home run in Game 3 of the Series, but Bush was a prime agitator. Creamer wrote in *Babe* that Bush and two other Cubs players were on the top step of their dugout in Wrigley Field, heckling Ruth as the game began. Ruth responded with a first-inning, three-run home run. In the fifth inning, with the score tied, Bush and his pals were yelling at Ruth again, and Creamer says Bush wound up taking a step or two onto the grass in front of the dugout after the second strike from Root to Ruth. Ruth held up two fingers or pointed to the outfield—nearly a century later it is still unclear, but what is certain is that he crushed an off-speed pitch over the wall in center field. Bush had his take on the incident, writing in a 1964 note that became a valued collectible: "Ruth was talking to me. At the time when he raised his right hand it is of my belief he pointed to center field. The only thing I am sure of he hit the next pitch in center field stands."

What is also certain is that Bush retaliated in the next game: In the first inning, he hit Ruth with a pitch. It was hardly out of character. Bush feuded with his manager on the Cubs, "Jolly Cholly" Charlie Grimm, and he was in the middle of some memorable on-field fights—most notably a month before Ruth's three-homer game, in April 1935, by which time he was a Pirate playing his old Chicago teammates. His punch—perhaps with a ring on his finger, according to a SABR article—laid open a six-inch cut on the jaw of Cubs pitcher Roy Joiner.

Red Lucas, the starting pitcher on May 25 for the Pirates, was about as good as Bush, who relieved him in the first inning, but he had the misfortune of playing for very bad Reds teams in the 1920s and '30s while Bush was pitching for good Cubs teams. Lucas had a 157–135 record (.538) with a 3.72 ERA (107 ERA+), while Bush was 176–136 (.564) with a 3.86 ERA (104 ERA+). The Reds were 301–467 (.392) in Lucas's best five-year stretch, in which he led the league in complete games three times and went 70–74 (.486) with a 109 ERA+.

He was no longer a workhorse by 1935, but he remained an anomalously good-hitting pitcher—Lucas batted .318 that season (and over .300 six times) and .281/.340/.347 with an OPS+ of 85 for his career. Managers loved that; he was used as a pinch-hitter 506 times and actually held the record for pinch-hits (114) until Smoky Burgess passed him in 1965. Lucas also had good defensive skills and was used occasionally at other positions. After the Reds traded him to the Pirates, he compiled a 14–0 record against his old team.

Ruth could have had a shot at another home run on May 25—then we would have all memorized "715" for years—but McKechnie took him out in the bottom of the seventh. His replacement, Joe Mowry, was portrayed, after a fashion, in the 1948 movie *The Babe Ruth Story*, but in a scarcely recognizable way. As the writer Bill McCurdy related on his baseball blog *The Pecan Park Eagle*, the movie took great dramatic license. It shows Ruth singling, stumbling on his way to first base and concluding that it was time to retire. He would leave the game, for good, with a hit, if not a home run. Movie Babe signals for a pinch-runner—a young player who had previously talked trash to him, but now seemed sheepish about it. The Babe consoles him, of course.

The reality is that Mowry, a frequent late-inning defensive replacement, went in for Ruth in the bottom of the seventh inning in right field on

May 25, not as a pinch-runner. (Ruth's last at-bat in the game was a home run anyway.) McCurdy wrote that there was no evidence that Mowry had ever badmouthed Ruth. And Ruth played five more games. In his actual finale, Ruth batted once and grounded out to first. No pinch-runner needed.

THIRTEEN

June 2
The Day Lou Gehrig Died

Lou Gehrig played his last baseball game on April 30, 1939. He was clearly a shell of his once-robust self, and that 0-for-4 game left him with a .143 batting average for the season in eight games. Two and a half months later, Gehrig was told he had amyotrophic lateral sclerosis, on June 19—his 37th birthday. Two weeks later, on the Fourth of July, he gave his "luckiest man on earth" speech between games of a doubleheader at Yankee Stadium. And less than two years later, the Iron Horse, the player known for never missing a game, died on June 2, 1941.

Gehrig was only one of 28 Major Leaguers who have died on June 2. Most had nondescript careers, but a few were notable ballplayers. And another slugging first baseman from New York had his career—and life—cut short by disease. Here's a look at some of those players.

Dave Orr, died June 2, 1915, at 55. He played organized baseball from 1883 to 1890, mostly for the New York Metropolitans. Orr was a hulking first baseman, listed at 5 feet 11 inches and 250 pounds, who led the American Association (then a Major League) in batting at .354 as a 24-year-old rookie. In his brief career, he also led the league in RBIs once, slugging percentage twice, hits twice and—remarkably, given his size—triples twice. One year, he hit 31 triples, still the second-highest total. (It wasn't a Metropolitans thing; they had only 72 overall, seventh in an eight-team league.) He also led League first basemen in fielding percentage once. At age 30, by then playing for the Brooklyn Ward's Wonders in the Players League, he hit .371 with 124 RBIs. A few weeks after the season ended, however, he suffered a stroke while playing in an exhibition game, according to his SABR *Bio Project* biography, leaving his left side paralyzed. He survived, but died at 55 of heart disease.

Johnny Mize, died June 2, 1993, at 80. He played from 1936 to 1953, for the St. Louis Cardinals, the New York Giants and the New York Yankees. Another big first baseman (6-2, 215), who was nicknamed the Big

Cat, Mize was one of the National League's foremost sluggers—he led the league in home runs four times (topping out at 51), slugging four times and RBIs three times from the late '30s into the early '50s despite missing three seasons serving in World War II. He also led the league in intentional walks three times, batting average once and—excuse me if this sounds ridiculous again for another big guy—triples once. He struck out infrequently (career high of 57), and, despite his size, rarely grounded into double plays. In the late '40s and '50s, the Yankees had a knack for acquiring veterans who played vital roles as they won pennant after pennant. Mize was purchased from the Giants in late 1949 for $40,000, and in 1950 he hit 25 home runs for the Yankees in 305 plate appearances as they won the American League by three games. He was an All-Star at age 40, although inexplicably, really, and was selected for the Hall of Fame by a veterans committee.

Bruce Kison, died June 2, 2018, at 68. He pitched, mostly for the Pittsburgh Pirates and the California Angels, from 1971 to 1985. Kison was a 21-year-old rookie in the Pirates' bullpen in the 1971 World Series, a midseason call-up after going 10–1 in Class AAA. In Game 4, the Pirates, trailing the Baltimore Orioles, two games to one, fell behind by 3–0 early. Kison had mostly started for the Pirates, but he was called on in relief and pitched 6 1/3 shutout innings, allowing one hit, as Pittsburgh rallied to win, 4–3. That tied the Series, which the Pirates went on to win. He also pitched for the Pirates' 1979 World Series champs (also against the Orioles), but he never reached stardom. Kison dealt with elbow and shoulder injuries and never pitched 200 innings in a season; he said he hurt his arm throwing 92 innings of winter ball after the 1971 World Series. But he did land a lucrative free-agent contract in 1980 with the Angels. Laugh at the numbers now, but this was big money: $160,000 a year for five years, a $750,000 signing bonus and $800,000 deferred.

Gene Woodling, died June 2, 2001, at 78. He played the outfield for six teams from 1943 to 1962. His career spanned from pre-integration to expansion (he was an Opening Day starter for the expansion Senators in 1961 and was a 1962 Met). He earned his renown—and five World Series checks—as a Yankee, but grated at the occasional platooning by Casey Stengel. Woodling, a left-handed hitter, had as many as 500 plate appearances only once with the Yankees. He could always hit—he leaped into professional baseball by batting .398 as a 17-year-old minor leaguer, hit .313 as a 38-year-old with the Washington Senators and still batted .274 with some walks as a 40-year-old with the Mets. And he hit .318 in all those Series with the Yankees. Woodling's career numbers were .284/.386/.431, and he was thought of highly enough that he earned down-ballot MVP votes six times. An oddity: He was part of a 17-player trade between the

Yankees and the Baltimore Orioles—a deal that sent Don Larsen to New York.

Preston Ward, died June 2, 2013, at 85. He played from 1948 to 1959. Indulge me. Preston Ward does not belong on this list based on his accomplishments, but for some reason I liked his 1959 Topps baseball card and the "first base–third base" position he was accorded. Although he played mostly first base, Ward did play third and all three outfield positions. His career numbers were not much—.253/.326/.380 with 50 home runs—but as a teenager he looked as if he might be something special. He turned pro at age 16 during World War II. At 17, he hit .325 with a .426 on-base percentage in the Piedmont League. He batted .325 again when he was 19, with 17 home runs, 21 triples and 30 doubles. He certainly impressed the Dodgers, who won the pennant in 1947 but made him their Opening Day first baseman in 1948 (the previous first baseman, Jackie Robinson, had moved to second).

Ward was not the starter for long, however; he hit an empty .260 and was shipped out to Mobile while some guy named Gil Hodges took over at first base. From a starter on a defending champion, he became a utility player on a succession of bad teams—the Chicago Cubs (terrible), the Pittsburgh Pirates (terrible), the Cleveland Indians (pretty good heading quickly to mediocrity) and the Kansas City Athletics (terrible). He was hitting .338 for the Indians in 1958 when he was traded to Kansas City along with Roger Maris. After the 1959 season Maris was dealt to the Yankees ... and Preston Ward's career was over.

Skinny O'Neal, died June 2, 1981, at 82. He pitched in 1925 and '27. Oran Herbert O'Neal merits this list even less than Preston Ward, but who can resist a player nicknamed Skinny? Which he must have been, as he was listed at 5–11 and 160. His Major League career amounted to almost nothing—25 1/3 innings with a 9.30 ERA for the Philadelphia Phillies in 1925, and five innings with a 9.00 ERA for the Phillies in 1927. His decade-long minor league career was noteworthy for moving around so much during the season. Three times he played for three teams in one year, and another season he played for four teams. Can you imagine a summer moving from Bloomington, Illinois; to Okmulgee, Oklahoma; to Salina, Kansas; to Sapulpa, Oklahoma?

Andrés Segovia and Bo Diddley also died on June 2. Bo Diddley, a Hall of Famer in his own right, had a lot of hits, too.

Fourteen

June 15

Why Is There a Trade Deadline? Blame New York

Almost since the owners of baseball teams signed the first player to a contract, the have-nots of ownership have sought ways to keep the haves from cornering the market on talent. Trades were prohibited early on. Waiver rules were eventually added so that the successful teams could not prey so easily on the bottom feeders. The farm systems that were developed beginning in the 1930s were a means to develop players without having to pay large sums to acquire them from minor league teams. Move ahead a generation, and baseball instituted "bonus baby" rules, putting harsh penalties on the payment of large signing bonuses to amateur players in an effort to keep teams like the Yankees from buying up the best of the lot. A decade later, instituting the amateur draft was supposed to make the best young players available to the worst (often poorest) teams.

One more link in this chain was the trade deadline. Half a century of professional baseball passed without one. But that would change when frustration with the New York teams led the other baseball owners to restrict in-season trading.

In the early 1920s, the New York Giants ruled the land, and the New York Yankees wanted to. After three consecutive second-place finishes that grated on Manager John McGraw, the Giants won the National League pennant every year from 1921 to 1924, capturing the World Series in '21 and '22. Buoyed by wealthy owners, the Yankees averaged a tick over 96 wins a year from 1920 to 1923, lost two Series to the Giants and finally broke through with a championship in 1923.

The other teams in baseball tired of the money being tossed around by the Yankees' owners, Jacob Ruppert and Tillinghast L'Hommedieu Huston, and the maneuverings of the Giants' owner, John Brush, "a master of backroom intrigue with his fellow owners," according to his SABR *Bio Project* biography. Beginning in the mid- to late teens, the New York

Fourteen. June 15

franchises kept making midseason or late-season trades to bolster their pennant runs.

On August 15, 1917, the Giants traded for pitcher Al Demaree. He was ordinary, but the Giants won the pennant. On July 17, 1918, the Giants purchased pitcher Fred Toney; three days later, they bought the contract of another pitcher, Bob Steele. Toney excelled, Steele was pretty much league average, and neither could keep the Giants from finishing second.

On December 18, 1918, the Yankees made their first swap with the Harry Frazee-owned Boston Red Sox. The Red Sox, fresh off a World Series victory, dealt the Yankees two past-their-prime pitchers and a former star outfielder who had missed the season serving in the Navy. But their sell-off to the Yankees had begun ... and continued on July 29 and 30, 1919, when they consummated a trade for star pitcher Carl Mays. The Yankees still couldn't win the pennant, finishing third in the year of the Black Sox.

On August 1, 1919, the Giants struck again, acquiring pitcher Art Nehf, who was tremendous (9–2, 1.50 ERA), from the Boston Braves, but not enough to win the pennant. In January 1920, the Yankees completed the deal for Babe Ruth. Not midseason, but that was enough. The Yankees did not make another deal all season. On June 7, 1920, the Giants traded for the future Hall of Fame shortstop Dave Bancroft from the sixth-place Phillies, although they still came home second, by seven games. In December 1920, the Yankees again picked the Red Sox's pocket, landing the future Hall of Fame pitcher Waite Hoyt in a trade.

In 1921, the Giants picked up outfielders Casey Stengel (July 1, a character) and Irish Meusel (July 25, a star). They were in second place at the time, but won the pennant by four games and then whipped the Ruth Yankees in the World Series. On December 20, 1921, the Yankees relinquished a great-field, little-hit shortstop, Roger Peckinpaugh, and three nondescript pitchers for an ungodly haul from the Red Sox: top-notch pitchers Sad Sam Jones and Bullet Joe Bush and reliable shortstop Everett Scott (who went on to set the consecutive-games record that Lou Gehrig would break).

That is a lot of wheeling and dealing, and it brings us to 1922, when the New York teams made midseason deals with the Boston teams that left the rest of the Major Leagues fuming. On July 23, the Yankees traded flotsam and jetsam to bring in Joe Dugan to fill a hole at third base. Brian Cronin wrote in *The Los Angeles Times* in 2011 that Dugan, acquired by Boston from the Philadelphia Athletics, was with the last-place Red Sox in large part because Frazee was trying to prove to the other AL owners that he wasn't dealing with *only* the Yankees. His resolve didn't last the season, as the $50,000 that came with the players from New York was too tempting. That proved the suspicions of other owners, that Frazee had acquired Dugan only so he could sell him to New York.

The Yankees were two and a half games behind the surprising league leaders, the St. Louis Browns, at that point, but they won the pennant. Dugan replaced 36-year-old Home Run Baker and banjo-hitting Mike McNally at third base, and with him playing every game, the Yankees finished 41–19, a .683 clip. "The other teams were apoplectic," according to Cronin, who added that the AL president, Ban Johnson, "wanted to ban midseason trades altogether."

The pot was about to be stirred more, by the Giants. A week later, they snagged pitcher Hugh McQuillan for a minor league pitcher, a rookie pitcher who never played another Major League season and a veteran pitcher whom the Braves would waive two and a half weeks later. McQuillan's victory on August 12 put the Giants in first place by half a game, and he won five of six decisions through September 9. The Giants wound up winning the pennant.

And their opponents decided enough was enough. The American League owners had pushed through a rule in 1920 banning trades and sales, and beginning in 1921, it was August 1. But the Yankees beat the deadline by a week. The National League's deadline was August 20.

The other owners took their proposal for a midseason trade deadline to Commissioner Kenesaw Mountain Landis, Cronin wrote, and he chose June 15 at the suggestion of Barney Dreyfuss, the Pittsburgh Pirates' owner. And the trade deadline stayed June 15 until 1986, when it was moved back to July 31. As for the immediate effects? The Yankees did not make a single in-season trade in 1923, and the Giants made only one, which had no impact. Both teams won their pennants anyway.

FIFTEEN

June 21

The Boys of Summer, and the Summers Boys

Roger Kahn embedded the phrase "the boys of summer" in the baseball lexicon, although he appropriated it from a Dylan Thomas poem that begins: "I see the boys of summer in their ruin." The poem is not about light and warmth and any sort of good vibrations/summer of love sentiment; the last verse begins: "I see you boys of summer in your ruin. Man in his maggot's barren." Nor is Kahn's book overstuffed with sunny characters. Even the chief protagonist, beyond Kahn himself, Jackie Robinson, confronts rage and worry and despair in middle age. Kahn's boys of summer must manage physical tragedy (Roy Campanella), personal loss (Clem Labine, Robinson), unabated bitterness (Duke Snider, Carl Furillo, Billy Cox), wariness (George Shuba). The most summery personalities—Preacher Roe and especially Carl Erskine and Pee Wee Reese—stand out in the dugout full of

Ed Summers was a pioneer of the knuckler, but he called it "a finger-nail ball" (National Baseball Hall of Fame, Cooperstown, NY).

aging athletes' angst that Kahn found as he visited old Dodgers across the country.

There apparently is no escaping that hint of melancholy in *The Boys of Summer*. Don Henley borrowed the title for his 1984 hit, and the lyrics—by Henley, with music by Mike Campbell, of Tom Petty and the Heartbreakers—riff on the passing of youth, too. (Henley was 37 when he wrote the song—the same age Robinson was when he retired from baseball.) Whether it's old flames or old ballgames, Henley's lyrics ring true: "I can tell you, my love for you will still be strong, after the boys of summer have gone."

But if the sunshine fades when you have lived that life as a ballplayer, as a musician—pastimes of the young—there is plenty of it left for the rest of us, who look on from the outside or back from many years. Baseball fills our summers, and over the years, some guys named Summers have filled box scores. It's Summers time.

Ed Summers, pitcher, 1908–12. Born in December. The mists of history have obscured who invented the knuckleball. Eddie Cicotte, the Chicago White Sox/Black Sox pitcher, often gets credit, but perhaps undeservedly so. Toad Ramsey of the Louisville Colonels threw a sort of knuckleball from 1885 to 1890, the Armory Power Pitching Academy says, although it may have been more of a knuckle curve. Ed Summers's SABR *Bio Project* profile says he began using a knuckler in the minors in 1907 after learning it in one of the previous two seasons from a longtime minor league pitcher named Frosty Thomas. (Frosty and Summers—what a pairing!) Summers *was* a teammate of Cicotte with Indianapolis of the American Association in 1906, and for *The Neyer/James Guide to Pitchers*, Rob Neyer found a quote from Cicotte that Summers "deserves a full share of the credit" for coming up with the knuckler.

Depending on the source, though, Cicotte may have tutored Summers or Summers may have tutored Cicotte. In *K: A History of Baseball in Ten Pitches*, Tyler Kepner says Cicotte credited Summers "with developing the pitch in its modern form." John Thorn and John Holway wrote in *The Pitcher*, however, that Cicotte and teammate Nap Rucker worked it out while playing for Augusta in the South Atlantic League in 1905. The (Mostly) Complete List of Knuckleball Pitchers leans into the Cicotte-Rucker story, but it also says that Lew (Hicks) Moren, who pitched in the Majors beginning in 1903, may have had a hand, or fingers, in the pitch's invention. The same names keep coming up: Neyer's list of the four most likely inventors were Rucker, Moren, Cicotte and Summers. It's convoluted and confusing, but this was Neyer's conclusion: "I think that Cicotte came up with the knuckleball (perhaps with the help of Rucker, in 1905), and Summers figured out a different (if not better) way of getting something like the same results." What I think: Neyer may be right, but no one will ever really know.

Whoever invented the knuckler, they passed along the knowledge. Armory Pitching says a player from the Blue Ridge League, Charles Druery, taught the knuckler in 1917 to Eddie Rommel, who used it with great success with the Philadelphia Athletics. (As an example of just how mysterious knuckleball history is, Kepner refers to this tutor as Cutter Drury, a first baseman-outfielder, who, as it turns out, played in the Blue Ridge League in 1920, Rommel's rookie season in the Majors.) A lot of pitchers learned the knuckleball: In its Pitcher Census of more than 1,000 hurlers from the 19th century until 2004, *The Neyer/James Guide to Pitchers* lists at least 120 hurlers who threw the knuckler at least occasionally.

Beyond who threw it, there is what to call the pitch. Summers did not call his a knuckleball, but a "finger-nail ball," because he—like most knuckleball pitchers—gripped the ball with his fingertips, not his knuckles. (Cicotte did use his knuckles.) The (Mostly) Complete List of Knuckleball Pitchers says that many of the pitchers known for throwing a knuckleball before World War II may well have been throwing a knuckle curve, for which Burt Hooton earned renown in the 1970s. Relying on his "finger-nail ball," Summers had an excellent rookie season in 1908, going 24–12 with a 1.64 ERA (145 ERA+) as his Detroit Tigers won the pennant. But in Game 1 of the World Series against the Chicago Cubs, he faced another opponent: the rain, his SABR biography says.

Rain is a knuckleballer's nemesis. "It's like throwing water balloons," knuckleballer R.A. Dickey said of gripping a knuckler in the rain after a 2012 start for the New York Mets, *The New York Times* reported. Steven Wright, a knuckleballer with the Boston Red Sox, said that rain was a "huge factor" in a 2016 loss to the Houston Astros, MLB.com said. "It got to the point where I couldn't keep anything dry, which, you're trying to throw a pitch with your fingertips, it makes it a little slippery, hard to get a finger pressure," he said. Summers managed early on in that 1908 Series opener as the rain waned, but when it returned, he may have decided he had to give up on his knuckler, his SABR biography says. His other pitches clearly didn't work: Summers yielded five runs in the ninth inning, and the Tigers lost, 10–6. They lost the Series, too.

Throwing a knuckleball in the best of conditions can be unnerving. "You really have to have a lot of balls to throw the pitch," Kevin Pucetas, who relied on the knuckler through nine minor league seasons, told *The Guardian* in 2016. "It's a scary thing. You're 60 feet away from the best hitters in the world, and you're throwing a pitch at 65 mph. If it doesn't do anything there at the plate, if it doesn't separate, you can get your head taken off." It doesn't help when your arm gives out, even for a pitcher throwing something as slow as a knuckler, as Summers's did for good in 1912.

Champ Summers, pinch-hitter, outfielder and first baseman, 1974–84. Born in June (six days before summer). His father nicknamed John Junior Summers II "Champ" as an infant, and if he was never quite a champion, he was always a scrapper. Summers was dealt to Cincinnati just after the Big Red Machine's World Series glory years. After his manager there, Sparky Anderson, moved on to Detroit, Summers also became a Tiger, but he was gone by the time the Tigers were World Series champions in 1984. Despite an 11-year career in the Majors, his real renown was for battling, not batting. Summers, a Vietnam veteran, had numerous fights as a kid because of his nickname, according to his SABR *Bio Project* profile, and again as a Major Leaguer. In 1980, Larry Hansgen recalled in *The Dayton Daily News* upon Summers's death in 2012, Summers and his Tigers teammate Richie Hebner kept punching White Sox players during a brawl that neither was a part of to begin with. The TV cameras never turned away.

His most notorious scuffle occurred on August 12, 1984, and stemmed from his San Diego Padres' game-long animosity toward Atlanta Braves pitcher Pascual Perez. With the very first pitch of the game, Perez, who generally had good control, hit Alan Wiggins in the ribs. The announcers speculated that it was payback for Wiggins's bunting for base hits the day before. Every time Perez came to bat, the Padres threw close to him—Ed Whitson buzzed him three times in Perez's second time up, earning an ejection. Finally, in the eighth, Perez was backing away from the plate even as Craig Lefferts was winding up, but Lefferts nailed him anyway, and a lengthy brawl was on. Summers was restrained from getting to Perez, who had a bat in hand, by the Braves' Bob Watson. But, with Perez by then in the Braves' dugout, Summers broke away from the scrum and sprinted toward the pitcher, only to be stopped by Bob Horner and a couple of fans who spilled out of the stands. "It was crazy," Summers's CBS obituary said.

Lonnie Summers, catcher, outfielder and third baseman, 1938. Born in August. Lonnie Summers played awhile in the Negro leagues, but he played for years in the Mexican League, where he was often known as Sommers. And became known as the father of Jesus Sommers, the only player to accumulate 3,000 hits in the Mexican League. Jesus played 27 seasons in the Mexican League, amassing 3,004 hits in 2,908 games. He also played 1,290 winter league games in Mexico, racking up another 1,073 hits. Jesus was not known as a home run hitter, and neither was his father. "Lonnie was one of those big, strong ballplayers who hit powerful line drives," Chico Renfroe, an Atlanta-based sportswriter and former Negro league player himself, told *The Los Angeles Times* in 1990. "He hit some of the most screaming line drives you've seen in your life."

Fifteen. June 21

Tack Summers, outfielder and third baseman, 1923–28. Born in June (four days into summer). One website mentions Tack Summers—given name Smith—as in the running for one of the 10 best players on Cleveland's various Negro league teams. Summers didn't hit as a 23-year-old in Chicago, but when he resurfaced in Cleveland three years later, he did. He batted .294 for the Cleveland Elites in 1926 and .355 for the Cleveland Hornets in 1927, but nothing could help those teams, which *Baseball Reference* lists with Negro National League records of 8–40–1 and 13–36. In 1928, Summers's team was called the Cleveland Tigers, and while they still weren't any good (20–59), he was no longer much of an offensive threat (.258). The best Cleveland teams were the Buckeyes in the 1940s, but there were also the Tate Grays, the Browns, the Cubs, the Stars, the Giants, the Red Sox and the Bears. Other than the Buckeyes, only one of Cleveland's NNL teams—the 23–22 Cubs in 1931—had a winning record.

Kid Summers, catcher and left fielder, 1893. Birthdate unknown. The 1893 St. Louis Browns fielded Dad Clarkson, Kid Gleason (who was only two months younger than Dad) and Kid Summers, who was the youngster of the lot at age 25. Summers played in only two games—on August 5 and 6—as a catcher for three innings one day and an outfielder for five innings the other. He made an error at each position. He did go 1 for 2 and was hit by a pitch as a batter. Summers spent the rest of that season with Chattanooga of the Southern Association, 1894 with Toledo of the Western League and 1895 with Chattanooga and Mobile. He died that October after an accident at his home in Toronto.

Their name wasn't Summers, but summer was in their names:

Don August, pitcher, 1988–91. Born in July. The team that the United States sent to the Olympics when baseball was added for the Los Angeles Games in 1984 included Division I All-Americans like Mark McGwire, Barry Larkin, Will Clark and Chris Gwynn. And a Division II right-hander, Don August. It was quite a summer for August, who earned an Olympic victory with a sterling relief effort against South Korea in a game in which he had not expected to pitch. August almost passed on trying to make the Olympic team, he said in a 2016 interview with USA Baseball. He was invited to a Saturday morning tryout, but "I was a lazy college kid who wanted to sleep in." However, his coach at Chapman College, Paul Deese, said, "Oh, you're going." August went, was invited to another tryout, and eventually made the team with all the big names.

June Greene, pitcher and pinch-hitter, 1928–29. Born (fittingly) in June. Julius (June) Greene had a June game to forget, though. On June 5, 1929, against the Reds, he faced 19 batters while pitching two innings. Ten of them got base hits, and two walked. Twelve of them scored. That's a good way to wind up with an 18.38 career ERA.

Gerald June Perry, first baseman and outfielder, 1983–95. Born in October. There was nothing middling about June for him; it was his second-best month as a hitter, with a .277/.342/.394 line in 600 times at bat. In 1988, the year he finished fifth in batting in the National League at .300, he burned up June—.423/.442/.549 for the month. June 2009 was not so kind; he was fired that month as hitting coach of the Cubs.

Sixteen

June 29

The Moonlight Grahams of the Majors

Imagine if the editors of the *Baseball Encyclopedia* had listed an obscure New York Giants outfielder from 1905 as Archibald Graham. Or Archie Graham. Or even Doc Graham. Would Bill Kinsella have noticed his name? But Moonlight Graham—*that* name caught the attention of Kinsella, a Canadian author with a distinctive love of baseball and fantasy. He lifted the bare facts of Graham's baseball story (one game, no at-bats, a long line of zeroes in the *Encyclopedia*) and the fleshed-out story of his life after baseball (a small-town physician living hundreds of miles from the nearest Major League team) and turned Moonlight Graham into a compelling figure in his novel *Shoeless Joe*. Without *Shoeless Joe*, there would have been no *Field of Dreams*. Without Moonlight Graham in either work, the delight and plight of a player who reached the Major Leagues, only to have the dream end without a time at bat, might not resonate so deeply with fans of the game fascinated with the human psyche.

Moonlight Graham was but one of 64 players through 2022, not counting pitchers who pitched in a single game, whom *Baseball Reference* lists as having had Moonlight moments: one game, no at-bats. (This also does not count Negro league players, whose careers were recorded with much less care and specificity.) Their moments ranged from 1885 to 2021, although it is easy to imagine that other 19th-century players had a one-game/no-plate-appearance record that was never captured in print.

Predictably, such players were more numerous in the early decades of the modern game, with the largest number—more than a quarter of the Moonlights—coming and going in the 1910s: 17 players. Moonlights were fairly frequent through the 1920s, then began to diminish in the 1930s (perhaps because farm systems, introduced then, more formalized player acquisition and development) before a resurgence in the 1940s and 1950s, no doubt abetted by World War II and perhaps the Korean War. In the expansion era, Moonlights have nearly vanished: only 10 of them have appeared since expansion began in 1961. Here's a breakdown by decade:

1880s: 1	1930s: 3	1980s: 2
1890s: 1	1940s: 10	1990s: 0
1900s: 5	1950s: 7	2000s: 2
1910s: 17	1960s: 3	2010s: 0
1920s: 10	1970s: 2	2020s: 1

It's interesting to see what kind of players were viewed as so dispensable. An overwhelming number—25—were used only as pinch-runners, and 18 were catchers in their sole appearance without a time at bat. (A few pitchers either played the field or pinch-ran in their only Major League experience, never taking the mound; talk about feeling cheated.)

Some of the Moonlights played for a World Series champion, more of them for a tail-ender. Some were bonus babies who, for one reason or another, did not fulfill their promise; others were amateurs pulled off local sandlots to fill out the roster. Some had famous names thanks to higher-profile brothers; at least one Moonlight played under an alias (an appropriate word given his criminal profile). Thanks to Bill Kinsella for making Moonlight magic. And for helping to make a single game without out a single plate appearance so memorable. Here are the Moonlights of the game.

The 19th Century

Sandy McDermott, 29, second baseman, Baltimore Orioles, June 18, 1885. The 1885 Orioles played in the American Association, considered a Major League, and finished 41–68–1, last of the eight teams and 36½ games out of first place. They were last in the league in batting average, on-base percentage and slugging percentage (although their batters did lead the league in walks). The team was seventh in ERA and second in errors made. This was the team that McDermott could play for only briefly at second base, and without a time at bat. He finished his career with a couple of teams in the Ohio State League, the Akron Acorns and the Columbus Buckeyes. What a league! It also included the Kalamazoo Kazoos, the Steubenville Stubs, the Zanesville Kickapoos and a team from Sandusky alternately called the Suds, Sands and Maroons.

Phil Wisner, 25, shortstop, Washington Nationals, August 30, 1895. Perhaps not a Moonlight Graham despite the record book. The *Sporting Life* of September 7, 1895, says Wisner was one of three local amateurs given a chance to play in a late-season game against the St. Louis Browns. Baseball records do not indicate Wisner's having a plate appearance, but they do say he played four innings at shortstop (with three errors and an assist), from which you would infer he had to have batted. And a box score in *Sporting Life* shows him going 0 for 1. (It also renders his name as Wesner. There is no official record for a Phil Wesner.) A side note on the state of the National League then: Nine of the 12 teams had winning records. The bottom three—Washington, St. Louis and the Louisville Colonels—finished 117–273, a .300 winning percentage. The second-place team was the Cleveland Spiders. Four years later, in the final season for that League with 12 teams, the Spiders and St. Louis had common ownership, the good players were all packed on the roster for St. Louis (by then known as the Perfectos), and Cleveland finished 20–134. In 1900, Cleveland and Louisville were among the four teams contracted out of the League.

The 1900s

Henry Stein, 31, catcher, St. Louis Cardinals, October 14, 1900. Stein was born in Hannibal, Missouri, a generation after Mark Twain grew up there, so perhaps it is appropriate that he seems like a fictional character. He caught in a game for the Cardinals without batting, but details of his appearance are lacking. *Baseball Reference* says he was a 30-year-old *left-handed* catcher—a detail remarkable given how little else is known about this outing, which was the final game of the season for St. Louis. This was baseball at the time: The Cardinals had a 19-game homestand, followed by a 25-game road trip that season. Henry Stein is a better-known name in the video world: He was the protagonist in the five-chapter survival horror video game *Bendy and the Ink Machine*.

Frank Mahar, 23, outfielder, Philadelphia Phillies, August 29, 1902. In these early days of baseball, teams did curious things. Late in the season, the Phillies, bound for next-to-last in the National League, signed Mahar from an amateur team in Massachusetts and put him in the starting lineup against the even worse Giants. His SABR *Bio Project* biography tells his woeful tale: During warmups, a fly ball bounced off the bleachers and hit Mahar "on the mouth, cutting his lip and face very badly," *The Philadelphia Record* reported. He played the top of the first in left field but had to come out of the game and was taken to a hospital, where he received several stitches in his lip. *The Record* reporter was not dazzled with what he had seen, writing that Mahar (or "Maher"; the paper misspelled his name) "is a frail-looking young man, and his actions do not impress one as though he would prove to be fast enough for a major league." Or a minor league. Mahar never played another professional game.

Moonlight Graham, 27, right fielder, New York Giants, June 29, 1905. Archibald Graham's family called him Archie, as did many of his teammates. Sportswriters often called him Doc, as he was attending medical school, but a few called him Moonlight. In 1905, well before the start of the season, *The New York Evening World* wrote, "Dr. Archie Graham, who is to join the Giants as soon as he completes his examinations at the Baltimore Medical College, is known as 'Moonlight' because he is supposed to be as fast as a flash." Still, he would have been an unknown footnote in baseball history but for the author W.P. (Bill) Kinsella, who made Moonlight Graham famous.

Graham, who had become a longtime, small-town doctor, died in 1965; some years later, Kinsella received a copy of the *Baseball Encyclopedia* (first published four years after Graham's death) from his father-in-law. Kinsella was perusing the *Encyclopedia* when he became intrigued by the entry under Graham. Not Peaches Graham (he wasn't from Georgia) or Skinny Graham (he was 5 feet 7 and 181) or Tiny Graham (he was 6–2), but Moonlight Graham, who had a 1 listed for games played followed by an entire string of 0s. Ben Walker of *The Associated Press* quoted Kinsella in 2005: "I found this entry for Moonlight Graham. How could anyone come up with that nickname?" He borrowed the name and Graham's story—one Major League game, no at-bats, and a long medical career in the Minnesota boondocks—for a character in his novel *Shoeless Joe*, which was published in 1982. That was the basis for the same character in the 1989 movie *Field of Dreams*, indelibly portrayed by Burt Lancaster.

The book was among Kinsella's great successes, and although he stewed over the movie as it was being made, he liked the film, which was a considerable success, with catch phrases lifted straight from the novel. ("If you build it, he will come." "Go the distance.") And suddenly, Moonlight Graham's modest career seemed like a success. Before his Moonlight moment, he had spent four seasons in the minor leagues. He graduated from medical school in May 1905 and was called up by the Giants, who kept him on the bench. He may have been dealing with an injury sustained while playing football for the University of Maryland, his SABR *Bio Project* biography says.

Finally, on June 29, with the Giants leading the Brooklyn Superbas, 10–0, Manager John McGraw inserted Graham in right field for the last two innings. He was on deck when the third out was made in the top of the ninth. After his one game, he sat on the bench for another week before his contract was sold to the Scranton Miners. Graham played another three seasons of minor league ball while continuing medical studies and eventually embarking on his medical career. He practiced in Chicago but moved to Chisholm, Minnesota, in the Iron Range, thinking the climate would help his chronic respiratory problems, his SABR biography says. Veda Ponikvar, whom Graham treated when she was a girl in Chisholm and who formed a bond with him when she ran the local newspaper, told *The Associated Press* she knew him for almost half a century, but said he never explained his nickname. Or boasted about his baseball days.

Charlie Fallon, 24, pinch-runner, New York Highlanders, June 30, 1905. Fallon had his Moonlight moment the day after Moonlight Graham had his. Fallon, an outfielder, ran for catcher Deacon McGuire in the ninth inning. He spent the rest of the season, his first in pro ball despite the advanced age of 24, with Hartford, where he played for four years.

Cecil (Cy) Neighbors, 27, left fielder, Pittsburgh Pirates, April 29, 1908. Neighbors would have been a curious addition to the Pirates' 1908 roster. The team won 91 games the year before, finishing second, and was stronger in '08, winning 98 games but finishing tied for second, a game back of the Cubs. (Yes, three teams accounted for 99, 98 and 98 victories in the National League that year.) Neighbors had hit only .268 in '07 as an outfielder in the Southern Association. But he was in Chicago with the Pirates when player-manager Fred Clarke, an eventual Hall of Famer, took himself out of the game for a pinch-hitter and then inserted Neighbors to play left field. He returned to the minors for the rest of the season and 10 more. When he was about 80, according to an obituary in *The News Tribune,* the newspaper in his hometown, Tacoma, Washington, he did carpentry work on a ballpark for the minor league team. It was built in 42 days and, although renovated, is still in use.

The 1910s

Danny Mahoney, 22, pinch-runner, Cincinnati Reds, May 15, 1911. Not to be confused with the Dan Mahoney who played for the Reds two decades earlier and died at the age of 39 by drinking carbolic acid, a death ruled suicide. An article in *The Sporting Life* indicated that Danny Mahoney might have lost his eligibility in college—it reported Notre Dame, although Mahoney attended the College of the Holy Cross—by signing a contract with the Reds. After his Major League experience pinch-running, he played fewer than 200 minor league games.

Jack Smith, 18, third baseman, Detroit Tigers, May 18, 1912. You could call Jack Smith a thief. Or a crook. Or a scab. Even, if you were literal about it, a Major League third baseman for two innings in 1912, although that was because of one of the most bogus games in Major League history. You couldn't really call him Jack Smith, though, as his real name was John Joseph Coffey. An article in the Spring 2023 *Baseball Research Journal* about the game in question says the 18-year-old Smith—or Coffey—had been sentenced to the Pennsylvania Industrial Reform School not quite two months earlier on a larceny charge and may have played the game under the assumed name because he was supposed to be at the reform school, not the ballpark.

If Smith/Coffey and his appearance all seem a little shady, then the game of May 18, 1912, was perfect for him. It was the game for which the Tigers fielded a team of strike-breakers to avoid a fine from the American League and a forfeit after Ty Cobb's teammates refused to play in the aftermath of his suspension for beating up a fan. Accounts of the lead-up to the assault vary, depending on the source (Cobb and allies or the fan). Charles Leerhsen's biography *Ty Cobb: A Terrible Beauty* discusses how rowdyism and abuse from fans were a problem at the time, resulting in numerous incidents in which players, managers or coaches went after fans. At a game a week earlier in New York, a Highlanders fan known for heckling Cobb, Claude Lucker (that's according to Leerhsen; the name is sometimes rendered as Luecker or Lueker), had verbal exchanges with Cobb that led the Tigers star to jump into the stands and pummel him. This was no ordinary loudmouthed fan, however. Lucker had only three fingers, all on one hand, because of an accident in his old job as a pressman for *The New York Times*.

According to the *Baseball Research Journal* account, "A bystander yelled to Ty, 'Don't kick him, he's a cripple and has no hands,' to which Cobb replied, 'I don't care if he has no feet.'" The American League president, Ban Johnson, was at the game and suspended Cobb indefinitely. The Tigers played their next game, on May 17, without him, but his teammates wrote a letter to Johnson saying there would be no game on May 18 unless Cobb was reinstated. "If players cannot have protection we must protect ourselves," the letter said. Johnson told the Tigers' owner, Frank Navin, that if he did not field a team on May 18, the Tigers would be fined $5,000 (more than $150,000 in 2024 dollars).

Navin told the manager, Hughie Jennings, to put a team on the field, *Baseball Research Journal* says, but Jennings was not inclined to do so until the opposing manager, the Athletics' Connie Mack, encouraged him to round up a backup squad of Philadelphia-area sandlot players just in case. (There may have been a financial incentive; not playing the game would have meant giving up the bigger revenue from a Saturday game at Shibe Park.) The Tigers warmed up, Leerhsen wrote, but then would not take the field without Cobb, so Jennings's backup squad, made up of young college and sandlot players and aging coaches, did. Leerhsen quotes Arthur (Bugs) Baer, a future sportswriter who was a bench player for the fill-ins, saying, "Any ballplayer who could stop a grapefruit from rolling uphill or hit a bull in the pants with a bass fiddle was given a chance of going direct from the semipros to the Detroits with no questions asked."

The game went as you might expect: The Athletics won, 24–2, knocking out 26 hits (all against Al Travers, a 20-year-old St. Joseph's College junior who pitched a complete game) and stealing 10 bases. Mack was not merciful; he played mostly his starters, and Eddie Collins stole five bases (most of them while 48-year-old Deacon McGuire was catching). The scabs were paid anywhere from $10 to $50, newspaper accounts said, and the regular Tigers were fined, initially $100. Eventually, Cobb accepted a 10-game suspension, and the fines were reduced to $50. Smith had his Major League moment, but during World War I he spent time in the county jail, *Baseball Research Journal* says. He later worked as a writer for a publishing company and as an insurance agent.

Fred Walden, 21, catcher, St. Louis Browns, June 3, 1912. Walden's adult life was tied to St. Louis. He played his one Major League game in St. Louis, catching an inning for the Browns, who would lose 101 games, in a 13–4 loss to the Senators. The next year, he was a backup catcher for the St. Louis Terriers in the Federal League the season before it became a Major League. He later served in World War I and worked in a newspaper pressroom. He was living in Jefferson Barracks, Missouri, a decommissioned Army base near St. Louis, part of which was converted to low-cost housing, when he died.

Homer Thompson, 21, catcher, New York Highlanders, October 5, 1912. It was the last game of the season, and Homer Thompson was a late-inning replacement at catcher for his one and only game. His brother Carl, normally a pitcher, was a pinch-runner in the game. It was Carl's only Major League season, too, but he managed eight games. He *did* come to bat—13 times, going 3 for 10 with a couple of walks. The Thompsons had also been teammates at the University of Georgia.

Joe Evers, 21, pinch-runner, New York Giants, April 24, 1913. Joe played his one game for the pennant-winning Giants; his brother, Johnny, who was 10 years older, was starring for the third-place Cubs. Joe, a middle infielder, pinch-ran for a catcher and then was replaced. He spent the rest of the season at Class B Terre Haute, and over eight seasons he never rose above Class B. He was a pro basketball player longer, 12 seasons, in the days well before the NBA. He played in the New York State League, for the champion team from Troy, New York, his hometown, and the Pennsylvania State Basketball League, plus one season in the Metropolitan Basketball League. He was listed at 5 feet 9 inches and 135 pounds, which made him larger than his famous brother, who was said to have been 100 pounds or so when he broke into pro ball. Joe, whom the Troy newspaper said was one of the top bowlers in town, died two years after Johnny.

John Merritt, 18, outfielder, New York Giants, September 27, 1913. John McGraw, like other managers of the era, would occasionally want to take a look at a young ballplayer over a period of time. These tryouts sometimes turned into Major League appearances—much like Moonlight Graham's. And John Merritt's. Merritt was actually a pitcher who had finished up a 14–16 season in Class D ball when McGraw's Giants took him on. Merritt never got to pitch, but with a week left in a pennant-winning season, he was slipped into left field for two innings. Merritt couldn't hit, but he did win 215 minor league games over 14 seasons, with a 119–86 record in eight seasons in the American Association. He just never got the ball in the Majors.

Sam Brenegan, 23, catcher, Pittsburgh Pirates, April 24, 1914. Little in *Field of Dreams* sounds more implausible than Brenegan's life in baseball. The headline on a *Buffalo News* article from May 12, 1914, paints a pretty good picture of it: "Loafs Himself Out of Major League." *The Racine (Wisconsin) Journal-News* was no kinder with its headline: "HE WAS TOO LAZY/Catcher Sam Brenegan Released by Pittsburgh—Has Hook Worm." (No, I don't know what that means. Nothing ever says he had hookworm, or any other disease.) This from a player who had impressed reporters in spring training and "was declared to be a whale behind the bat and a bear at throwing."

The *Buffalo News* article began,

> Catcher Sam Brenegan, who loafed a job away, has been released by Pittsburgh to the Portland, Ore. Sam had a job cinched until he broke into the game one afternoon out at Forbes Field. He failed to deliver and was at once marked for decapitation. Brenegan is the catcher who allowed a wild pitch to roll to the wire screen and then failed to go after it. A few minutes later, he was guilty of a passed ball and again he loafed on the job while runners scampered around the bases.

The website Diamonds in the Dusk says Brenegan replaced the starting catcher in the sixth inning and allowed a passed ball, which a newspaper account said split his finger, and a wild pitch. (*The Dickson Baseball Dictionary* says that for years, a catcher who was hit hard on the hand by a ball was said to "have pulled a brenegan.") *Pittsburgh Baseball History* says he walked after the passed ball. With one out in the seventh, Brenegan did not hustle after a wild pitch, and the runner on first made it to third. Manager Fred Clarke then took Brenegan out of the game, the Pittsburgh newspaper article said, and "since then Brenegan has taken no part in the Pirates' activities other than to warm up a pitcher occasionally." *The Sporting Life* said spacious Forbes Field might have been a factor in Brenegan's dilatory play behind the plate, noting that he had played in Petersburg, Virginia, where the backstop was only 30 feet from home plate but that at Forbes Field it was 140 feet.

The Sporting Life said the team owner, Barney Dreyfuss, excused Brenegan's play, saying that it sometimes took new players awhile to become accustomed to Forbes Field. *Baseball Reference's Bullpen* says: "According to Sam's obituary, he had told a writer that he had been out drinking the night before, and in his only major league appearance muffed a foul fly ball, which angered manager Fred Clarke. When Sam also got angry, it was the end of his major league career." When he was released, Diamonds in the Dusk wrote, "the general consensus of the Pirates management is that the big catcher lacks 'ambition and sand' for success at the major league level." Or the minor league level. When he was released by the Spokane Indians in 1916, a newspaper account said he was "discouraged easily." In an exhibition game in 1916 for Terre Haute against the Pirates, Pittsburgh stole so easily that he became frustrated and stopped trying to throw out base stealers, Diamonds in the Dusk says.

The next year he was playing in Ohio for the Dayton Veterans, and *The Dayton Herald* wrote on June 23: "Sam Brenegan will have to put in several hours each morning finding where second base is located if he repeats his demonstration of throwing again. In two days Sam has thrown the ball to center field while trying to catch base runners." On July 4, *The Herald* wrote, "Although Sam is a hard worker and can hit, his bonehead plays have cost the Vets more games than his hitting has ever won." Three days later he asked for his release and said, "The Devil must be in me and everything is going wrong."

Tom Burr, 20, center fielder, New York Yankees, April 24, 1914. Burr was one of eight Major Leaguers to die while serving in World War I. He was actually a pitcher, but was inserted into the game as a pinch-runner amid several shifts by Manager Frank Chance in a ninth-inning rally and wound up playing center field in the 10th inning without having a play.

Ralph Shafer, 20, pinch-runner, Pittsburgh Pirates, July 25, 1914. Shafer was the Pirates' second Moonlight Graham of 1914. Sam Brenegan was the first, in April, and Shafer came and went with less drama. He had been signed out of the University of Cincinnati, and although he spent most of the season splitting time among three teams in the Class D Ohio State League, he was in New York in late July as Pittsburgh took on the league-leading Giants and Christy Mathewson. Shafer ran for a pinch-hitter in the eighth inning. He and his wife, Elsa, were physical education teachers, and Ralph was a longtime coach and referee, according to her obituary in *The Akron Beacon Journal*.

Ray Shook, 26, pinch-runner, Chicago White Sox, April 16, 1916. How did Shook ever earn even a few days with the White Sox? He had spent five years catching in the minors, the low minors, and not hitting or playing regularly. In 1915, he batted .189 for the Racine Belles in the Class D Bi-State League. (He did meet and marry his wife, Mabel, there.) Yet he was in Chicago to begin the season in 1916, and five games into the season, he pinch-ran as the White Sox tried in vain to rally against the future Hall of Famer Eddie Plank. Shook played out the season, and his career, in Rockford, Illinois, in the Three-I League.

Duke Kelleher, 22, catcher, New York Giants, August 18, 1916. Kelleher graduated from Princeton in the spring of 1916 and wound up with the Giants, getting into the ninth inning of an 8–1 victory over the Cubs. It was a game for nicknames: Duke; his batterymate, Pol Perritt; Giants second baseman Laughing Larry Doyle; and Three Finger Brown, the Chicago pitcher.

Ollie Welf, 27, pinch-runner, Cleveland Indians, August 30, 1916. Welf was a pitcher who had control problems and an outfielder who did not hit well in four seasons in the Class D Cotton States League from 1910 to 1913, but he surfaced three years later deep in the season with Cleveland as a pinch-runner. It was a .500 team that year, with a future Hall of Famer (Tris Speaker), a future scoundrel (Black Sox member Chick Gandil), a second baseman famous for one play (Bill Wambsganss, who had an unassisted triple play in the 1920 World Series), a shortstop famous for one time at bat (Roy Chapman, who died after being hit on the head with a pitch in 1920), an outfielder with an outlandish, yet accurate, nickname (Braggo Roth, who was infamous for his boasting), a pitcher with an outlandish, yet accurate, nickname (Pop-boy Smith, who was a soda vendor at a minor league ballpark as a teenager), another pitcher with a wildly inaccurate nickname (Shorty Des Jardien, who was 6 feet 4 inches tall) and a pitcher named for the president when he was born (Grover Cleveland Lowdermilk, born two years before the infinitely more famous Grover Cleveland Alexander).

Johnny O'Connor, 24, catcher, Chicago Cubs, September 16, 1916. The season was winding down when Rowdy Elliott went out to catch the bottom of the first against the Phillies. A foul tip split his finger, which was bad news for the Cubs, whose two regular backups, Jimmy Archer and Art Wilson, were sitting in the stands with injuries of their own, *The Philadelphia Inquirer* reported. Out came O'Connor to catch, but only for an inning; *The Inquirer* said Wilson limped to the clubhouse to suit up and replace O'Connor. O'Connor is the next-to-last native of Ireland to play in the Majors, *Baseball Reference's Bullpen* says.

Ivan (Pete) Bigler, 24, pinch-runner, St. Louis Browns, May 6, 1917. The 1917 Browns, who featured a young first baseman named George Sisler, had five players with one-game careers: Bigler, Tom Richardson, Ed Murray, Otto Neu and George Pennington, according to SABR's *Bio Project* biography of Bigler. Richardson had an at-bat, as a 33-year-old pinch-hitter in the eighth inning of a rainy second game of a doubleheader. Murray, a 22-year-old shortstop, played two innings and got one at-bat—he struck out—before being lifted for a pinch-hitter. George (Kewpie) Pennington, who was 20, pitched the ninth inning of an 11–0 blowout loss—a no-hitter by Eddie Cicotte; Pennington yielded a hit but no runs. Only Neu was also a one-game, no at-bat position player, a 22-year-old shortstop. In Bigler's sole game, he was inserted in the seventh inning as a pinch-runner for a batter who hit for pitcher Eddie Plank; in the top of the inning, a reliever took Bigler's spot in the lineup. Bigler spent nearly the first month of the season with the Browns, who would finish 57-97-1 with the worst offense in the American League, but that was his only game.

Arch Reilly, 25, third baseman, Pittsburgh Pirates, June 1, 1917. The Pirates acquired Reilly from the minor league Newport Reds in mid–April 1917, but he never got in a game until June 1. And then, he played only the ninth inning, recording a force out at third to conclude the inning. He was on deck when the game ended, and the next week he was back in the minors. Reilly's college coaching career was almost as short as his Major League playing career. At his alma mater, Marshall College, he coached one season of baseball (8–8, 1920), football (8–0, 1919) and basketball (2–5, 1918–19).

Otto Neu, 22, shortstop, St. Louis Browns, July 10, 1917. Neu *did* come to bat in a "big league" setting: on an episode of *The Simpsons*. In *Homer at the Bat* on February 20, 1992, a fictional Neu plays right field for the Smithers Contemporaries against the Burns Anachronisms—and hits a bloop single. (He also made an error.) Real life was also unbelievable: Neu, along with Ivan Bigler, was one of *two* Browns in 1917 who made their only Major League appearance and did not get to bat. He replaced shortstop Doc Lavan in the middle of a 17-inning game, but when his turn to hit came up, he was replaced by Armando Marsans. Neu was from Springfield, Ohio, and of course the Simpsons live in a fictional Springfield.

Jesse Baker, 24, shortstop, Washington Senators, September 14, 1919. It was Ty Cobb's fault that Baker never came to bat. Baker, who was 5 feet 4, weighed 140 pounds and was called Tiny, started the Senators' September 14 game against the Tigers. But, as the baseball historian and illustrator Gary Cieradkowski recounts, Cobb spiked Baker on a steal of second with two out in the second inning. The papers said the injury was not serious, but it was enough to knock him out of the game. Born Michael Silverman in Cleveland in 1895, he played in a 1915 exhibition game against the Toledo Mud Hens as a tryout for Cubs Manager Roger Bresnahan; the box score shows no at-bats and one assist. He later surfaced not as Mickey Silverman but as Jesse Baker, in 1919 for the Richmond Colts of the Class C Virginia League. Senators Manager Clark Griffith got good reports on him and got the Colts to lend him Baker for a few games. He kept switching names back and forth and was later a fight promoter and a stunt double.

The 1920s

Jim Mahady, 19, second baseman, New York Giants, October 2, 1921. It was the last game of the regular season and three days before the beginning of the World Series—Babe Ruth's first as a Yankee—and John McGraw was unloading his bench against the Brooklyn Robins. He inserted four substitutes in the fifth inning, two more in the sixth, another two in the seventh and then made a final two lineup changes in the eighth. One of them was Mahady, a 19-year-old who had yet to play a professional game and would spend the rest of his career as a pitcher. In this game, however, he played second base and handled the only ground ball that came his way.

Elmer Pence, 22, right fielder, Chicago White Sox, August 23, 1922. Pence replaced the future Hall of Famer Harry Hooper in right field in the eighth inning against the Senators, but beyond that his baseball career—and his life—is a mystery. *Baseball Reference* shows no minor league numbers for him, although its Bullpen notes that there were some players listed only as Pence who played in the minors in that era. In fact, in 1922 an outfielder named Pence batted .294 in 46 games for Class C Lakeland, Florida, and an outfielder Pence is shown hitting .394 in nine games for the Class B team in Greenville, South Carolina. Another Pence—no first name, no position listed—played for Jackson, Mississippi, in the Class D Cotton States League in 1923. B-R Bullpen says that *Baseball Digest* listed Elmer Pence in 1962 as among numerous ex-Major Leaguers who were "lost," but he was quickly found and died six years later.

Leo Taylor, 21, pinch-runner, Chicago White Sox, May 3, 1923. Taylor was a shortstop in the semipro Idaho-Washington League for several years in the 1920s, but he cut his teeth as a pro with the White Sox. His one appearance: as a pinch-runner in the eighth inning in a loss to the Browns just three and a half years removed from Chicago's Black Sox scandal in the 1919 World Series. The 1923 White Sox weren't any good (69–85–2), part of a 15-year stretch in the American League's second division. The only other pro experience *Baseball Reference* shows for Taylor was in 1926 with the San Francisco Seals. They weren't any good either: 84–116.

Joe Bennett, 23, third baseman, Philadelphia Phillies, July 11, 1925. Bennett played the seventh inning against the Cardinals, recording one assist. Russ Wrightstone pinch-hit for him in the bottom of the inning with none out and runners on first and third but popped up; in the eighth, Wrightstone hit a grand slam, although the Phillies lost, 16–12. *Baseball Reference's Bullpen*, quoting *The Big Book of Jewish Baseball*, says Bennett said he was never paid for the game.

Mel Kerr, 22, pinch-runner, Chicago Cubs, September 16, 1925. Unlike most Moonlight Grahams, Kerr did something that actually showed up in a boxscore: He scored a run after being sent in to run for Tommy Griffith in the ninth inning of an 8–6 loss to the Boston Braves. Kerr could hit a little (.304 in the minors, although mostly in the low minors) and was fast (he once stole 80 bases in a season). But baseball probably was not his best sport. Accounts at different stages of his life note his prowess in road racing, track and field, tennis, basketball, rugby, bowling and golf. A rugby injury may well have cost him a shot at the 1924 Olympics track and field competition.

Jim Boyle, 22, catcher, New York Giants, June 20, 1926. Boyle caught the ninth inning of an 8–0 loss to the Pirates, replacing Paul Florence, who was playing his only Major League season. The Giants used seven catchers that year—they hit .198—and another of them, Jim Hamby, played only one game (going 0 for 3). But Hamby did play in 21 games the next year. Boyle went straight from Xavier University in Cincinnati to the Giants; his grandson Steve Rushin, a well-known writer at *Sports Illustrated*, wrote that Boyle was paid $250, minus a $30 deposit for his home and road uniforms. He retired after that season and went on to own an acclaimed restaurant in New York, The Browntown Beefery.

A website called *The Baseball Impurist* says Boyle was one of six players who played their only Major League game on June 20; Boyle, in 1926, was the most recent. "And while more than 900 men have appeared in one—and only one—game in the majors, Boyle did so without ever setting foot in the minors," Rushin wrote in *Sports Illustrated* in 2006. "'Not on the way up,' says his son, Patrick, 'and not on the way down.' It's an extraordinary trick, like painting one fresco on the Sistine ceiling without a ladder, but Jimmy Boyle remains an elusive figure, a less-celebrated version of Moonlight Graham, who made one appearance for the same Giants—and the same manager, John McGraw—in 1905."

Russ (Hack) Ennis, 29, catcher, Washington Senators, September 19, 1926. Ennis, on his seventh day with Washington, was the third catcher the Senators used against the Tigers, playing the ninth inning as Detroit rallied for two runs to win. The Senators had struggled to find a third-string catcher after sending theirs to the Yankees and finally landed Ennis, the MVP of his team in Elmira, New York. He served in the Army in both World War I and World War II.

Terry Lyons, 20, first baseman, Philadelphia Phillies, April 19, 1929. Lyons made the Phillies' Opening Day roster in 1929 without any professional experience, according to *Baseball Reference*. The 20-year-old rookie was not really needed that year, as first baseman Don Hurst played all 154 games and was quite good, batting .304/.390/.525 with 31 home runs, 125 RBIs, 80 walks and an OPS+ of 119. In the second game of the season, Hurst made his fourth consecutive out in the seventh inning and charged into the Giants' dugout after apparently hearing too much chatter. He was ejected, and young Lyons came on to play first base for two innings, making three putouts. The details of his short career are quite sketchy—11 games later that season in Class B, another 12 the next year in Class C. He died under unusual circumstances, according to *Baseball Almanac*, after a dentist in Dayton, Ohio, began to knock him out to extract several teeth; he fell unconscious and was dead on arrival at a hospital at the age of 58.

Dan Jessee, 28, pinch-runner, Cleveland Indians, August 14, 1929. Jessee was inserted as a pinch-runner in the eighth inning of Cleveland's 17-inning loss to the Athletics. Willie Hudlin replaced him in the lineup and pitched the final nine innings. Boston's starter pitched all 17 innings and won despite giving up 20 hits (all singles): Lefty Grove. Jessee was the baseball coach at Trinity College in Connecticut for more than 30 years (he also coached football and squash) and wrote an instructional book, *Baseball*, that had multiple printings.

The 1930s

Eddie Hunter, 28, third baseman, Cincinnati Reds, August 5, 1933. Hunter played the final inning of a 2–1 loss to the Cardinals. He spent three seasons in the Class D Mississippi Valley League—one report says he was on the restricted list in the middle of that stretch, with no explanation—before heading home to the Cincinnati area, where he was playing in a local league. The Reds, beset by terrible finances and a run of injuries, were scrambling to field enough players for a pair of weekend doubleheaders against the Cardinals, according to *The Local Boys: Hometown Players for the Cincinnati Reds*. "The team is now so utterly without reserve strength that a couple of local athletes were called on yesterday to be used in case of emergency," the book quotes *The Cincinnati Enquirer*. Those two were Hunter and a guy named Hap Bohl, bolstering a roster that had only 16 players available.

Hunter sat on the bench as the Reds broke a 10-game losing streak in the opener, played in Game 2 and then signed a contract before the Sunday doubleheader. But he did not play, and then, with four days off before their next game, the Reds went out and signed a 20-year-old minor leaguer, Tony Robello, whose Major League career lasted only 16 games. Hap Bohl never got in the game, although he managed some low-level minor league teams for the Reds. By 1939—when the Reds were in the World Series—Bohl was playing the outfield for the Beeco Monuments in the Tristate Semipro League in Cincinnati, *The Enquirer* reported.

Bob Daughters, 22, pinch-runner, Boston Red Sox, April 24, 1937. In Boston's home opener, Daughters was sent in to pinch-run in the 10th inning with the Red Sox trailing the Yankees by two runs. With Daughters on third with the bases loaded and one out, a groundout scored him, but the Red Sox could not tie the game. He had signed with the Red Sox after apparently flunking out of Holy Cross. He made the team out of spring training, but was sent down to Class C in mid–May. He was released the next year, with his SABR *Bio Project* profile noting that his subpar defense and weak arm were among the reasons. His daughter, the biography reports, said that Daughters had hurt his arm or collarbone while in Boston and could no longer throw well—a problem for a third baseman and outfielder. The SABR biography says that Daughters, who was known as Red, took in Moe Berg, the ex-ballplayer and likely spy, when he was homeless and alcoholic for a couple of months sometime after World War II. "Coincidental or not, Red's brother Don was active in World War II intelligence work and spent most of his life in South America after the war."

Harry O'Neill, 22, catcher, Philadelphia Athletics, July 23, 1939. Two former Major Leaguers were killed while serving in World War II—O'Neill, who was shot by a sniper at Iwo Jima, and Elmer Gedeon, whose plane was shot down over France, according to *Spartan Seasons: How Baseball Survived the Second World War*. O'Neill had signed with the Athletics in June 1939 after his graduation from Gettysburg College, his SABR *Bio Project* biography says, and was basically a bullpen catcher until he was sent in to replace Frankie Hayes behind the plate in the eighth inning of a 16–3 loss. Four innings earlier, another 22-year-old college man, pitcher Jim Schelle from Villanova, made *his* Major League debut. He had more of an impact than O'Neill, but it was lamentable: Schelle hit the first batter he faced, gave up a single to the next and then walked the following three batters before being relieved. It was his only Major League appearance, giving him a career ERA of infinity.

The 1940s

Buddy Hancken, 25, catcher, Philadelphia Athletics, May 14, 1940. Hancken caught the bottom of the ninth of a 9–7 victory over Cleveland. *Baseball Reference's Bullpen* says he was kept on the Athletics' roster in 1940 because he had experience catching the knuckleball and the team had two knuckleballers. When they were sent to the minors, so was he. Hancken later spent 34 years with the Astros, as a bullpen catcher and in the front office in ticket sales, his obituary in *The Seattle Post-Intelligencer* said.

Chip Marshall, 21, catcher, St. Louis Cardinals, June 14, 1941. In 1941, the Cardinals had two good catchers, Gus Mancuso and Walker

Cooper, even after dealing a hot young catching prospect, Mickey Owen, for Mancuso and a lot of money. Mancuso and Cooper split time pretty evenly to start the season, but then Cooper broke his shoulder in a home-plate collision on May 18. Mancuso was 35 and suddenly was *the* catcher, catching 36 consecutive games from May 16 (just before Cooper was hurt) through June 20, starting 34 of them. After Cooper's injury, Mancuso was not the starter only once in that streak, when Don Padgett, a catcher who had been moved to the outfield to get his bat in the lineup (he had hit .399—yes, .399—in 257 plate appearances in 1939), started once. Mancuso came in late in that game anyway.

St. Louis finally brought in a new third-stringer, Marshall, even though he was hitting .167 at Class AAA Sacramento. His contribution: He ran for Mancuso in the eighth inning against the Dodgers on June 14 and caught the ninth (he snagged a foul pop-up). Marshall was sent back to Class AAA, and, although Padgett caught some more, the Cardinals rode Mancuso hard until Cooper could come back. And it showed: Mancuso was hitting .395 when his consecutive-game streak began, .231 when it ended. He batted .172 in that stretch, with a single home run and 9 RBIs, and .204 over the final four and a half months of the season as the Cardinals slipped out of first place and finished two and a half games behind the Dodgers for the pennant.

Jack Aragón, 25, pinch-runner, New York Giants, August 13, 1941. *Baseball in Wartime* says Aragón was the Giants' batting practice catcher in 1941, when he played in his only Major League game. In the second game of a doubleheader, he ran for 40-year-old catcher Gabby Hartnett with two outs in the ninth inning in a 3–1 loss to the Braves. The next batter, Morrie Arnovich, made an out to end the game. *Baseball in Wartime* says that when Aragón was playing for the Class AAA Louisville Colonels in 1945, he broke his leg in a collision at the plate; fans in Louisville gave him 50,000 pennies ($500) as a gesture. His father, Angel Aragón, was briefly a utilityman for the Yankees in the teens.

Hank Schmulbach, 18, pinch-runner, St. Louis Browns, September 27, 1943. World War II led to some unusual happenings in baseball. Schmulbach was an 18-year-old from East St. Louis, Illinois, who was a pre-med student and second baseman at Washington University in St. Louis in 1943. For some reason, his college team wound up playing a game in August—even *The St. Louis Post-Dispatch*, which reported on the game, called it unusual. Also unusual: Schmulbach pitched that afternoon. He was signed by the Browns later in the season and was used as a ninth-inning pinch-runner. He scored the tying run as St. Louis rallied to win the second game of a doubleheader—and *The Associated Press* incorrectly called him Carl Schmulbach.

Sixteen. June 29

Mike Kosman, 26, pinch-runner, Cincinnati Reds, April 20, 1944. Kosman pinch-ran in the seventh inning of a 1–1 game against the Cubs, but he was long out of the game by the time his spot in the lineup came up in the ninth inning. He did not play professional baseball until he was 26, spending the 1944 season in the Southern Association except for his one game with Cincinnati. He had played three seasons at Indiana University, through 1941, and was an assistant coach at IU the next year, according to a university archive. His whereabouts in 1943 were unclear. He played one more season in the minors, proving that for him, a walk was really as good as a hit. He walked in more than 20 percent of his minor league plate appearances and actually had more walks than hits, 181–179.

Garth Mann, pinch runner, 28, Chicago Cubs, May 14, 1944. In the top of the eighth inning, the Dodgers used a pitcher, Cal McLish, as a pinch-runner; he scored. In the bottom of the eighth, the Cubs used a pitcher, Mann, as a pinch-runner; *he* scored. Six days later, he was optioned back to the minors. His nickname was Red. Red Mann. Appropriate for a sport full of Red Man chewing tobacco.

Gene Patton, 17, pinch-runner, Boston Braves, June 17, 1944. They should have called it Patton's Army. The Patton family of Coatesville, Pennsylvania, had nine boys, and Gene was the youngest. When he was 12, *Baseball in Wartime* said, his older brothers formed a baseball team and stuck the young'un in right field. (The Pattons' six sisters formed a basketball team, *Baseball in Wartime* wrote, good enough to beat the local high school team.) His name was Gene Tunney Patton, named for the heavyweight boxing champion Gene Tunney. Gene outgrew the Patton outfield to sign with the Braves as an infielder after graduating from high school; days later, he pinch-ran in the bottom of the ninth and was forced out at second. His career was hampered by bouts of rheumatic fever. The '44 Braves had another 17-year-old one-game wonder, Harry MacPherson, who pitched a single inning that August.

Ray Medeiros, 18, pinch-runner, Cincinnati Reds, April 25, 1945. Medeiros was two weeks shy of his 19th birthday when the Reds used him to run for pitcher Bucky Walters in the eighth inning of their seventh game of the season. One of Medeiros's teammates was 46-year-old pitcher Hod Lisenbee, who had already been pitching professionally for two years when Medeiros was born. Heck, Lisenbee, then 50, was still pitching professionally the year after Medeiros's baseball career ended.

John Corriden, 28, pinch-runner, Brooklyn Dodgers, April 20, 1946. With the Dodgers trailing by a run in the bottom of the seventh in their fourth game of the season, Corriden ran for Billy Herman and scored the go-ahead run. He was replaced in the eighth on defense by first baseman Howie Schultz. His father, John (Red) Corriden, was a Major League infielder and a Dodgers coach in 1946. Corriden père became a Yankees coach in 1947; Corriden fils played across the river in Jersey City and drifted out of baseball after two more seasons.

Otis Davis, 25, pinch-runner, Brooklyn Dodgers, April 22, 1946. In the bottom of the ninth, Davis pinch-ran for Eddie Stanky as the Dodgers staged a two-run rally to force extra innings. Davis was replaced by reliever Hugh Casey. Davis, an outfielder known for his speed, had aggravated an old high school knee injury on a slide during a fouled-off bunt attempt, and he was soon sent down to Class AAA to rehab, but he reinjured his knee and managed to play only nine games. He spent the next two seasons slipping down the minor league food chain. From his SABR *Bio Project* biography:

> What baseball did for me was give me something to talk about. It gave me another identity. "Moonlight" Graham played the field, but he never got to bat. I'd like to have batted. But I could have gone 1 for 1, or I could have struck out, like Walter Alston did. … Think about this. What if Eddie Stanky had struck out? If he doesn't get on base, what happens to my shot at the big leagues?

The St. Petersburg Times wrote about Davis and the day in his Major League life in 1994:

> When he dreams at night, he dreams about playing baseball, about sitting on the bench, about standing in the on-deck circle and studying the pitcher. The dream always ends before Otis Davis gets to the plate. He never did. He never will. He never swung a bat for the Brooklyn Dodgers, never wore a glove. He can't even remember the number he wore. Still, he made it the Major Leagues. Forty-eight years ago this week, Otis Davis earned his line in *The Baseball Encyclopedia*.

Bob Mavis, 31, pinch-runner, Detroit Tigers, September 17, 1949. After hitting .300 for six consecutive seasons in the minors, Mavis earned a call-up to Detroit late in the season. His reward: one pinch-running appearance in the ninth inning. At least he played in Yankee Stadium. Any chances of staying in Detroit evaporated over the winter when the Tigers acquired the talented if troubled Jerry Priddy from the Yankees to play second base; they didn't need a 32-year-old like Mavis with no Major League résumé. "I got a 'cup of coffee,' but I never got any cream," he told Jim Sargent of SABR in a 2004 interview. "Still, the Lord gave me the opportunity to play baseball, and I have no regrets. I spent 47 good years in the game as a player, minor league manager and scout."

The 1950s

Bob Scherbarth, 24, catcher, Boston Red Sox, April 23, 1950. Walt Dropo had an exemplary rookie season in 1950—a batting line that would just about have fit in Ted Williams's career (minus 100 walks). Dropo hit .322/.378/.583 with 34 home runs and 144 RBIs. He batted .400 with six homers in his first 14 games, helping Boston go 10–4. But Dropo spent the first two-plus weeks of the season at Class AAA Louisville because the Red Sox felt compelled to keep a third-string catcher, Bob Scherbarth. Boston's starting catcher, Birdie Tebbetts, was dealing with a finger injury, and his backup, Buddy Rosar, was sidelined with injured ribs, so in the sixth game of the season, Scherbarth replaced Tebbetts in the sixth inning. When it came his turn to bat in the eighth, however, Scherbarth was pinch-hit for. A week later he was back in Louisville, and days later Dropo was raking in Boston. "The managers and coaches said they were really grateful that I came up to help them out," Scherbarth said in his SABR *Bio Project* biography. "Even though I didn't play or anything, they got me in one inning just so I'd get my name in the book."

Frank Verdi, 26, shortstop, New York Yankees, May 10, 1953. Verdi played in 1,916 minor league games. He managed in 2,683. But his Major League experience was one game. One unusual game. Verdi entered it against the Red Sox in the sixth inning at shortstop. In the top of the seventh, the Yankees rallied, batting around, bringing Verdi up with the bases loaded and two out. He stepped into the batter's box, as *Sports Illustrated* later recounted, only to have the Red Sox change pitchers. He stepped back in, only to have Yankees Manager Casey Stengel call time and send up a pinch-hitter. When the cutdown to 25 players came a few days later, Verdi was sent back to the minors for good. Earlier in Verdi's one game, Boston first baseman Billy Goodman, incensed over what he thought was a bad call at first, charged the umpire, who threw him out of the game. But not before a teammate, Jimmy Piersall, had restrained him with a bear hug so hard that Goodman was sent for X-rays, fearing he had sustained broken ribs. (He hadn't, but strained cartilage sidelined him for several days.) To top off the day, the Yankees' feisty Billy Martin, responding to accounts of the team's recent brawl with Browns catcher Clint (Scrap Iron) Courtney, was quoted, pants apparently on fire, in *The New York Times* saying, "I never started a fight in my life."

Fred Marolewski, 24, first baseman, St. Louis Cardinals, September 19, 1953. Marolewski was a big, right-handed, low-average, power-hitting first baseman in the Cardinals' organization. He was also the same age as Steve Bilko, a bigger, right-handed, higher-average, power-hitting first baseman in the Cardinals' organization. Bilko's promise never really paid off in the Majors, but he was in Marolewski's way, except for one late-season game in 1953. Bilko was removed for a pinch-runner in the 11th inning, and Marolewski took over at first in the 12th. He was on deck when the game ended. He told MLB.com in 2017: "You get a chance, and if you're lucky you get to play. If you're not lucky, you don't. Sometimes you've got to be in the right place at the right time. That's it."

Chris Kitsos, 26, shortstop, Chicago Cubs, April 21, 1954. It was early April 1954, Ernie Banks's rookie season, and he was struggling. He was batting .158 when Eddie Miksis, a nondescript hitter himself (.236 career average with a 62 OPS+) pinch-hit for Banks. Kitsos then took over at shortstop in the bottom of the eighth and had assists on two ground balls. And his Major League career was over. Kitsos had starred against top national competition while in high school, playing in the inaugural Hearst Sandlot Classic, a game sponsored by *The New York Journal-American* that pitted a New York team against a U.S. team. Kitsos drove in an early run in the game and then tied it up with a two-run single that led to extra innings; he scored the game-winner in the 11th.

John Oldham, 23, pinch-runner, Cincinnati Reds, September 2, 1956. Oldham was a pitcher with an uncertain idea of the strike zone, walking 6.0 batters per nine innings in the Pacific Coast League in 1955. He was 9–6, though, and the Reds gave him a raise to $5,000 for 1956, he told the website *This Great Game*. "Back in those days, if you signed a contract for more than $4,000, they had to carry you on their 25-man roster, and that's why I was with the big team in 1956," he said. In spring training, however, he got his draft notice; was inducted into the Navy; was given a medical discharge before the season ended; and returned to the Reds. Never to pitch. He ran for hulking Ted Kluszewski in the third inning in an early-September game and "was definitely excited but also scared at the same time," he told *This Great Game*. "Don't get picked off, I told myself. Our shortstop Roy McMillan popped out and I returned to the bench. I never imagined that would be the end of my MLB playing career." He warmed up in the bullpen a few times, but that was as close as he came to being a Major League pitcher. He was the college coach for Dave Stieb and Dave Righetti.

Nick Testa, 30, catcher, San Francisco Giants, April 23, 1958. In 1957, a decade into his professional career, Testa was catching for the Dallas Eagles in the Class AA Texas League. Baseball had been integrated for more than a decade, but racial problems persisted. For example, Shreveport, Louisiana, home of another Texas League team, had laws that prohibited Black and white athletes from competing against one another, so when Dallas played at Shreveport, its Black players could not take the field. In 1957, that included Willie McCovey and Tony Taylor. The local law left Dallas with only eight position players for a four-game series in Shreveport, so Testa wound up playing third base, according to his SABR *Bio Project* biography. The next year, he made the Giants out of spring training for the team's first season in San Francisco. He was a pinch-runner as the

Giants used 24 players in an 8–7 victory over the Cardinals; three weeks later, he was released and made the bullpen coach. His one game ended on Daryl Spencer's home run—with Testa on deck.

Jack Feller, 21, catcher, Detroit Tigers, September 13, 1958. He drove in the winning run in the pennant-clincher on the last day of the 1958 season for Augusta, Georgia, in the Class A South Atlantic League before receiving a surprise call-up to Detroit, according to his SABR *Bio Project* biography. He was given No. 19—the same number as Cleveland star Bob Feller—and caught the ninth inning of Jim Bunning's 13–2 victory over the Orioles. He became a junior high teacher and high school coach for 26 years.

The 1960s

Mickey Harrington, 28, pinch-runner, Philadelphia Phillies, July 10, 1963. Harrington was a baseball standout at Mississippi Southern College (now the University of Southern Mississippi), but he may have been a better basketball player. He turned down scholarships from Kentucky, which a year earlier had won a national championship, and Duke, according to his obituary in *The Hattiesburg (Mississippi) American*. A 6-foot-4-inch forward, he started all four seasons. After then serving in the Army, he had offers from the NBA, including the Minneapolis Lakers, and Major League Baseball, his obituary said. He was a solid singles-hitting outfielder (career .293 in the minors) with minimal power and few walks, so he languished in the minors with the Phillies, who were going nowhere, and the Angels, an expansion team. In 1963 he was finally called up in midseason by the Phillies, whose strength was their outfield, with Johnny Callison, Tony Gonzalez, Wes Covington and backup Don Demeter all hitting well. He was inserted as a pinch-runner for Roy Sievers in the bottom of the eighth of a 10–2 blowout victory over the Giants. He advanced to second but seems to have been the final out of the inning on a 1-6-5 double play. In his 60s and 70s, Harrington, by then an administrator at his alma mater, was an accomplished cyclist and triathlete.

John Sanders, 19, pinch-runner, Kansas City Athletics, April 13, 1965. Sanders was in the last class of high school seniors who were not subject to the amateur draft that baseball instituted in 1965. He picked up a $20,000 bonus from the Athletics. Later, he was the head coach at the University of Nebraska for 20 years, with nearly 100 of his players getting drafted. His Cornhusker players included first-round pick Darin Erstad. Sanders had an abbreviated first year in pro ball because of an injury, but he was put on the Athletics' 40-man roster, *RIP Baseball* says, along with a long list of other young rookies: outfielder Joe Rudi, 20; pitcher

Jim (eventually Catfish) Hunter, 19; third baseman Skip Lockwood, 18, who was quickly converted to a pitcher; catcher Rene Lachemann, 20; and pitcher Don Buschhorn, 19. Sanders was just another young hopeful crowding a roster that unsurprisingly lost 103 games. He pinch-ran in the seventh inning against the Tigers—*RIP Baseball* says he joked, "I was asleep on the bench, and the manager woke me up to go in"—but within three weeks, when rosters had to be cut to 25 players, he was waived.

Ralph Gagliano, 18, pinch-runner, Cleveland Indians, September 21, 1965. He ran for Larry Brown in the ninth inning of a 7–4 loss to the Yankees. It was the only game he played at any level that year, according to *Baseball Reference*; he had played 75 games at Class A Dubuque in 1964 and then was back in Class A in 1966 before losing the next three years to military service. He was the younger brother of Phil Gagliano, also a light-hitting infielder. Ralph was on a Topps Indians 1965 Rookie Stars card with pitcher Jim Rittwage, whose career spanned only eight games in 1970. Ralph had received a bonus of $40,000 to $60,000 to sign with Cleveland, which outbid the other 15 teams, according to Phil Gagliano's SABR biography.

The 1970s

Bart Zeller, 28, catcher, St. Louis Cardinals, May 21, 1970. It was hard to get Joe Torre out of the lineup in 1970. He tied for the league lead in games played with 161. He batted .325/.398/.498 with an OPS+ of 137. When Torre wasn't catching, a young Ted Simmons was, after he finished a stretch in the Army Reserves and a short stint in the minors and was called up in late May. But in the bottom of the ninth inning on May 21, with Torre out of the game for a pinch-runner, Zeller got his one chance. And in his one inning behind the plate, the Cardinals gave up a run and lost to the Phillies, 4–3. Shortly after Simmons arrived in St. Louis, Zeller, only 28, became a Cardinals coach. "When I played Little League, all I—all everyone—wanted to do is play baseball, and I was lucky enough to do that," Zeller said, according to *Baseball Reference's Bullpen*.

Gary Hargis, 22, pinch-runner, Pittsburgh Pirates, September 29, 1979. With the Pirates in a pennant race, Hargis pinch-ran in the 13th inning on the next-to-last day of the season, but he was stranded at second. "You keep thinking, 'Just let me get in one game so my name can get into the book,'" he said in a 2005 interview with *The Lubbock (Texas) Avalanche Journal*. "When you do, it's just like the movie. Your eyes light up, you never want the night to end." He had spent the season at Class AAA Portland in the PCL as an error-prone middle infielder, hitting with little power and not much on-base ability (eight walks in 406 plate appearances for a .292 OBP). Hargis received a $250 World Series share for his brief appearance.

The 1980s

John Lickert, 21, catcher, Boston Red Sox, September 19, 1981. The 1981 season was an odd one, torn apart by a strike, after which Major League Baseball decided on pairing division winners of the first and second halves in the playoffs. Two National League teams, the Expos and the Reds, had the best overall records in their divisions but didn't advance because neither had won a half-season title. Lickert, who was called up after his Pawtucket team's season ended, fell into this messy situation in a game against the Yankees. New York had won the first half's title but was well back in the second, yet on its way to the playoffs and the World Series. It was a big game for the Red Sox, however, who were only a game out of first place. Boston called on three catchers that night as it rallied in the eighth to take the lead. In came the untested Lickert for the ninth, and Mark Clear got the save. The Red Sox failed to reach the postseason, however, and Lickert failed to make it back to the Majors. "I'm probably the only guy who has 17 zeroes in the record book," Lickert told *The New York Times* in 1999, and at least with that comment he struck out, as this list shows.

Bob Hegman, 27, second baseman, Kansas City Royals, August 8, 1985. Hegman took George Brett's place in the lineup, but at second base, for the ninth inning of a 10–3 victory over the Tigers. The game was originally scheduled for August 5, but MLB players went on strike for two days, mainly over salary arbitration, and the game was played as the opener of a doubleheader. The Royals began the day in second place, five games out of first, but won the division with a 36–23 finish. In 2005, when he was asked by *The Star-Ledger* of Newark, New Jersey, whether he had received a World Series ring, Hegman replied: "Heck, all I got was a $100 check. I should have kept it and framed it, but I had to eat." Twins Almanac says Hegman said he was called up when shortstop Buddy Biancalana was hurt and was sent back down when Biancalana got healthy. Hegman was the starting point guard for four years at St. Cloud State, averaging 9.4 points a game. He grew up in Sauk Rapids, Minnesota, about a three-hour drive from Moonlight Graham's Chisholm.

The 2000s

Pedro Santana, 24, second baseman, Detroit Tigers, July 16, 2001. Santana was once the No. 11 prospect in baseball, and he hit for a pretty good average every year of his professional career. Except in 2001. That year, he struggled in his first exposure to Class AAA, finishing with a .227/.274/.299 line. As usual, he hit with little power and did not walk much, although he flashed speed and good judgment on the bases, successfully stealing in 36 of 44 attempts. Yet despite his offensive problems, that was the year the Tigers called Santana to the Majors. They needed an infielder, with shortstop Deivi Cruz hurt and third baseman Dean Palmer getting injured. Santana replaced second baseman Damion Easley in the bottom of the eighth of a 9–1 loss to the Reds. He caught a pop fly and did not come to bat in the ninth. Five days after his call-up, Santana was sent back to Toledo when Cruz came off the disabled list. He went on to become a hitting instructor at the Santos Baseball Academy.

Joe Hietpas, 25, catcher, New York Mets, October 3, 2004. Hietpas caught the final two innings of the final game of the season, an 8–1 Mets victory over the Expos in their final game representing Montreal. "At the time, you don't look at it as your one missed opportunity for an at-bat. It's the start. It's not the finish," Hietpas said in a 2015 interview with the *Louisville Courier-Journal*. "I played long enough after that and had every chance to earn my way back, and I just didn't." He earned a law degree from Northwestern in 2012, according to his SABR *Bio Project* biography.

The 2020s

Jack Kruger, catcher, Los Aneles Angels, May 26, 2021. It never looks like a Moonlight moment. Kruger was 26 when the Angels called him up to replace a catcher who had sustained a concussion, according to *The New York Times*. He was slipped into that night's game in the top of the ninth of an 9–4 loss to the Tampa Bay Rays—a Major Leaguer at least, and certain his first game would not be his last. The next day, when a team executive approached him, Kruger told *The Times*'s Kurt Streeter, he said he was expecting an "attaboy." Instead, he was told he was being designated for assignment—if no other team picked him up, the Angels could return Kruger to the minors. Three days after he was an Angels catcher, Kruger was a Rangers minor leaguer, with Class AAA Round Rock. He was still there in 2022, suffering through a dismal season, after which he became a free agent. He remained one: Kruger retired from baseball and began an internet career, his Moonlight moment intact.

Seventeen

June 30

The First Modern No-Hitter (Maybe)

No-hitters are not exactly a rarity—Major League Baseball had certified 322 of them, from 1876 and the first professional Major League to 2023—but to pitchers at any level, they are special. The thought of a no-hitter is special even to pitchers at any level who just missed a no-hitter. Do you think that Tom Seaver ever forgot Jimmy Qualls, or that Mike Mussina didn't remember Carl Everett? Will Armando Galarraga ever get over umpire Jim Joyce's botched call? (Heck, I still remember the high bouncer over my outstretched glove that Tim Lasher hit to spoil a no-hitter when I was a chunky, 12-year-old right-hander in the Irvington Little League in Indianapolis.) After the most recent no-hitter, by Michael Lorenzen of the Philadelphia Phillies in August 2023, he said, "It was incredible." Fifteen months earlier, after his no-hitter, the Los Angeles Angels' Reid Detmer said: "It's just something I've dreamed ever since I was a little kid. I didn't think it would ever happen." That is a pretty common sentiment, unless, perhaps, you were Nolan Ryan or Sandy Koufax or Bob Feller.

No-hitters are not even a sign of excellence. Jim Maloney of the Reds threw a no-hitter (and a shutout) despite walking 10 batters, although he did go 10 innings. A.J. Burnett of the Marlins pretty much matched that (including the shutout) with nine walks in his nine-inning "gem." Five pitchers have walked eight batters, yet finished with a no-hitter.

And no-hitters don't guarantee much of anything anyway. Virgil Trucks of the Tigers pitched two no-hitters in 1952 and still had a 5–19 record despite those two victories. And Lorenzen was left off the Phillies' wild-card playoff game roster despite pitching his no-hitter less than two months earlier. His 6.81 ERA in his other 10 games with Philadelphia may have influenced that decision.

Leaving a pitcher off the postseason roster despite throwing a no-hitter that year *is* unusual, although not without precedent if you go back far enough in baseball history. George (Iron) Davis of the 1914

Miracle Boston Braves was a little-used, 24-year-old right-hander who had pitched in only three games that season when Manager George Stallings tapped him to start the second game of a doubleheader on September 23. The Braves were leading the National League by only one and a half games, but they were playing their third doubleheader in four days. (Clearly there was no players union.) Davis, whom *The Boston Globe* called "the collegian of the moist ball delivery," walked five batters—three in one inning—but never allowed the Phillies a hit. He made four more starts down the stretch as the Braves pulled away, with middling success—2–2, 3.45 ERA (in the Deadball Era, remember). But when it came to the World Series against the heavily favored Athletics, Davis was apparently not on the roster. *Baseball Reference*'s list of Boston players in the Series shows the 15 who played and four who did not appear. Davis's name is not among them.

The no-hitter was one of only seven Major League wins for Davis, but that is far from the fewest victories for a pitcher with a no-hitter. Bobo Holloman, for example, threw a no-hitter in his first start with the 1953 St. Louis Browns but wound up with only three career wins. (If later we would say Bo Knows, perhaps then we could have said Bobo No-nos.)

There are dozens of unlikely no-hit pitchers, including the one who threw—or may not have thrown—the first no-hitter in the modern era, after the two current Major Leagues were established, in 1901. *Baseball Reference* shows Pete Dowling of the Cleveland Blues (later Naps/Indians/Guardians) pitching a no-hitter on June 30, 1901, against the Milwaukee Brewers (later St. Louis Browns/Baltimore Orioles). So does *Retrosheet*. Major League Baseball, however, does not.

The unsettled status of Dowling's game began immediately.

In the seventh inning of the game in Milwaukee, Dowling gave up a sharply hit ground ball by Wid Conroy to third baseman Bill Bradley. Dowling's SABR *Bio Project* biography says that the wire-service article that newspapers nationwide used, plus an article filed by a correspondent to *The Plain Dealer* in Cleveland, called it a scratch single. But *The Milwaukee Journal*, *The Cleveland Press* and *The Cleveland Leader* all called it a no-hitter, with an error by Bradley. The SABR bio says: "The most plausible explanation for the divergence is that the official scorer, who was probably a Milwaukee sportswriter, changed the hit to an error after the game had ended. The wire service and *Plain Dealer* stories weren't corrected, and it is likely that at the end of the 1901 season relatively few people considered Dowling's June 30 outing a no-hitter." Fast-forward to 1969, though, and the first edition of *The Baseball Encyclopedia* said Dowling had thrown a no-hitter. The confusion did not end there, however; *The Baseball Encyclopedia*'s next nine editions did not list Dowling's game among American League no-hitters.

Dowling certainly was not the pitcher you would have expected to throw any league's first no-hitter. His career record in the Majors was 39-64 (.379). He allowed 992 hits in 916 innings (and walked more batters than the normal turn-of-the-century pitcher). His four Major League seasons included records of 13-20, 13-17 and 12-25. He also had a thoroughly documented drinking problem, and 1901 was his last season in the Majors. He died at the age of 28 in 1905, while pitching in a semipro league in Oregon. His SABR profile says Dowling bought a train ticket but did not board the train. He decided to walk along the tracks before stepping onto the tracks and being killed by an oncoming train that had no chance to stop. *The Seattle Times* wrote days later: "It was a sad ending to a brilliant career. He was as tender hearted as a woman and generous to a fault but he could not let liquor alone and his end was a tragic one."

If you don't count Dowling's game, the first no-hitter in the modern era came 15 days later—by Christy Mathewson. He had a fantastically better career, of course, but he had his own tragedy. Mathewson, who had been exposed to mustard gas while serving in World War I, later contracted tuberculosis and died at age 45 in 1923.

Major League Baseball counts the very first no-hitter as George Bradley's, as the St. Louis Brown Stockings defeated the Hartford Dark Blues, 2-0, on July 15, 1876. The National League was only three months old, and the game was not what we know. Pitchers threw from a "box"—two 12-foot lines from 45 to 48 feet from home plate, the Major League historian, John Thorn, wrote in *A Brief History of the Pitching Distance* on Medium in 2015. Batters could also direct whether they wanted the ball thrown high or low. Yet Bradley pitched a no-hitter. This was not entirely out of line in this early version of the professional game, as Bradley compiled a 45-19 record (he did not lead the league in wins) with a league-best 1.23 ERA and a league-leading 16 shutouts while pitching 573 innings. He threw all but four of his team's innings. And while his ERA looks Gibson-like, he yielded 3.60 runs a game; his team did, after all, make 268 errors in 64 games.

Thorn notes that the front of the pitcher's box was moved back to 50 feet in 1881; in 1887, a running start was outlawed; and in 1893, the box was eliminated, and a pitching rubber was installed at the distance we know now, 60 feet 6 inches. In reality, Thorn says, the introduction of the pitching rubber did not make a pitcher throw an extra 10 feet. Throwing from a rubber rather than in a box with a front line like one for the javelin throw, a pitcher would stride four to four and a half feet—so a pitch would cover a distance more like 56 feet. The journalist and baseball historian Bill Deane, Thorn adds, says it was "actually 4'3½" shorter, as the pre-1893 distance was measured from the center of the (plate) instead of the rear point, as it is today." (The blog 19th Century Base Ball points out another wrinkle: Pitchers threw from flat ground, not a mound, which was not introduced until the early 20th century.) No surprise, batting averages rose 35 points in 1893 and 29 more in 1894.

As a result of the changes in the pitchers' box, Bumpus Jones of the Cincinnati Reds was the last pitcher to throw a no-hitter at the shorter distance, a 7–1 victory over the Pirates on October 15, 1892. It was the last game of the season, and the Pirates may not have been particularly enthused about a season-ending road game against a rookie.

That was Jones's only Major League start in 1892 (after a 24-3 season for the Joliet Convicts/Aurora Indians in the Illinois-Iowa League). The new distance did not help Jones, who pitched only seven more Major League games, all in 1893, while racking up a 10.19 ERA. He pitched his last Major League game on July 14 that year for the New York Giants, walking 10 batters in four innings.

Although there was a no-hitter thrown in 1893, the offensive explosion in 1894—the league batted .309—coincided with an absence of no-hitters. In fact, there was a four-year gap—until Cy Young hurled a no-hitter in 1897 and no-nos became a regular feature again. Although not always evenly. Let's look at no-hitters by decades:

1870s: 1	1950s: 18
1880s: 26	1960s: 34
1890s: 15	1970s: 31
1900s: 20	1980s: 13
1910s: 29	1990s: 31
1920s: 9	2000s: 15
1930s: 8	2010s: 40
1940s: 13	2020s: 19

Other than the 1870s, the decade with the fewest no-hitters was the '30s, and Johnny Vander Meer of the Reds threw two of them in back-to-back starts in 1938.

There are other no-hitter quirks. Don Larsen (1956) and David Wells (1998), who pitched the first two perfect games in Yankees history, both attended Point Loma High School in California. But even they can't match the no-hit history of Fullerton Union High in California. The baseball team has sent four pitchers to the Major Leagues, and all four of them have thrown no-hitters: Walter Johnson (yes, that Walter Johnson), Steve Busby, Mike Warren ... and Michael Lorenzen.

Eighteen

July 4
Born to Diamond Glory

George Steinbrenner is probably the most prominent figure in baseball born on the Fourth of July. He was not shy about mentioning when he was born, either. Curiously, two other renegade sports team owners were also born on the Fourth: Peter Angelos and Al Davis. Not for nothin', so was Meyer Lansky. But enough about shady characters (although we will come back to Steinbrenner later). There were 62 Major Leaguers born on the Fourth of July—including 19 born in the 19th century. Maybe mothers were more patriotic then. Here's a look at some of those star-spangled babies.

Ed Armbrister, born 1948. Played 1973–77. Ed Armbrister went to bat in the regular season 302 times in his career, but he is known for one at-bat in the 1975 World Series. Here's a *New York Times* account of a 10th-inning sacrifice bunt attempt on which Armbrister stutter-stepped out of the box while Boston Red Sox catcher Carlton Fisk tried to make a play in Game 3 against the Cincinnati Reds. "The Reds had a man on first with no one out when the hitter, Ed Armbrister, laid down a bunt in front of the plate." He and Fisk became entangled, and Fisk threw the ball away trying for a force at second. The umpire, Larry Barnett, said: "I ruled that it was simply a collision. It is interference only when the batter intentionally gets in the way of the fielder." Except the rulebook made no mention of intent. Fisk said: "I don't know what the damn rule is, all I know is that he ran into me. If that's not interference, then I don't know what is."

No surprise, but Reds Manager Sparky Anderson had a different view: "I can only say that whenever you hit a ball, you have the opportunity to run to first base." The call stood, and the Reds won the game and the Series. Although Armbrister had only one sacrifice bunt in the regular season in 1975 in 72 plate appearances—talk about your part-time players—Joe Morgan called Armbrister the best bunter he had ever seen, according to one obituary of Armbrister in 2021. He certainly was not the best hitter (a career slash line of .245/.307/.377), base runner (he was 15 for

25 stealing in the Majors) or fielder (career fielding percentage of .925 versus a league average for outfielders then of .978). But he won two World Series rings. And a place in baseball history.

Coco Laboy, born 1940. Played 1969–73. A Montreal Expos executive once said that Coco Laboy had "a million-dollar name." Yet he most likely did not make $100,000 in a career that spanned five seasons. He was an original Expo, a 28-year-old rookie who had labored through 10 seasons in the minors. He was second in the 1969 Rookie of the Year voting for a .258/.308/.409 season in which he hit 18 home runs and drove in 83 runs. He homered on Opening Day and was the Expos' first hero—he hit .377 with three home runs and 14 RBIs in Montreal's initial month. But Laboy hit .239 with a .293 on-base percentage the rest of the season. The next year was worse: .199/.254/.299 with five home runs in 476 plate appearances. He drifted in and out of the minors, and in his final year, going to bat for the Expos only 33 times, he hit .121/.237/.242. His career obscured noteworthy connections. One of the scouts who signed him out of Puerto Rico was Alex Pompez, a native Cuban who had owned a Negro leagues team and, as a scout for the Giants, mined the Dominican Republic. Well after Laboy's playing career ended, his SABR *Bio Project* biography says, he was credited with scouting Edgar Martinez. And he had the great name, although how José Alberto became Cocó is hazy. He said his mother nicknamed him—but he did not know why.

Mickey Welch, born 1859. Played 1880–92. Smiling Mickey Welch was a Hall of Fame pitcher who, in one of his best seasons, had a very tough two weeks. In August 1884, he was hit on the hip by a line drive by Dan Brouthers, one of the game's top batters. A few days later, while batting, Welch was hit on the head with a pitch (remember, no batting helmets then). Two days later, he struck out the first nine batters he faced. But soon after that he was hit by another batted ball that knocked him to the ground. Still, he finished the year 39–21, pitching 557 1/3 innings as a 24-year-old for the New York Giants. The 557 1/3 is not a typo, but an artifact of an unimaginable era. Welch competed mostly in an era when a pitcher released the ball 50 feet from home plate and later 55 feet 6 inches. His rookie season, when the pitcher was only 45 feet from the plate, he threw 574 innings and completed all 64 starts while compiling a 2.54 earned run average—which was below average. Welch and Smiling Tim Keefe combined to win 76 games for the 1885 Giants (apparently a happy team). Welch was one of the first 300-game winners … and 200-game losers (307–210). His career was effectively over when he was 30. He was said to have avoided hard liquor—but not beer, about which he wrote this couplet: "Pure elixir of malt and hops/Beats all the drugs and all the drops."

Vinny Castilla, born 1967. Played 1991–2006. Do you know who hit the most home runs in the Majors by a Mexican-born player? Yes, Vinny Castilla. His total of 320 homers is more than double the total of any other Mexican player. Didn't hurt that he played his prime years in Denver. In one five-year stretch in which he was loved by fantasy players, Castilla hit 191 home runs. He batted .300 or better in four of those years and drove in 100-plus runs four times. Then he was traded to the Tampa Bay Devil Rays for a couple of rosin bags and stopped hitting … until the Rockies signed him as a free agent four years later. At the age of 36, he hit 35 bombs and drove in 113 runs. Maybe he was a product of the mile-high Denver air, but Castilla did hit in the postseason, too: .350/.409/.617 with five homers in 66 plate appearances, all in division series. And he is third on the Rockies' career list of home run hitters.

Chuck Tanner, born 1928. Played 1955–62. You know Chuck Tanner as a manager. He skippered more than 2,700 games in the 1970s and '80s. He calmed the waters for Dick Allen's monster 1972 season with the Chicago White Sox. He led a Charlie Finley Oakland Athletics team that stole 341 bases. He was traded to Pittsburgh (as a manager, mind you) for catcher Manny Sanguillén, then guided the Lumber and Lightning Pirates to a World Series title in 1979. (Those Pirates teams had sluggers Willie Stargell and Dave Parker, but they also stole between 180 and 260 bases each year from 1977 to '79.) He helped strong personalities excel (Allen, Parker) and underused talents thrive (he converted the knuckleballer Wilbur Wood into a starter, and a star). But you probably don't know about Chuck Tanner as a player.

For nine years, he swung the bat in the minors, hitting .300 at every level. When he made it to the Majors in 1955, he did not have much of a role. The Braves had the 21-year-old Henry Aaron, swift center fielder Billy Bruton and the solid veterans Bobby Thomson and Andy Pafko in the outfield. First base was foreclosed by the thumpers Joe Adcock and George Crowe. Yet among those sluggers, it was Tanner who, on the first big-league pitch he saw, homered, as a pinch-hitter on Opening Day. The next game, he cracked a pinch-hit single. The next game, he pinch-ran and scored. Nothing he did, however, could get him into the lineup. Tanner did not start a game until the Braves' 30th of the season. That first pitch was the season's highlight—career's highlight, pretty much. Dogged by Achilles' problems (and his .261/.323/.388 career slash line), he retired as a player at age 33. He hit 21 home runs. But that first one was memorable. Only 31 players have homered on their first pitch. Curiously, 16 of them have done so since 2000; from the inception of baseball in the 1800s through 1999, only 15 had. Even more curiously, eight of these first-pitch sluggers were pitchers.

José Oquendo, born 1963. Played 1983–95. If you are an older Mets fan, you may remember José Oquendo as a young shortstop who could not hit. He batted .213 playing 120 games as a 19-year-old for the Mets, then

.222 at age 20. But if you are an older St. Louis Cardinals fan, you definitely remember Oquendo as Ozzie Smith's slick partner in the middle of the infield, where they were both well-above-average gloves and improved singles hitters (although Ozzie could also steal a base). After being traded to the Cardinals (mostly for another infielder who couldn't hit; remember Angel Salazar?) and scuffling in Class AAA, Oquendo suddenly began hitting in the Majors in 1986 (.297 with some walks). He was a jack of all trades for two seasons, and I do mean all: He played eight positions in 1987 and all nine in 1988, with more playing time while continuing to hit for average and to walk. Manager Whitey Herzog called Oquendo "the Secret Weapon." He spent four seasons as the primary second baseman alongside Smith. His playing career was over at age 31 (a .317 slugging percentage even playing Whitey Ball was a problem), but he was the Cards' third-base coach for most of two decades.

Jim Beattie, born 1954. Played 1978–86. Jim Beattie had an athlete's pedigree. He was a high school baseball and basketball star, leading the South Portland High School Red Riots to the Maine basketball championship. He walked on in basketball at Dartmouth, where, as a 6-foot-6-inch junior, he averaged 14 points a game. He quit basketball, though, to concentrate on baseball, excelling sufficiently to become a fourth-round draft pick of the New York Yankees in 1975. By 1978, he was a rookie in New York, but his championship pedigree did not cut him any slack with George Steinbrenner. In June 1978, the Yankees were seven games back of the Boston Red Sox (and you know it was going to get worse) when Beattie—who had pitched only 12 innings in the previous three weeks—was tapped to start against the Red Sox at Fenway Park. It did not go well: two-plus innings, five hits, three walks and five runs in the Yankees' 9–2 loss. Before the game was even over, Steinbrenner had Beattie demoted to Class AAA Tacoma and called him "gutless."

But not talentless. Beattie was recalled in July, and in September he won four starts with a 2.70 earned run average as the Yankees famously rallied to tie the Red Sox and then win a one-game playoff. He won Game 1 of the ALCS and threw a complete-game victory in the World Series. "I'd been up against a lot trying to be a successful Major League Baseball player," Beattie told *The Hartford Courant* in 2003. "You get a lot of failures, and you learn to bounce back from them. This was just another one. I didn't duck my head and go down and pout about it. I worked hard and got back to the big leagues. You have to keep on bouncing back." Beattie became general manager for the Seattle Mariners, the Montreal Expos and the Baltimore Orioles. And he learned a lesson from his experiences with Steinbrenner. "I've never released a player or sent a player anyplace else telling a kid he can't play," he told *The Courant*. "Young players change so much during their careers. All I've said is, 'We can't give you an opportunity right now, and good luck.'"

Bobby Malkmus, born 1931. Played 1957–62. If you collected 1959 Topps cards, as I did, you had more Bobby Malkmus cards than even the Malkmus family would have wanted. He was an infielder who could pick it with the best of them, apparently, but he could not hit: .215/.265/.301 in a year's worth of plate appearances (625) over six seasons. He was good enough to be called up to the 1957 Milwaukee Braves, who went on to win the World Series, but not good enough to stick for more than 13 games. Yet in 1961, when he hit .231/.276/.327 (a 62 OPS+ if you're scoring at home), he received an MVP vote playing for the Phillies, who went 47-107-1. An autographed 1959 Topps card of his has a biblical notation, John 1:12. That verse, in the King James version, reads: "But as many as received him, to them gave he power to become the sons of God, even to them that believe on his name." Power at bat was not given to Malkmus, however—he hit eight Major League home runs.

Hal Lanier, born 1942. Played 1964–73. Hal Lanier knows how hard baseball can be. Although he played for 10 seasons in the Major Leagues, he was never a threat at the plate. He hit .228/.255/.275, and yes, he played in the '60s Deadball Era, but he really was that bad a hitter. His OPS+ was 50—basically half of a league-average hitter's. He became a manager and learned all over again how hard the game can be. He was hired to manage the 1986 Houston Astros, and he guided them to a 96-66 record and one of the most thrilling National League Championship Series yet played, against the eventual World Series champion Mets. "Ralph Houk told me during the 1986 winter meetings: 'That wasn't very smart, winning in your first year. You never win your first year. Win your second or third year; you'll be around a lot longer,'" Lanier told *The Tampa Bay Times* in 1994. "Well, I won my first year, and I think the (Astros) owners believed we should've won every year. That's not how baseball works."

No, it isn't. His Astros were 76–86 in his second year, falling from a half-game out of first place on August 24 by going 11–26 to finish the season, 14 games back. Lanier was 82–80 in his third season, sinking from a half-game out of first on August 9 to 12 games back at season's end. There was no fourth season. "I was a, umm, firm manager," he said, which worked when he won but wore thin when he didn't. Also, he had pegged the offense on stealing more bases (the Astros did, going from 10th in the league with 96 in 1985 to fourth in the league with 163 in '86), but the game was moving from the Whitey Ball he had learned under Whitey Herzog in St. Louis to Power Ball. In 1987, everyone bashed more home runs (Wade Boggs hit 24! Larry Sheets hit 31!), but the Astros slugged fewer. Lanier did, however, bring Yogi Berra to the Astros as bench coach.

Nineteen

July 6

An All-Star Game Is Born

Early 1933 was a grim time. That March, unemployment in the United States reached 30 percent of the civilian work force. "There is no doubt that 1933 was the worst year, and March the worst month for joblessness in the history of the United States," a U.S. Department of Labor history of the Depression said. But things were about to look up, at least briefly. "After four years of depression and deflation, the United States experienced a rapid turnaround recovery in the spring of 1933," Andrew Jalil and Gisela Rua wrote in a 2015 Federal Reserve Board study, *Inflation Expectations and Recovery from the Depression in 1933: Evidence from the Narrative Record.* "From March to July, industrial production rose by 57 percent. No other period in U.S. history has experienced such a sudden upswing in economic activity."

It was in this window of optimism that Arch Ward, sports editor of *The Chicago Tribune,* hatched an idea to match that sunny outlook: an all-star game between the American and National Leagues. Ward and other area sports editors were approached by officials of the World's Fair in Chicago, known formally as A Century of Progress Exposition, about an athletic event for it. (Some sources say that the mayor approached *The Tribune*'s publisher, Colonel Robert McCormick, who passed him along to Ward.) Ward's idea was for a game of the top players from the AL and NL—"a game of the century," he called it. That may have overstated history a bit—as the Baseball Hall of Fame notes, there was an exhibition benefit of Major League stars including Ty Cobb, Walter Johnson and Tris Speaker in 1911, and John Thorn, Major League Baseball's official historian, points to a 1903 game between African American teams as perhaps the first all-star game to be played in-season between professionals.

An actual all-star game between the Major Leagues had been floated as far back as 1915 by F.C. Lane, the editor of *Baseball Magazine,* the Hall of Fame says, but earned no support. Nearly two decades later, Ward's proposal did not draw unanimous support immediately. All eight American League teams voted yes, but three National League teams voted no, with scheduling concerns paramount in their reasoning. As Ward described in an article on May 19, 1933, in *The Tribune* announcing the game, the NL owners came around after teams agreed to rejigger their schedules to fit in an all-star exhibition on July 6. The game would be in Comiskey Park.

As wary as the Major Leagues were, the Negro leagues were enthusiastic about an all-star game. That very July, two sportswriters—Roy Sparrow of *The Pittsburgh Sun-Telegraph* and Bill Nunn of *The Pittsburgh Courier*—proposed a game. Encouraged by Gus Greenlee, owner of the Pittsburgh Crawfords, they arranged the first East-West All-Star Game, to be played at Comiskey as well, but in September. It was an immediate hit, with the historian Larry Lester saying it would become "the pinnacle of the Negro League season. It was an all-star game and a World Series all wrapped into one spectacle."

For the Major Leagues, details still had to be worked out before their All-Star Game could be played. Ultimately, the League presidents chose two umpires from both the AL and the NL. They decided to use the American League baseball—said to be livelier—for the first four and a half innings before switching to the NL ball. There remained concerns about whether the game would draw well; it *was* the Depression, and the White Sox had even half-filled 52,000-seat Comiskey Park only twice all season—both times for doubleheaders.

And then teams had to be selected. Ballots were printed in 55 papers (including, for some reason, *The Times* of Streator, Illinois, a town of 14,000 about 80 miles southwest of Chicago). Managers also had a vote. Ultimately, 18 players were chosen for each team. Proceeds went to a charity for retired players; the All-Star Game's players received not a penny.

Carl Hubbell of the New York Giants and Lefty Grove of the Philadelphia Athletics were announced as the starting pitchers, but the managers, John McGraw of the Giants and Connie Mack of the Athletics, changed their minds the day before the game and went with Bill Hallahan of the Chicago Cubs and Lefty Gomez of the New York Yankees. (Hubbell and Grove did pitch, in relief. Hubbell, who had pitched an 18-inning shutout four days earlier, threw two scoreless innings; Grove pitched the last three innings.)

Attendance worries proved unfounded, as the game drew 47,595 fans. Still, as lauded as the game was, there was no guarantee it would become an annual affair. Some team owners were hesitant despite the crowd and the hoopla surrounding the game and the $50,000-plus in gate receipts, at $1.10 a ticket.

Davis J. Walsh, a sportswriter for the *International News Service* whose work was syndicated nationally, five days after the game wrote scathingly about the owners' reluctance.

> Of course, it was somebody else's idea in the first place, but that's exactly why it ought to be a good thing for baseball, which has no ideas, all told, and is exceedingly proud of it. Anyhow, there is reason to believe that before the end of the week the baseball people will be subjected to a new and more elaborate plan in connection with an all-star, interleague game, the original idea having been an admitted success. The original idea, it may be added, proved a positive pleasure to 49,000 witnesses and hundreds of thousands of listeners and readers, and, as a result, was very repugnant to the baseball people.

The baseball people got over it. They approved a follow-up, and in 1934, a crowd of 48,368 attended the second All-Star Game, at the Polo Grounds. And of course it became an annual affair. The American League won the first All-Star Game, 4–2, using just 13 of the 18 players on the squad. Other than pitchers, the only reserve the AL employed was outfielder Sam West, who replaced Babe Ruth for the ninth inning. The National League used every player but Giants pitcher Hal Schumacher. Here's a look at those first All-Stars, running through the lineups.

National League

Pepper Martin, Cardinals, third base. In the 1960s, consensus was that Pie Traynor was the greatest third baseman ever. Yet Pepper Martin was voted in as the starting third baseman for the first All-Star Game. Traynor was on the back end of his career (age 34), and Martin was having the best season of his career. It may have helped that St. Louis had a population that was nearly 20 percent larger than Pittsburgh's and thus a larger voting pool.

Frankie Frisch, Cardinals, second base. In his book *The Politics of Glory: How Baseball's Hall of Fame Really Works*, Bill James makes a case for how Frankie Frisch's influence on the Veterans Committee (along with that of his ex-teammate Bill Terry) wrecked the standards for the Hall of Fame. Frisch was a star on Giants teams of the '20s and Cardinals teams of the '20s and '30s, and the ledger of his teammates in the Hall is long. When I was a kid, Frisch's reputation was still one of an excellent, fiery ballplayer, but I suspect that now, his reputation is as the guy who stacked the Hall with his cronies. It's a shame, because he could play; in his book, James compares him to Roberto Alomar (on a caffeine high).

Chuck Klein, Phillies, right field. The Baker Bowl in Philadelphia was made for Chuck Klein. When he came up to the Majors after barely

400 minor league at-bats, he could already hit and with some power. But as a left-handed hitter with the Baker Bowl's right-field fence sitting only 280 feet away, Klein was in a perfect situation. After hitting .360 with 11 home runs in his first half-season in Philadelphia, he started cranking out video-game numbers. Over the next five years, he batted .359 with 180 home runs and 232 doubles. And boy, did the Baker Bowl help. In those five years, he hit .423 with 122 homers at home and .290 with 56 homers on the road. (He had only one more at-bat at home but 202 more hits!) His worst slugging percentage at home was .734; his best on the road was .583. He led the National League in home runs and total bases four years out of five. Then he was traded to the Cubs, and he transformed from Babe Ruth into Paul O'Neill.

Paul Waner, Pirates, right field. The story has often been written that the 1927 Pirates were psyched out before the World Series started by seeing those vaunted Yankees take batting practice. But what could have psyched out Paul Waner that year? Nothin'. In his second season in the Majors, he hit a league-leading .380. He also led the league in hits (237), total bases (342), RBIs (131) and triples (18). He scored 114 runs and hit 42 doubles and 9 homers (Forbes Field did not yield many home runs). His middle name was Glee, changed from John when Paul was 6 in honor of an Uncle Glee who had given him a shotgun. (At age 6!)

Chick Hafey, Reds, left field. Bill James wrote this of Hafey's poor eyesight: "He wore thick glasses, even on the field, and a teammate of his, Andy High, once told me that Hafey's eyes were so bad that he often couldn't make out letters on street signs or in the train station. High said he couldn't imagine what Hafey would have hit had he been able to see." His SABR *Bio Project* biography says he began wearing glasses in his sixth season, 1929. Two years later he won a batting title. He is derided as a subpar selection for the Hall of Fame, but he did bat cleanup in the first All-Star Game.

Bill Terry, Giants, first base. John McGraw *was* the New York Giants for the first third of the 20th century. He became their manager in the middle of the 1902 season, taking over a losing team that he guided to 106 wins and a pennant two years later. Over three decades, he won the NL pennant 10 times and the World Series three times. But by 1932, he was old and ailing and, eight years removed from his last pennant, managing his worst team since '02. He resigned after 40 games, with a 17–23 record. In stepped Bill Terry, his star first baseman. The Giants did not improve much that year, but the next season, Terry led them to a World Series championship. For which he received minimal acclaim. Many of the New York writers grew to dislike him, his SABR *Bio Project* biography spells out. Westbrook Pegler called him a "cold man." Joe Williams painted him as "hostile, cold and arrogant," his SABR biography says, in part because he refused to give reporters his home phone number. He called reporters "$25 a week clerks." The writers exacted some revenge; Terry, the last National Leaguer to hit .400 (.401 in 1930), retired in 1936, but was not voted into the Hall of Fame until 1954.

Wally Berger, Braves, center field. In 1930, Wally Berger set a Major League record for home runs by a rookie, 38; the rest of the Boston Braves team hit 40. In 1933, he hit 27 of his team's 54 home runs. In 1935, Berger batted .295/.355/.548, leading the league in both home runs (34) and RBIs (130); the rest of the Braves hit 41 homers. The Braves were so bad—38–115—that the next year they had a new name, the Bees.

Dick Bartell, Phillies, shortstop. A young Dick Bartell and an established Pie Traynor were teammates for three years on the Pittsburgh Pirates, and although Traynor would be voted into the Hall of Fame and was years later acclaimed as the greatest third baseman ever, Bartell was no fan. Bill James (also no fan) wrote in *The New Bill James Historical Baseball Abstract* that Bartell thought Traynor "was a selfish player. 'He had some deficiencies that you weren't aware of unless you played next to him,' said Bartell. 'When making a throw to second base he would lob the ball like a shot put instead of throwing it.'"

Pie Traynor, Pirates, pinch-hitter. Pie Traynor did not pinch-hit much—27 times in his career, according to *Baseball Reference*—but his PH numbers are an excellent match for his numbers as a regular: .320 batting average for both, with a .360 on-base percentage as a regular and a .370 as a pinch-hitter. He made this All-Star at-bat count—he doubled off Lefty Grove. He played in one more All-Star Game, in 1934, and went two for five with a stolen base, two runs scored and an RBI.

Carl Hubbell, Giants, pitcher. From July 17, 1936, to May 27, 1937, Carl Hubbell didn't lose any of the 27 games he pitched in, and he won 24 of them—16 to close out the '36 season, eight to start 1937. He also saved two games, and Win No. 24 came in two shutout innings of relief. He did not earn a decision in only one of his 24 starts in that stretch, a game in which the Giants rallied to win in the ninth inning after he was removed for a pinch-hitter in the seventh. He pitched 207 2/3 innings in his winning streak, with a 1.82 ERA. Once the streak was over, Hubbell lost four decisions in a row and began the mortal portion of his career. Through the streak, he had a 182–98 record (.650 winning percentage) with a 2.77 ERA; afterward, a 71–56 mark (.559) and a 3.46 ERA.

Tony Cuccinello, Dodgers, pinch-hitter. How Tony Cuccinello made the All-Star team is a bit of a head-scratcher. Cuccinello, the second baseman for a Brooklyn Dodgers team that would finish 65–88, was hitting below .200 as late as May 20. By the All-Star Game, he was still hitting only .243. But there he was, pinch-hitting in the first All-Star Game (he struck out). He became more renowned for the closest race for a batting title in the Majors, in 1945, losing out in the end to Snuffy Stirnweiss of the Yankees by .0000866. And with, apparently, some chicanery. Cuccinello, whose average had been fading over the final month, missed out on one last chance to raise his average when his White Sox team was rained out on the final day of the season. Stirnweiss, meanwhile, had two hits … and then was awarded a third when an error was changed to a hit. Some accounts say the official scorer—from *The Bronx Home News*—made the change only after learning of the White Sox's rainout. On September 7, Cuccinello, a 37-year-old who didn't play quite full time, was hitting .321 with Stirnweiss at .297. But Cuccinello went 9 for 44 (.205) the rest of the season, while Stirnweiss batted 34 for 89 (.382), getting past Cuccinello, .3085443 to .3084577.

Jimmie Wilson, Cardinals, catcher. In 1933, Jimmie Wilson was an All-Star catcher in St. Louis. His Cardinals had played in the World Series in three of the previous five years. But after that All-Star season, Wilson was shipped to the futile Philadelphia Phillies, where he became a player-manager with no chance of seeing the World Series. His five Phillies teams went 280–477, a .370 clip. "His main accomplishment as Philadelphia manager was converting Bucky Walters to a pitcher; that, or surviving," Bill James wrote in *The New Historical Baseball Abstract*. Well, he didn't survive; he was gone with two games left after his Phillies went 46–103 in 1938. Walters was another story. Wilson persuaded him to move from third base, where he didn't hit much, to the mound, where he became a star. Just not in Philadelphia. After a trade to the Reds, he nearly pitched his way into the Hall of Fame.

Lefty O'Doul, Giants, pinch-hitter. There's a movie to be made about Frank (Lefty) O'Doul. He said he was taught baseball fundamentals by the woman who was his school's coach when he was a kid. He was a pitcher and was signed by his hometown team in the Pacific Coast League, the San Francisco Seals. He and George Halas played together trying to make the Yankees' roster. He struck out Babe Ruth twice in an exhibition game— and then gave up a homer to the Babe. He wound up being optioned back to the minors, where he was the PCL's Shohei Ohtani (or maybe Babe Ruth) in 1921, going 25–9 with a 2.39 ERA in 312 innings on the mound while batting .338 with 5 home runs in 146 at-bats. He hurt his arm and so became a full-time outfielder, batting .392, .375, .338 and .378 in four PCL seasons. Finally, at age 31, he earned a regular job in the Majors and immediately hit .319 for the Giants. The next year he won a batting title, hitting .398 with 32 home runs, 152 runs and 122 RBI. Three years later, at age 35, he won a second batting title, at .368. He didn't play quite 1,000 games in the Majors but hit .349—better than Ruth, better than Ted Williams, better than Gehrig.

He was by his own account a terrible fielder. According to his SABR *Bio Project* biography, after a guy signed O'Doul's name to a bad check in a bar, he told the bartender: "The next time somebody comes in here and says he's me, take him out in the back and have somebody hit a few balls to him. If he catches them, you know he's a phony." He managed for two decades in the PCL after his playing days (although he played a little into his mid–40s) and was an ambassador for baseball in Japan, which he visited often. He was such an avid golfer that while managing San Diego in the PCL, he requested in his contract that he be allowed to play a round of golf a day. Maybe he had sights on the 19th hole: O'Doul had a well-known bar in San Francisco, Lefty's, that remained open until 2019.

Gabby Hartnett, Cubs, catcher. Leo Hartnett was tagged with the nickname Gabby because he was so quiet as a young player, his SABR *Bio Project* profile says. Yet he became known as a chatterbox when he was behind the plate. (The only other Major Leaguer nicknamed Gabby, Charles Street, also was a catcher and, his protestations to the contrary, was something of a chatterbox himself.) "Gabby was always jabberin', and he didn't let a pitcher take his mind off the game," Walter Johnson, his old batterymate, told *The Associated Press* in 1931. "When we got in a tight spot Gabby was right out there to talk it over with me." They were very different players—Street "never hit much," Johnson said, while Hartnett hit for average and for years held the career record for homers by a catcher. Both went on to become short-lived but successful managers; Hartnett won one pennant in three seasons, Street two pennants and a World Series in six seasons.

Bill Hallahan, Cubs, pitcher. His nickname was Wild Bill, and Bill Hallahan earned it. He led the National League in walks three times and was in the top 10 three other times in a 12-year career. He also led the league in wild pitches three times. Hallahan curbed his wildness a bit in midcareer, getting his walks per nine innings under 4.0 for five seasons, but perhaps at the cost of his strikeout pitch; after leading the league in K's in 1931 and '32, his strikeout rate dropped. He was built a little like Billy Wagner—a short left-hander—who was considered one of the hardest throwers in the National League.

Lon Warneke, Cardinals, pitcher. If there were a Nickname Hall of Fame, Lon Warneke would be in it. He was lovingly called the Arkansas Hummingbird by St. Louis sportswriters, especially J. Roy Stockton of *The St. Louis Post-Dispatch*. Stockton bestowed the nickname on Warneke, who was from Mount Ida, Arkansas (at the time a town of 500), "because he throws a fast ball that sings as it darts past hostile bats," as he wrote in

1937. Bill James said that the nickname came from Warneke's humming and singing with a band headed by teammate Pepper Martin, but Stockton really did write that.

Woody English, Cubs, pinch-hitter-shortstop. The most controversial moment of Woody English's career came after the 1932 regular season. His Cubs won the pennant and had to divvy up their World Series shares, and as *The New Bill James Historical Abstract* relates, English oversaw the meeting at which the players voted. Rogers Hornsby had been the team's much-despised manager for the first four months of the season but was fired; the players refused to vote him a share. Mark Koenig had been acquired in mid–August from the Tigers and, replacing light-hitting Billy Jurges, batted .353 and played good defense in 33 games. His reward? A half-share from his Cubs teammates. These decisions drew criticism from all over. Hornsby filed a complaint with Commissioner Kenesaw Mountain Landis. Koenig's ex-teammates on the Yankees (who played the Cubs in the World Series that year) said he deserved a full share. Landis ruled against Hornsby; he didn't overrule the Cubs' vote on Koenig. English had explained to Landis that the vote had to be unanimous, English's SABR *Bio Project* profile said, and two Cubs said no. One of them was Billy Jurges.

Did Not Play

Hal Schumacher, Giants, pitcher. Hal Schumacher was a star for three years, from ages 22 to 24, and he had pitched for three pennant-winning teams by the time he was 26. A sore arm began to bedevil him at 25, and he never finished with the kind of career that would get him to the Hall of Fame. He did make it to Cooperstown in the end, but sadly; he died in a hospital there, about 40 miles from his hometown in New York, at the age of 82.

American League

Ben Chapman, Yankees, left field–right field. Forget, if you can, how unlikable Ben Chapman was. As manager of the Philadelphia Phillies, he race-baited Jackie Robinson badly (retold in *The Boys of Summer* and portrayed in *42*). Once upon a time he was a star outfielder for the Yankees. In his first three seasons, beginning at age 21, he finished in double figures in doubles, triples and home runs. Beginning in his second season, he led the league in steals three consecutive years (though he also led in being caught all three years). Chapman got into it everywhere. He feuded with Babe Ruth (he said Ruth was over the hill, which, even if true, was impolitic);

got into a fight with a Senators pitcher who was upset that Chapman had spiked his second baseman two days in a row; and knocked down catcher Birdie Tebbetts after verbal back-and-forth following a called third strike. *The Washington Post* reported that Chapman tried to hit an umpire with a throw moments after the ump called him out. (Unpleasant matched set: The Yankees traded Chapman to the Senators for outfielder Jake Powell, who later, as Steve Wulf of ESPN.com wrote, told a radio interviewer who asked how he stayed in shape in the off-season, used a racial slur to say, "I beat [Blacks] over the head with my blackjack." Bill James gave Powell his "Cap Anson Award" for the 1930s.)

Charlie Gehringer, Tigers, second base. Lefty Gomez of the Yankees nicknamed Charlie Gehringer the Mechanical Man. "You wind him up in the spring and he goes all summer," Gomez said. "He hits .330 or .340 or whatever, and then you shut him off in the fall." Not far off. Here's a 10-year run of hits: 193, 215, 201, 119 (hurt, played 101 games), 184, 204, 214, 201, 227, 209. Here's a 10-year run of runs: 107, 131, 144, 67 (hurt), 112, 104, 135, 123, 144, 133. Here's a 10-year run of doubles: 29, 45, 47, 24 (hurt), 44, 42, 50, 32, 60, 40. He once reached double figures in triples six years out of seven. From ages 24 to 37, he hit below .300 once—at .298.

Babe Ruth, Yankees, right field. In 1933, Babe Ruth was in his 20th season in the Majors. He had already hit 670 career home runs by the All-Star break. He was voted into the lineup, and who would complain? Not the players. "We wanted to see the Babe," Bill Hallahan, the National League starting pitcher, said, according to *Baseball Almanac*. "Sure, he was old and had a big waistline, but that didn't make any difference. We were on the same field as Babe Ruth." Ruth did not disappoint: He hit the first All-Star Game home run, a two-run shot in the third inning.

Sam West, Browns, center field. Sam West was a fading veteran outfielder when the Washington Senators released him after the 1941 season, in which he had batted only 49 times, hitting .270 with no extra-base hits. But his career average in more than 1,700 games was .301. And then he signed with the Chicago White Sox. West went 35 for 151 for a .232 average … which dropped his career average to .299. Had he accumulated two more hits or 12 fewer at-bats, his average would be in the record books as .300.

Lou Gehrig, Yankees, first base. His famous streak of consecutive games was 2,130. But if you think about it, the streak was 2,170, as Lou Gehrig played in all 34 World Series games of the Yankees and six consecutive All-Star games. Superfluous aside: Derek Jeter impressed me at the Baseball Writers Association of America dinner in February 2000. He sat next to Teresa Wright, the 81-year-old actress who portrayed Eleanor Gehrig, Lou's wife, in the movie *Pride of the Yankees*. Wright was moving gingerly on the dais, and Jeter, who was 25 and hot stuff, casually but carefully walked her off the platform, his hand on her elbow, chatting with Wright the whole way.

Al Simmons, White Sox, center field–left field. If I didn't know better, I'd say Al Simmons was the first of a series of star players named Simmons—Al, Curt, Ted, Andrelton. But I know better: Al's real name was Szymanski. Well, Al's real name was Aloysius Szymanski. He was by far the best Aloysisus in the game (he batted .334 with 2,927 hits). No matter what name, Simmons was not the most pleasant fellow—the historian Donald Honig wrote, "King of his league's right-handed hitters for a decade, he was an elitist who bullied rookies, manifested a chilly disdain for lesser mortals, and even on occasion questioned the wisdom of Mr. Mack"—his manager with the Philadelphia Athletics, Connie Mack. But in Mack's later years, he kept one photo in his office: of Simmons.

Jimmy Dykes, White Sox, third base. In 1960, Jimmy Dykes was managing the Detroit Tigers and Joe Gordon was managing the Cleveland Indians when the teams did what no other Major League teams had apparently done before: On August 3 they swapped managers. The Indians were 49–46 (.516) and in fourth place under Gordon; the Tigers were 44–52 (.458) and in sixth place under Dykes. *The New York Times*'s account included: "About three weeks ago, Bill DeWitt, Detroit's general manager, and Lane"—Frank Lane, the Indians' general manager who was notorious for his frequent trades—"talked over the telephone. Both teams were slumping, and DeWitt said to Lane, 'We've been trading players, why don't we trade managers?'" So they did. To no great effect, however. The Indians went 26–32 (.448) under Dykes, the Tigers 26–31 (.456) under Gordon. The only maneuver close to this that *The Times* could come up with also came in 1960: Manager Charlie Grimm was bounced to the Cubs' radio booth … and radio announcer Lou Boudreau became the manager.

Joe Cronin, Senators, second base. Player-managers once were not at all unusual. In the 1920s and '30s, several had considerable success. Frankie Frisch won two pennants and a World Series with the Cardinals as a player-manager. Bucky Harris also won two pennants and a Series, with the Washington Senators. Charlie Grimm won two pennants as a player-manager with the Cubs. Rogers Hornsby won a World Series with the Cardinals and maybe a portion of one with the Cubs. Chicago fired him in 1932 with the Cubs sitting 53–46; Grimm took over in August, leading Chicago to a 37–18 record and the actual pennant. And then there was Cronin, who was nicknamed The Boy Wonder for capturing the A.L. pennant in 1933, when he was also the team's star shortstop. (After the 1934 season, he also married the niece of the Senators' owner, Clark Griffith.) Pete Rose was the last player-manager, in 1986.

Rick Ferrell, Red Sox, catcher. How disheartening would this be if you were Rick Ferrell? He caught more than 1,800 games, but his brother Wes, a pitcher, hit 10 more career home runs than Rick ... in 5,700 fewer plate appearances. Ferrell was traded to the Red Sox by the Browns a month into the season. He was an All-Star eight times, including at age 38 and 39.

Lefty Gomez, Yankees, pitcher. There are a million Lefty Gomez stories, and it is worth looking them up. But here's a Lefty Gomez fact: Gomez was a notoriously weak hitter, batting .147 for his career with no home runs in 1,024 plate appearances—but he drove in the first All-Star Game's first run, with a second-inning single.

General Crowder, Senators, pitcher. OK, we have to know: Why was he called General? According to his SABR *Bio Project* biography, Alvin Floyd Crowder was pitching in the minor leagues in 1925, and pitching a lot—he was called into service (heh heh) 59 times. A Gen. Enoch Crowder had instituted a draft lottery for the Army in World War I, and thus Alvin became General. He was a pretty fine pitcher, too, and the Senators worked him hard in 1932 and 1933. In '32, with Walter Johnson as manager, Crowder pitched a league-high 327 innings and went 26–13, 3.33 (129 ERA+). The Senators finished third, though, and Johnson was replaced by Joe Cronin, a 26-year-old player-manager, who squeezed another 299⅓ innings out of Crowder, who at age 34 finished 24–15, 3.97 (105 ERA+) as Washington won the pennant. He was done as a top-flight pitcher, though he played another three seasons.

Earl Averill, Indians, pinch-hitter. This Cleveland Indians slugger was from Snohomish, Washington, and was sometimes called in the press the Earl of Snohomish. But his son Earl was not; he was sometimes called Junior, although he wasn't really a Junior. He was Earl Douglas; his father was Howard Earl. There *was* another Earl of Snohomish, however—Earl Torgeson, a longtime first baseman, mostly in the '50s. Bob Feller played with both the elder and younger Earl Averill.

Lefty Grove, Athletics, pitcher. Did you notice that there were three players called Lefty in this game? According to *Baseball Reference*, there have been dozens and dozens of players nicknamed Lefty. Even a manager, Lefty Phillips. B-R doesn't show anyone nicknamed Righty.

Did Not Play

Bill Dickey, Yankees, catcher. When Bill Dickey went into the service after the 1943 season at age 36, he had exactly 200 Major League home runs. It was not unreasonable to think his career was over. But after two years in the Navy, the 39-year-old Dickey returned to play 54 games as a league-average hitter—who knocked out two more homers. Famously, both Dickey and Yogi Berra wore No. 8, which was retired for both of them.

Wes Ferrell, Indians, pitcher. Wes Ferrell and his brother Rick were teammates for five seasons with the Red Sox and the Senators, and Rick caught Wes in 140 games. Wes won 25 games with Rick as his catcher for the 1934 Red Sox. They were opponents far longer. Rick was 12 for 42 against his brother for a .286/.382/.452 slash line (OPS of .814)—better than he hit against the rest of the league.

Jimmie Foxx, Athletics, first base. A guy who would hit 534 home runs was a bench-warmer for the All-Star Game? Yup. Hard to move that Gehrig out of the lineup. Foxx was, along with Hack Wilson, the inspiration for Manager Jimmy Dugan in the movie *A League of Their Own*. Foxx served as manager one season in the All-American Girls Professional Baseball League, with the Fort Wayne Daisies, in 1952—a year after his induction into the Baseball Hall of Fame. The Daisies won the pennant. And Foxx "could still hit a ball," one of his players said years later.

Oral Hildebrand, Indians, pitcher. Orel Hershiser I know. But Oral Hildebrand? Never heard of him. And he and I are both from Indianapolis and he is buried in the suburb where my parents lived for years. He had, from this distance, a forgettable 10-year career, with an 83–78 record and a 4.35 ERA. *Baseball Reference* lists his best modern comps as Gil Meche and Cal Eldred, and who will remember them in 90 years? When Hildebrand was a high school freshman, the star of the team was Chuck Klein. Klein pitched, not Hildebrand, who played the outfield. Klein never pitched in the Majors (but did hit 300 homers); Hildebrand never homered in the bigs.

Tony Lazzeri, Yankees, second base. Tony Lazzeri hit 60 home runs in a season before Babe Ruth did. As a 21-year-old playing for Salt Lake City in the Pacific Coast League, he hit exactly 60 homers in 1925. Of course, he played 197 games. (His Major League high was 18.)

Twenty

July 17
Stopping Joe DiMaggio

Seeds for the end of Joe DiMaggio's hitting streak in 1941 were planted that June. In the second game of a doubleheader at Memorial Stadium in Cleveland on June 1, DiMaggio barely kept his streak alive at 18 games when, in his fourth and final time at bat, he singled off the glove of third baseman Ken Keltner. DiMaggio had pulled the ball down the line, and Keltner was moving to his right when the ball ticked away. "He could go to his right better than anyone," Cleveland ace Bob Feller said of Keltner, but it was not enough that June day.

A month and a half later, on July 17, DiMaggio was back in Cleveland before a crowd of 67,468, having hit in every game since. As was the case in June, the grounds were damp because of rain the day before. Feller said he would have relished the opportunity to stop DiMaggio's epic streak at 56—he was 18–4 with a 3.01 earned run average at the time—but he was scheduled to pitch the next day. The task fell to a far more pedestrian pitcher, Al Smith, "a lefty who held no particular terror," as Richard Ben Cramer wrote in *Joe DiMaggio: The Hero's Life*.

No terror? Smith looked like a treat. DiMaggio had singled in three times at bat against Smith that season, and over his career DiMaggio battered Smith. He went 16 for 42 with 10 walks and four home runs for a .381/.509/.714 line. He reached base eight of the first nine times he faced Smith and 10 of the first 12. Smith walked him three times in one 1940 game. No terror, indeed. In fact, Smith and the pitcher who wound up relieving him on July 17, Jim Bagby, were about as close to league average as you could find—in 1941 or for their careers. Smith was 12–13 that season with a 103 ERA+; over his 12 seasons, he was 99–101 with a 99 ERA+. Bagby, whose father, Jim Sr., won 31 games for Cleveland's 1920 World Series champions, registered a 97 ERA+ in his career and a 97–96 record. To that point in the 1941 season, DiMaggio was 8 for 24 with three walks and two homers against Bagby. The last time Bagby had faced him, DiMaggio hit a homer to deep left field.

All that indicated that DiMaggio could be expected to hit the ball hard. Ken Keltner certainly expected it. He often played a deep third base. "He played as deep at third as the situation allowed, whatever the situation was," the Yankees' Johnny Sturm said in *Streak: Joe DiMaggio and the Summer of 1941*. Keltner also "had the best arm at his position in baseball," Sturm said.

Remembering the June 1 game, Keltner positioned himself deep at third DiMaggio's first time up on July 17. "Deep? My God, he was standing in left field," DiMaggio said. Keltner also knew that DiMaggio tended to pull the ball hard against left-handers (like Smith). Against that bastion of defense, DiMaggio hit the ball sharply down the line; as he recalled to the Baseball Hall of Fame, Keltner backhanded the ball on the third or fourth hop, well onto the grass in foul territory. "I couldn't get out of the box quickly because of the rains the day before, and Ken's throw just nipped me," DiMaggio said.

DiMaggio walked his next time up (and Smith was booed by his hometown crowd). He told Michael Seidel, author of *Streak*, that Keltner's positioning became more exaggerated as the game wore on. Keltner, Seidel wrote, said he wanted "to get an extra step's worth of time because of the damp field; he also wanted to hold any hit that got past him to a single." In the seventh inning, Keltner played even closer to the line, so the ball hit by DiMaggio, though in a similar spot as the shot in the first inning, was closer to him. Again, he backhanded the ball and threw a rope to first to retire DiMaggio. Keltner told Seidel that the throws were more difficult than the stops. "The plays at first base were bang-bang close," *Sports Illustrated* wrote in a retrospective in 2011, "and DiMaggio believed that the damp ground (it had rained heavily the night before) had slowed his stride, costing him."

Keltner led American League third basemen in assists that year, but those were the two that everyone remembered. They were hardly foreordained, however. *Sports Illustrated* noted that DiMaggio could have gamed the Cleveland defense, but chose to attack it straight up. "Keltner played DiMaggio on the edge of the outfield grass," *SI* wrote. "On either at-bat Joe could have dropped down a bunt and made it to first base at a trot. That was just not something he would do, not even with The Streak on the line." Sturm, DiMaggio's teammate, was clear about that, too. "Joe would never bunt," he told Seidel, "and Kenny knew it."

Not just The Streak was on the line; the game and the pennant were as well. The Yankees led, 4–1, after scoring twice in the eighth inning as they endeavored to keep Cleveland at bay in the American League race. Up came DiMaggio with the bases loaded and one out. Smith, having given up three consecutive hits and a walk, was replaced by Bagby, an infrequent reliever. It was only his third appearance out of the bullpen that season, and he had not been stellar in the other two. In the first, he allowed three runs, three hits, a walk and a homer in three and two-thirds innings; in the second, he pitched an inning and two-thirds of shutout ball despite giving up two hits and a walk.

The count went to 1-1 before DiMaggio hit another sharp grounder. *The Tampa Bay Times* described that final at-bat, on the 50th anniversary of the game, like this: "With one out, and the bases full, the Yankee Clipper bounded Bagby's pitch toward shortstop. Lou Boudreau reacted to a nasty bounce, gloving Joe's hopper. He flipped to second baseman Ray Mack for a forceout, and the relay reached Indians first baseman Oscar Grimes a step ahead of DiMaggio."

No one knew for certain that The Streak was over. Cleveland rallied in the bottom of the ninth to cut the gap to 4–3. Had the Indians tied the score, the Yankees would have come to bat in the 10th with DiMaggio the fourth batter due up. But Yankees reliever Johnny Murphy closed out the game, and The Streak *was* over. DiMaggio was philosophical about the end, at least as quoted in the papers. "That play Ken made on me in the first inning when he went behind the bag for a backhand stop of a hard smash was a beautiful piece of work," DiMaggio said in *The New York Times*. "When they take 'em away from you like that, there's nothing a fellow can do about it. Anyway, it's all over now."

Before long, the narrative was that Keltner had stopped The Streak. That's what baseball histories I read said less than two decades later. But in the immediate aftermath, the pitchers were the focus. The next day's *New York Times* featured photos of Smith and Bagby, but not of Keltner. In the five headlines on the article about the game (yes, five!), none mentioned Keltner; the first subhead read, "Smith and Bagby Stop Yankee Star." Smith and Bagby are cited in the third paragraph of the article, Keltner the fourth.

Bagby was subdued about his role. He had a cleft palate and was self-conscious about it. "Rival ballplayers can be terribly cruel," his son Charles told *The Tampa Bay Times* in 1991, "and Dad told me about being bothered plenty of times when enemy dugouts would mimic his speech and poke fun at him." But his reticence was more than that. "My dad, a man too humble for his own good, was always surprised at his notoriety," Charles Bagby said. "Jim Bagby," *The Tampa Bay Times* wrote, "figured he'd just happened to be on the mound, and wondered why all the fuss."

The fuss was immediate but also lasting. Richard Ben Cramer wrote that with thousands waiting outside the players' gate, "Keltner and his wife had to walk through the crowd with police protection." Charles Bagby said: "Throughout my father's life, when some major-leaguer hit safely in

Twenty. July 17

20 or 25 games, the stories of the 56-game DiMaggio streak would resurface. Reporters always called Dad, asking him to flash back to that July night in 1941, and to recreate Joe's final at-bat." (DiMaggio never forgot either. "Once, when he met DiMaggio years later after both men had retired," *Sports Illustrated* wrote, "Joe signed a ball for Keltner, inscribing it 'To the culprit.'") The Streak had been stopped, but DiMaggio wasn't. Sixteen hours later, facing Bob Feller, DiMaggio singled and doubled, starting a 16-game hitting streak.

Twenty-One

July 21
The Last to Integrate

By the time Pumpsie Green integrated the Boston Red Sox's lineup on July 21, 1959, more than 100 Black players—African American and Latino—had played for the other 15 Major League teams. The four southernmost teams in the Majors—the Washington Senators, the Cincinnati Reds, the St. Louis Cardinals and the St. Louis Browns/Baltimore Orioles—had all integrated by 1954. Even the Yankees, haughty holdouts to

Pumpsie Green, the first Black player for the Boston Red Sox, with Manager Mike (Pinky) Higgins, who had vowed to keep African Americans off the roster (National Baseball Hall of Fame, Cooperstown, NY).

integration of their Major League roster, had brought up a Black player, Elston Howard, in 1955. Although the front office repeatedly said it could not find suitable Black players for their club in Boston, by the time Green pulled on a Red Sox uniform, Black or Latino players had won nine Rookie of the Year Awards and eight Most Valuable Player Awards in 12 seasons.

There had long been pressure on the Red Sox, owned by Tom Yawkey since 1933, to integrate. In 1944, a Boston city councilor, Isadore Muchnick, requested that the Massachusetts Commission Against Discrimination look into the Red Sox's hiring practices, on and off the field, wrote Bill Nowlin in his deeply researched book *Tom Yawkey: Patriarch of the Boston Red Sox*. But they resisted. And resisted. And resisted, until Green, a modest and modestly talented middle infielder, pinch-ran in the eighth inning in Chicago against the White Sox in Boston's 91st game of the '59 season. He played one inning in the field, at shortstop. As a result, every team in the Major Leagues had, at long last, employed a Black player.

The Red Sox did not have to be the last team to integrate and could have, in fact, been the first.

In 1945, in an effort to secure a tryout for a Black player, Muchnick threatened to pull the Red Sox's permit from the city for Sunday baseball, Jules Tygiel wrote in *Baseball's Great Experiment: Jackie Robinson and His Legacy*. (Sunday baseball was the Red Sox's biggest money-maker, and its loss "would have been financially disastrous," Nowlin wrote.) Eddie Collins, the team's general manager and a former Columbia University student, responded to Muchnick by writing, however credulously: "I have been connected with the Red Sox for twelve years and during that time we have never had a single request for a tryout by a colored applicant. It is beyond my understanding how anyone could insinuate or believe that all ball players, regardless of race, color or creed have not been treated in the American way so far as having an equal opportunity to play for the Red Sox."

A team with a recent history of indifferent success and no World Series championship since 1918 now had a very public request. Wendell Smith, a columnist for the widely read *Pittsburgh Courier*, a Black newspaper, produced not one but three Black ballplayers for a tryout: 26-year-old shortstop Jackie Robinson (a future Rookie of the Year, MVP and Hall of Famer), 28-year-old outfielder Sam Jethroe (a future Rookie of the Year) and 25-year-old second baseman Marvin Williams (who hit .382 in three World War II seasons in the Negro National League and would play professionally until he was 41). The players were taken to Fenway Park on April 16, 1945—the day before the Red Sox's season opened and after two days of postponement in the aftermath of President Franklin D. Roosevelt's death—for the grudging tryout. As Robinson recounted to Tygiel, he, Jethroe and Williams all hit the ball well during the 90-minute tryout. They never heard back from the Red Sox.

But the tryout may have put more than talented ballplayers on display. Clif Keane, a longtime, influential Boston sportswriter, years later said that he heard someone in the stadium yell during the workout, using a racial slur, to "get those [Blacks] off the field." It was unclear, he said, who yelled that, but he speculated at various times that it was Yawkey, Collins or Manager Joe Cronin. Absolutely clear was the Red Sox's lack of interest in signing a Black player, not then and not for years after. "It was an episode from which the reputation and perception of the franchise have never recovered," Howard Bryant wrote in 2002 in *Shut Out: A Story of Race and Baseball in Boston*.

Ten days earlier, the Brooklyn Dodgers had held their own grudging tryout for two Black players, in Bear Mountain, New York, where the Dodgers were preparing for the last season of World War II. Joe Bostic of *The Amsterdam News*, another African American newspaper, had shown up with no notice along with two Negro League players, pitcher Terris McDuffie and slick-fielding first baseman Dave (Showboat) Thomas. Bostic demanded that the Dodgers' Branch Rickey give them a tryout, Tygiel wrote; Rickey, angered at being placed in what he viewed as a no-win situation (and with unannounced plans of his own in mind), unhappily agreed. McDuffie and Thomas got no more response from the Dodgers than Robinson, Jethroe and Williams did from the Red Sox. The Chicago White Sox also held a tryout for Black players that led to nothing, Bryant wrote; Tygiel mentions tryouts of Robinson and pitcher Nate Moreland by the White Sox in 1942 and said the Pittsburgh Pirates "appeared ready to recruit Black ballplayers" in 1943. None were, of course, fruitful.

The tryout that mattered arrived on August 28, 1945, when Robinson worked out for Rickey and the Dodgers. Two months later, Robinson signed with the Dodgers' organization; the next season, he played for the Dodgers' Class AAA Montreal team, and a year later, he was playing and starring in Brooklyn.

Robinson's 1946 season concluded with his Montreal Royals playing the Louisville Colonels in the Junior World Series. Coincidentally, the Colonels were affiliated with the Red Sox, and Cronin, the Boston manager, excused the team's indifference to Robinson, Jethroe and Williams by saying, "We told them our only farm club available was in Louisville, Kentucky, and we didn't think they'd be interested in going there," Tygiel wrote. At the time of Robinson's Red Sox tryout in 1945, Louisville was in fact Boston's only team in Class AA, the highest level in the minors at the time, but it did have a team one rung lower in Scranton, Pennsylvania, according to *Baseball Reference*. (In 1946, Boston's top two minor league teams were in Louisville, then in the new Class AAA, and New Orleans, in Class AA. But Cronin's reference was to the arrangements in 1945. Also, the Red Sox had made the old Class AA Minneapolis Millers their farm team for several years beginning in 1937, and Yawkey bought a Pacific Coast League team, the San Francisco Seals, in 1955 in a futile effort to establish an American League foothold in the city and freeze out the National League. Clearly the Red Sox had the means to get a top minor league team where they wanted.) Cronin also claimed that players were not signed off tryouts in those days—although clearly Robinson's tryout with the Dodgers sealed his deal with Brooklyn.

The Red Sox's flimsy flirtation with Robinson did occur at a time when Major League Baseball's color line remained unbroken. But by 1949, seven Black players had made it to the Majors when the Red Sox sent a top scout, Larry Woodall, to Birmingham, Alabama, to check out a dashing young outfielder: 18-year-old Willie Mays. Although he was still in high school, Mays was playing on weekends for the Birmingham Black Barons of the Negro National League, who played home games at Rickwood Field—the same ballpark in which a Red Sox farm club, the Barons, also played. Glenn Stout and Richard A. Johnson, noted Red Sox historians, said that the Black Barons "promised Boston first crack at their players."

Woodall's scouting trip was a disaster. Rain wiped out three days on which Woodall never saw Mays. Woodall invoked a racial slur in saying he was "not going to waste my time waiting for a bunch" of Black ballplayers to perform. It is unclear whether Woodall ever saw Mays play, but what is certain is that he wrote what Bryant called "an unenthusiastic scouting report" for Cronin. Several accounts say that another Red Sox scout, George Digby, called Mays "the greatest single talent I have ever seen," but Boston did not pursue him. Mays himself had regrets about that. In a 1997 interview with Bryant, he said: "There's no telling what I would have been able to do in Boston. To be honest, I really thought I was going to Boston."

Think about the team Boston could have had in the late 1940s and early 1950s: Ted Williams, Jackie Robinson and Willie Mays. By the middle of the decade, as Williams and Robinson were aging, they would have been joined by Jackie Jensen. (Just look at one season, 1954, Jensen's first in Boston, for the outfield the Red Sox could have had: Williams batted .345/.413/.635, with an OPS+ of 201; Mays, .345/.411/.667, 175; and Jensen, .276/.359/.472, 117. Best outfield ever?) All four of those hitters won MVP awards. And the Boston defense, not known for superlative play, would have had superior defenders in Mays, Robinson and Jensen.

Perhaps the Red Sox felt secure in their success without such young, Black talent. They were 83-71-3 in 1947, lost the 1948 pennant in a playoff, lost the 1949 pennant to the Yankees by a single game and finished 94-60 and 87–67 in 1950 and '51. And yet in 1950, they did sign a Black player—not a potential young superstar, but an aging Negro leagues star: Lorenzo (Piper) Davis, a 32-year-old first baseman who fudged his age by several years ... and who happened to have managed Mays in Birmingham.

Davis's arrangement was for $7,500 upon signing and another $7,500 if he remained on the roster of the Red Sox's Class A farm team in Scranton on May 15, Bryant wrote. Two days before the deadline, Tygiel notes, Davis was leading the team in batting average, home runs, stolen bases and RBIs when he was called in to the general manager's office. Davis expected a promotion; instead, he was released, for "economical reasons," the general manager told him. It was a rationale Cronin repeated to Davis, who was rightfully skeptical. "I knew that was a joke," he told Tygiel, "because Tom Yawkey's one of the richest men in the East." The Red Sox in 1949 had set a club attendance record of nearly 1.6 million, and Tygiel said the team had made a profit in four of the previous five years. There was never a Major League payday for Davis, but he was quickly signed by the Oakland Oaks of the Pacific Coast League and starred there for five years.

The Red Sox may have turned a cold shoulder to Robinson, Jethroe and Williams in 1945, but other than, surreptitiously, the Dodgers, no other teams were moving to sign Black players either. They had been given little encouragement by Major League Baseball's longtime commissioner, Kenesaw Mountain Landis, who oversaw the color barrier until his death in late 1944, even though he had said in 1942, "Not now or at any time in the 21 years I have been high commissioner of baseball has there been any rule or understanding against the hiring of Negro players." It was only with a new commissioner, A.B. (Happy) Chandler, a former senator from Kentucky, that three teams integrated in 1947; a fourth in 1949. By 1950, even a Boston team integrated—the Braves, who signed Jethroe and suffered no appreciable backlash as he played not a mile from Fenway Park. Another Boston team integrated that year, too: the Celtics, who had the second Black player in NBA history, Chuck Cooper. The Celtics' dynasty, begun in the late 1950s, was built on Black stars like Bill Russell (signed in 1956), Sam Jones (1957) and K.C. Jones (1958). Willie O'Ree became the first Black player in the National Hockey League, playing for the Bruins in 1958–18 months ahead of Pumpsie Green's first game with the Red Sox.

But after Boston let Davis go in 1950, it was four more years before the Red Sox signed another Black player: Earl Wilson, a teenage catcher who was almost immediately converted to a pitcher who would go on to substantial success in the Major Leagues. (As a sign of the times—and the Red Sox—a scouting report on Wilson sent to the front office, according to his SABR *Bio Project* biography, said: "He is a well mannered colored boy, not too black, pleasant to talk to, well educated, has a very good appearance and conducts himself as a gentleman.") After Wilson was in the fold, the next Black player the Red Sox signed was Pumpsie Green.

Elijah (Pumpsie) Green grew up in Oakland and followed the Oaks. His favorite player, in fact, was Piper Davis, although his SABR *Bio Project* profile says he styled his game after the Oaks' first Black player, Artie Wilson, a shortstop who joined the Oaks in 1949 and led the PCL in hitting. Green signed with the Oaks out of junior college and was dispatched to Wenatchee, Washington ("the apple capital of the world," Green noted), in the Class A Western International League, where he hit .244 and fielded miserably at third base. After another season in Wenatchee, Green was demoted to Class C Stockton, California. In the middle of a season in which he batted .319 with 31 doubles, 11 triples, 12 homers and 31 stolen bases, Green had his contract purchased by the Red Sox.

Boston, the organization that had said it did not want to assign the 26-year-old Army veteran Jackie Robinson to a city like Louisville, wanted to assign the 21-year-old Pumpsie Green to Montgomery, Alabama, and a team called the Rebels. Green resisted and won; he finished out the 1955 season in Stockton. (Historical context: This was only a year after the Brown v. Board of Education decision by the Supreme Court and months before the bus boycott in Montgomery began.)

If Green was moving slowly toward Boston, attitudes in the organization were moving glacially. Nowlin says in *Tom Yawkey* that in the summer of 1955—about the time the Red Sox were purchasing Green's contract, by the way—a well-known scout, Ted McGrew, conducted a tryout in Georgia for Black players. Of the 500 players trying out, Nowlin wrote, only one seemed like a Major League prospect to McGrew, "but he wanted more money than the Red Sox thought he would be worth and he signed with another club." That same summer, the Red Sox gave an $85,000 signing bonus to a 17-year-old white catcher, Jim Pagliaroni, capping a half-decade in which the team spent more than $600,000 to sign eight amateur players—bonus babies to the rest of baseball and the Gold Sox to those following Boston. That's about $7 million in today's dollars, for a team that did not want to spend to sign one Black player.

When the Yankees promoted Elston Howard that season, only three Major League teams remained all-white: the Philadelphia Phillies, the Detroit Tigers and the Red Sox. The Phillies were the team whose general manager, Herb Pennock (a former Red Sox pitcher), had told the Dodgers' Branch Rickey in harsh terms in 1947 that Brooklyn could not bring Jackie Robinson to Philadelphia to play. Rickey did, Phillies Manager Ben Chapman unleashed racist comments and, Howard Bryant writes, the National League president, Ford Frick, called Pennock demanding that he reprimand Chapman.

The Tigers were the last Major League team to sign a Black player to a minor league contract, Robert Kuhn McGregor wrote in *A Calculus of Color: The Integration of Baseball's American League*. They were owned for years by Walter O. Briggs, who, after taking control of the team in the mid-30s and renovating the stadium, enforced a ban on Black fans in the box seats, McGregor wrote. Briggs also vowed never to employ a Black player, and he died in 1952 never having done so. It took the family's sale of the team in 1956 and two more years of incubation before Detroit put a Black player on the field, in 1958—the Dominican Ozzie Virgil. Briggs's great-grandson wrote in a 2017 essay in *The Detroit Free Press* that Briggs was a racist, and he disavowed his great-grandfather's legacy.

These were the laggards the Red Sox trailed. And the Boston team was the one Pumpsie Green was hoping to ascend to. His play was good enough to earn promotions in the minor leagues, but not to the Majors. In his first season in the Red Sox's organization, Green hit .274 with a .406 on-base percentage, a 22-year-old shortstop who made 37 errors in the Class A Eastern League. The next year was more difficult: He batted .258, although with 81 walks, while splitting time between shortstop and second base (and committing 48 errors) for Oklahoma City. That meant playing in the Texas League, where he was not always welcome—even under the law. Green did not accompany his teammates to games in Shreveport, Louisiana, which had a law prohibiting whites and Blacks from playing together. A move up to Class AAA in 1958 allowed him to play in Minneapolis—at least he could suit up for all of his team's games—but he still wasn't putting pressure on the Red Sox to bring him up. Green batted .253, though with 107 walks.

On September 21, the Red Sox placed Green on their 40-man roster, but had they not done so, they would have risked losing him in that winter's draft. Still, he was on the cusp of the Major Leagues. Wilson might have been there ahead of him, but he was drafted into the military and spent the 1957 and '58 seasons in the Marines.

Green prepared for his first spring training with the Red Sox by hitting .306 in the Panama winter league. He was cautious about his role. "So far as I'm concerned, I'm no martyr. No flag carrier," Green said in *The Boston Herald*. "I'm just trying to make the ballclub, that's all."

When he took part in his first spring workout in Arizona, *The Boston Globe* reported, "The Boston Red Sox—in spring training, at least—today broke the color line." But the color line wasn't just baseball's; Scottsdale, Arizona, where the team's hotel was situated, did not allow Blacks to stay overnight, so Green had to go to Phoenix—eventually staying, coincidentally, in the same hotel as the San Francisco Giants, who had integrated a decade earlier. "From night to morning, the first Negro player to be

Twenty-One. July 21

brought to spring training by the Boston Red Sox ceases to be a member of the team he hopes to make as a shortstop," Milton Gross wrote in *The Boston Globe*. The team's response was to say that the Scottsdale hotel had run out of rooms.

(Accommodations for the players were a problem as baseball integrated; many hotels would not allow Black guests, even in Major League cities. Even as the game included more and more Black players, the issue persisted in spring training, in Florida and Arizona. The Dodgers moved to solve the problem early on, building their own facility, Dodgertown, in Vero Beach, Florida, as "a haven from southern segregation," Jules Tygiel wrote. "Black and white players could room together, eat together, and train together without interference from outside authorities." That was in 1948, but segregation remained entrenched into the 1960s. In 1961, for example, the St. Louis Cardinals' Black players could not stay at the same hotel in St. Petersburg, Florida, as the white players, which came to national attention—and the attention of the team's owner, Gussie Busch, according to an article at STLRedbirds.com, run by a longtime Cardinals fan, Richard Bray.

(When word of the situation became public, two hotels offered their facilities, and the Cardinals players—Black and white, even stars who had been staying in lusher accommodations elsewhere—lived together during spring training. The Cincinnati Reds and the Philadelphia Phillies fled segregated hotels in 1962, *The Tampa Bay Times* noted in a 2020 article, and by 1964, all the teams training in Florida were living in integrated hotels during spring training.)

Difficulties for Green did not exist only away from the ballpark. Boston's manager was Mike (Pinky) Higgins, a 50-year-old Texan and drinking buddy of Yawkey whose outlook on race relations was delineated by the writer Al Hirshberg. He quoted Higgins using a racial epithet to say, "There'll be no [Blacks] on this ballclub as long as I have anything to say about it." Yet Green began spring training like a potential standout, not a middling prospect, batting .444 in his first 11 games. Reporters covering the team voted him Red Sox Rookie of the Year. Under the rules of the time, the team could carry 30 players for the first month of the season. But Green was not convinced that he would make the team or that he was ready. Reflecting on his hot spring start, he said years later, "I knew that I wasn't that good." The Red Sox apparently concurred and optioned him back to Class AAA, with Higgins saying Green needed more seasoning.

If Green was now in Minneapolis, the controversy remained in Boston. The city's NAACP chapter filed a complaint with the Massachusetts Commission Against Discrimination. The team was skewered in the newspapers. The team responded that it would "make every effort" to employ a

Black player. The Red Sox's business manager, Dick O'Connell, acknowledged "that the team would be accused of racism 'until we have a Negro on our roster,'" Green's SABR biography says. (The problem persisted beyond the roster. Nowlin wrote in *Tom Yawkey* that at the time, the Red Sox had ever hired only one Black employee in any position: a Black cook who was gone after three weeks.) Green's own response: "I want to be judged like any other ballplayer. I don't want to be a crusader. I just want to play ball."

His further response was to play as he never had before. Used exclusively at second base by the Millers, he held his own defensively and batted .320 with 75 walks against 35 strikeouts in 432 plate appearances. The Red Sox, meanwhile, were terrible—31–42 and in last place when Higgins was fired as manager on July 3. Two and a half weeks later, Pumpsie Green was a Major Leaguer. And the Red Sox were no longer the only all-white team in Major League Baseball.

He started at second base the next day in Chicago, going 0 for 3 with a walk, and a week after his debut, he had a Black teammate when Earl Wilson was called up. After a 3-for-4 day at Detroit on July 31, Green was batting .313 with a .522 on-base percentage (thanks to six walks in 25 plate appearances) in his first seven games. After an extended road trip, he played his first game at Fenway Park on August 4 (going 1 for 4). He was still batting .306 on August 27 before his season began to unravel; Green ended the season in a 14-for-87 slump (.161) weighed down by a 0-for-24 finish.

Green was no savior for the Red Sox, but he played commensurate with his career minor league numbers. He batted .233/.350/.320 and played basically league-average defense, and the team went 44–36 under Billy Jurges, Higgins's replacement. Jurges said Green had worn down under a heavy workload, perhaps 200 games, in winter ball, spring training, the American Association and the American League.

There was much away from the ballpark that could have also worn Green down. Boston was not an easy city for any Black resident. Bill Russell, the Celtics star, eventually became vocal in his assessment of Boston as an intolerant city. Russell joined the Celtics in late 1956, and, Bryant wrote in *Shut Out*, he "was miserable in Boston, suffering from bouts of terrible loneliness and frustration at the racial climate of the city." Russell called the city "a flea market of racism." When Green—who grew up in the Oakland area, as Russell did—made it to Boston, Russell became a social mentor for the newly arrived ballplayer. Bryant wrote that Russell and K.C. Jones had Green to their homes for numerous meals, for example, and that Russell and Green "would drive around the city and Russell served as something of a tour guide, alerting the young Green to perilous areas of the city." A perilous climate did not end in the '50s. Or the '60s.

In the '70s, virulent demonstrations against court-ordered busing for the public schools erupted, further tainting the image of Boston, the so-called Athens of America and once a hotbed of the abolition movement.

It was in this unsettled environment that Green was trying to establish himself. If the Red Sox were expecting improvement in 1960, Green could not provide it. His offense was essentially the same (.242/.350/.338). His defense seemed better. But the team was not, getting off to a 14–21 start and drawing steady criticism in the papers by the end of May. On June 8, as Nowlin relates in *Tom Yawkey*, the team said Jurges was taking a three-week vacation because of doctors' recommendation. He did not get three weeks; two days later, he was fired—and Pinky Higgins, who had never left the organization, was brought back to manage. Higgins had enough confidence in Green that he moved him to shortstop for the final five weeks of the lost season. There was one significant gain that season: For the first time, the Red Sox traded for a Black player, Willie Tasby, an outfielder who played 113 games.

In 1961, Green had the best offensive season of his Major League career, batting .260/.376/.425 with an OPS+ of 114, as a part-time shortstop. His opportunity at second base had closed when the rookie Chuck Schilling, basically the same offensive player as Green, arrived and played better defense; he was third in the Rookie of the Year voting. Green spent much of the season as the only Black player on the Red Sox; Wilson was in the minors, Tasby had been drafted by the expansion Washington Senators, and Billy Harrell, another banjo-hitting infielder, played only 37 games.

The next season, Higgins was still managing and Boston was still losing, but Green was no longer playing regularly. He started only two of the first 50 games as the Red Sox had brought in Eddie Bressoud, a veteran shortstop who proved to be a vast upgrade offensively. The team also remained overwhelmingly white as Green and Wilson, back up with the team, were the only Black players. And after the season, Green was gone—traded to the New York Mets, with whom he finished his career in 1963 on a 51-111 team.

The Red Sox were still reluctant to add Black players, and they stumbled through the mid-60s. They were 76–85 in 1963 (Higgins had been moved to general manager) and had one African American player (Wilson) and two Black Latino players (Felix Mantilla and Roman Mejias). In 1964, their 72–90 team used Wilson and, briefly, outfielder Al Smith, along with Mantilla and Mejias. In 1965, the Red Sox were 62–100 with only Wilson, outfielder Lenny Green and Mantilla as players of color. That run of ruin finally led to Higgins's firing.

In came Dick O'Connell as general manager, and Nowlin generally credits him with changing racial attitudes within the organization. Some of it was immediately obvious, as the 1966 team—no great shakes at 72–90, but 10 games better, anyway—started three Black players in the infield: first baseman George Scott, second baseman George Smith and third baseman Joe Foy. Lenny Green was a backup outfielder, outfielder Jose Tartabull received plenty of playing time, Reggie Smith had a late-season call-up and Joe Christopher was around for a while. Although Christopher and Wilson were traded in midseason to Detroit, the pitching staff did have a Black reliever, John Wyatt, and starter, Jose Santiago.

The next year, 1967, was the Impossible Dream pennant-winning season. The Red Sox again had three Black starters in the field, in Scott, Foy and Reggie Smith, now a rookie center fielder, with Tartabull coming off the bench and Wyatt and Santiago in the rotation. Veteran catcher Elston Howard was acquired from the Yankees in early August for the stretch run. Integration was truly in place—20 years after Jackie Robinson integrated the modern Major Leagues.

But the attitudes within the organization and difficulties within the community did not end with Green's ascension and the addition of a few other Black players in the early 1960s. Earl Wilson thought management had not stood behind him after a bar in Lakeland, Florida, refused to serve him, Nowlin wrote. Closer to the game itself, the Red Sox had contended for years that they had scouted Black players, but with minimal success. In June 1965, at a time soon after the NAACP had threatened to picket the ballpark, Jack Mann of *Sports Illustrated* broached the subject of scouting Black players with Yawkey, who grew up in the North but spent much of his adulthood living in rural South Carolina. He responded:

> I have no feeling against colored people. I employ a lot of them in the South. But they are clannish, and when that story got around that we didn't want Negroes they all decided to sign with some other club. Actually, we scouted them right along, but we didn't want one because he was a Negro. We wanted a ballplayer.

Mann added that "the Aarons and Clementes and Olivas are still playing for other teams, despite the shook-up scouts."

Even in the Impossible Dream season of 1967, the link between the Red Sox, Yawkey and racism would not vanish. Jackie Robinson said late in the pennant race that he wanted to see Boston lose because Yawkey "is probably one of the most bigoted guys in organized baseball." The Red Sox did not lose the pennant race, but they also did not outrun race-related concerns. In 1974, Nowlin wrote, the Massachusetts Commission Against Discrimination began looking into complaints about its off-the-field personnel—"coaches, managers, front-office workers, ushers, ticket-takers, and refreshment vendors." Three years later, the commission settled discrimination complaints against the Red Sox, who pledged to bolster the organization's racial diversity. Soon after, Tommy Harper—a Black former player—was hired as a coach and for a job in the front office. But he was fired from the front-office position in 1979 after he told the commission that "the Sox had violated their pledge to improve the franchise's racial diversity," Bob Hohler wrote in *The Boston Globe*.

Harper was rehired, but in 1985 he was fired again. This time, he had talked to *The Globe*. At issue was the Red Sox's practice of issuing membership cards to an all-white Elks Club near their spring training site in Winter Haven, Florida, to white players but not Black players. Harper told *The Globe* that he had been aware of the practice since 1972 but that nothing had been done about it. The general manager in 1985 did something, severing the team's connection with the Elks Club. Harper told the author of the *Globe* article, Michael Madden, "I'm going to get fired for talking about this," and sure enough, nine months later, he was fired. The next month, Harper filed a discrimination suit. (He settled with the team out of court.)

And on it went. In 1991, *The Globe* detailed how challenging it was for Black fans at Fenway Park. And for Black players, too—in 2020, Torii Hunter, who played in the American League for 19 years, said he had been called "the N-word" a hundred times at Fenway. In a turnaround from decades past, the team acknowledged that he was correct: "Torii Hunter's experience is real."

That is a long history of racial grievance, much of it under Tom Yawkey, who owned the team for 43 years until his death in 1976. The question—unanswerable with absolute certainty now—is whether Yawkey created the atmosphere or allowed it. Yawkey bought the Red Sox in 1933 and was soon immersed in the casual racism of the game. Nowlin wrote in *Tom Yawkey* that two years later, at the annual winter meetings, Clark Griffith, the Washington Senators' owner, used a racial slur—recorded in the meetings' minutes—about the Black teams the Major Leaguers played during off-season barnstorming. (This attitude, and language, persisted among Major League difference-makers. As recounted in *George Weiss: Architect of the Golden Age Yankees*, Weiss, New York's general manager, was said to have told a group in 1952: "I will never allow a Black man to wear a Yankee uniform. Boxholders from Westchester"—a wealthy county just north of New York City—"don't want them. They would be offended to have to sit with" Black fans, although Weiss used the recurring slur.)

Two years after Yawkey bought the team, Nowlin wrote, he responded to a *Sunday Worker* reporter's request for comment about whether baseball had any rules preventing teams from hiring a Black player by wiring a note that included: "Have never given any thought to the matter." As the decades passed and the color line was broken elsewhere, the Red Sox still made no move to integrate. Nowlin further reported that in 1956, when *The Globe* pointed out that Boston was one of only three Major

League teams that were still all white (although with two Black players in the minors), Cronin, the general manager, said: "Pigment of the skin means nothing to us. We will not be pressured into signing a player merely because he is a Negro." This was, remember, nine years after the Major Leagues integrated.

Bill Nowlin indicated that he did not think Yawkey was racist, but was a benign overseer of an organization that he let others run and that firmly resisted integration. Others had a harsher view; Howard Bryant notes reporters who thought Yawkey was racist and that the Red Sox were referred to as "the plantation" and "the klavern." What is abundantly clear is that a small group of men whose lives were intertwined and whose racial attitudes were suspect were in charge of Red Sox player acquisition and management for three decades: Eddie Collins, Joe Cronin, Herb Pennock and Mike Higgins. Bryant wrote that "by letting men like Higgins, Cronin, and Collins define the racial attitudes of the Red Sox, those attitudes wound up defining him."

When Yawkey, a 30-year-old multimillionaire, bought the Red Sox, he immediately hired Collins, whom he had admired as a Hall of Fame player, to be his general manager. Cronin was an All-Star shortstop and player-manager for the Senators when Collins swung a deal in 1935 to acquire him that included a starting shortstop and $225,000 (that's $5 million in today's dollars). That same year, Collins made Pennock the director of Boston's farm system, a post he held for eight years. Collins also acquired Higgins, an All-Star third baseman who played two seasons for the Red Sox in the 1930s and was brought back for one final season for the Red Sox, in 1946.

Collins and Cronin were at Jackie Robinson's tryout and made no effort to pretend it was legitimate. Clif Keane said it was possible that Collins shouted the slur at the tryout. Nowlin quotes Clark Booth, a longtime newspaper and TV reporter in Boston, as noting that Collins was said to be "bitterly anti–Semitic as well as anti–Catholic." Pennock had moved to the Phillies, where he oversaw a team that voraciously confronted Robinson. Cronin replaced Collins as general manager in 1947 and elevated Higgins, whom Nowlin describes as "an unreconstructed racist," to be the Red Sox's manager. (In January 1959, Cronin became the American League president and was replaced as general manager by Bucky Harris, who may have made the eventual promotion of Pumpsie Green more likely, McGregor says in *A Calculus of Color*.)

The group included drinking buddies and hunting buddies of Yawkey, who was disinclined to totally get rid of employees like managers or general managers who had failed; he would recycle them in the organization. Take Pinky Higgins. With the Red Sox, he had middling success for four and a half seasons managing all-white teams—as he had vowed to maintain—and was fired in mid-1959, shortly before Pumpsie Green was brought up. But Higgins was kept on as a special assistant. Billy Jurges, his successor, was relieved as manager midway through the 1960 season—and back in the dugout went Higgins. He even was given some of the general manager's responsibilities, though not the title, after the season. He did get the title in 1962, after he had been fired again as manager. It was not until late in the 1965 season, in which Boston lost 100 games, that Higgins was booted out of the organization. The Red Sox immediately increased the number of Black Major Leaguers for 1966, and in 1967, of course, this more diverse (and more talented) team won the pennant.

Whatever Yawkey's actual racial sensibilities, he owned the team and could have set the tone, as Bryant and Nowlin both point out. And not just for the Red Sox. He was named to the American League's board of directors in 1935. He was a vice president of the League for years. He was also on a four-owner committee tasked with dealing with the Race Question; its report was never published, but Commissioner Chandler kept a copy, which, among other let-them-off-the-hook propositions, said that baseball was being pressured about Black players by those who were seeking to benefit themselves, not the players. The committee, led by the Yankees' Larry MacPhail, also said, "The individual action of any one Club may exert tremendous pressures upon the whole structure of Professional Baseball, and could conceivably result in lessening the value of several major league franchises."

The Red Sox were not one of those franchises. Yawkey bought the team and Fenway Park in 1933 for $1.25 million (nearly $30 million in today's dollars). He did pump millions more into it—without the benefit of seeing a World Series championship—but after the death of Yawkey and his wife, Jean, the team was eventually sold in 2002 for $700 million.

How Baseball Integrated

Crossing the Line: Black Major Leaguers, 1947–1959 details the Black players in the Major Leagues from Jackie Robinson to Pumpsie Green. Here's how teams integrated, by year.

1947: Brooklyn Dodgers, Jackie Robinson, Dan Bankhead. 1948: Roy Campanella. 1949: Don Newcombe. 1952: Sandy Amoros, Joe Black. 1953: Jim Gilliam. 1956: Charlie Neal, Chico Fernandez. 1957: John Roseboro, Rene Valdes. 1959: Tommy Davis, Maury Wills.

1947: Cleveland Indians, Larry Doby. 1948: Satchel Paige. 1949: Luke Easter, Minnie Minoso. 1951: Sam Jones, Harry Simpson. 1952: Dave

Pope, Quincy Trouppe. 1953: Dave Hoskins, Al Smith. 1954: Jose Santiago. 1955: Billy Harrell. 1956: Joe Caffie. 1957: Larry Raines. 1958: Jim (Mudcat) Grant.

1947: St. Louis Browns, Willard Brown, Hank Thompson. 1951: Satchel Paige. 1954 (as Baltimore Orioles): Joe Durham, Jay Heard. 1956: Charlie Beamon. 1957: Lenny Green. 1958: Willie Tasby.

1949: New York Giants, Monte Irvin. 1951: Willie Mays, Ray Noble, Artie Wilson. 1953: Ruben Gomez. 1956: Ozzie Virgil, Bill White. 1957: Andre Rodgers, Valmy Thomas. 1958: Felipe Alou, Orlando Cepeda, Willie Kirkland, Leon Wagner. 1959: Willie McCovey, Jose Pagan.

1950: Boston Braves, Sam Jethroe. 1951: Luis Marquez. 1952: George Crowe, Buzz Clarkson. 1953: Billy Bruton, Jim Pendleton. 1954: Hank Aaron, Charlie White. 1955: Humberto Robinson, Roberto Vargas. 1956: Wes Covington, Felix Mantilla. 1957: Juan Pizarro. 1959: Lee Maye.

1951: Chicago White Sox, Bob Boyd, Sam Hairston, Minnie Minoso. 1952: Hector Rodriguez. 1953: Connie Johnson. 1955: Earl Battey. 1958: Al Smith.

1953: Chicago Cubs, Gene Baker, Ernie Banks. 1956: Solly Drake. 1958: Tony Taylor. 1959: George Altman, Don Eaddy, Billy Williams.

1953: Pittsburgh Pirates, Carlos Bernier. 1954: Curt Roberts. 1955: Lino Dioso, Roberto Clemente, Roman Mejias. 1957: Bennie Daniels. 1958: RC Stevens. 1959: Joe Christopher, Al Jackson.

1953: Philadelphia Athletics: Bob Trice. 1954: Vic Power, Joe Taylor. 1955: Hector Lopez.

1954: St. Louis Cardinals, Tom Alston, Bill Gleason, Chuck Harmon, Brooks Lawrence. 1956: Charley Peete. 1957: Frank Barnes. 1958: Ruben Amaro, Ellis Burton. 1959: Marshall Bridges, Bob Gibson, Dick Ricketts.

1954: Cincinnati Redlegs, Nino Escalera. 1955: Milt Smith, Bob Thurman. 1956: Curt Flood, Frank Robinson, Pat Scantlebury. 1958: Orlando Pena, Vada Pinson.

1954: Washington Senators, Carlos Paula. 1955: Julio Becquer.
1955: New York Yankees, Elston Howard. 1959: Hector Lopez.
1957: Philadelphia Phillies, John Kennedy. 1958: Pancho Herrera.
1958: Detroit Tigers, Ozzie Virgil. 1959: Jim Proctor.
1959: Boston Red Sox, Pumpsie Green, Earl Wilson.

TWENTY-TWO

August 4
Birds Versus Baseballs

When Flaco, a Eurasian eagle-owl that had escaped from the Central Park Zoo, died after crashing into a Manhattan building in February 2024, New Yorkers responded as if a beloved local celebrity had passed. A celebrity had, in an avian way, having survived the heights and haunts of New York for nearly a year. Perhaps he survived that long because he avoided Yankee Stadium and Citi Field. Bird versus ball has a long and occasionally unpleasant history. If the rare collision of a baseball and a bird has been frustrating for the player, it has sometimes proved fatal for the living, breathing flying object.

Let's start with perhaps the best-known incident. On August 4, 1983, Yankees outfielder Dave Winfield had finished his warmup throws before the bottom of the fifth inning at Toronto's Exhibition Stadium, when he threw the ball back to the ballboy by the right-field line. The one-hop throw covered 75 or 80 feet ... and then hit a lethargic seagull in the neck, according to Adrian Fung's account for the Society for American Baseball Research. It was a fatal blow. Fans booed and threw rubber balls at Winfield. Cursed him, too.

While Flaco was honored with spontaneous memorials in Manhattan, the Toronto seagull was covered with a towel by the ballboy and carried off the field. Winfield covered his heart with his cap, *The New York Times* reported. Hours later, Winfield was taken away as well—by plainclothes officers, who met him in the dugout, to a Toronto police stationhouse. He was charged with animal cruelty, punishable by up to six months in jail and a $500 fine upon conviction. (Beyond the charge of general "animal cruelty," seagulls were a protected species in Canada.) "I definitely thought it wasn't errant," a Toronto police constable, Larry Savage, said, according to *The Washington Post*. The dead gull was taken to a veterinary hospital for a necropsy, *The Post* said, after lying on a table in the clubhouse for an investigation. Unnecessary, Savage thought: "In order to find a cause of death, though that seems sort of ridiculous." The Blue Jays' general manager, Pat Gillick, posted a $500 bond (and Winfield was asked to sign autographs, *The Times* said).

There were chuckles about a bird's demise happening against the Blue Jays (although it never happened to the Cardinals or the Orioles). And the "fowl ball" headlines were predictable. Even Winfield's teammates got in on the act. *The New York Times* said infielder Roy Smalley, Jr., suggested two headlines: "Winfield 2 for 4 with a Birdie," he said, or "Winfield Pleads Gullty." Winfield did not, in fact, plead guilty (or gullty), as a week later the charge was dropped.

As it turned out, Winfield's throw hit a bird that may have been terminally ill. The professor of wildlife pathology who performed the necropsy said the gull was sick and "was one of these young birds that was going to die within a week or 10 days," Fung wrote. The bird Randy Johnson hit with a pitch was healthy. It was just unlucky.

On March 24, 2001, Johnson, then with the Arizona Diamondbacks, hurled a fastball to the San Francisco Giants' Calvin Murray in a spring training game. A bird, thought to be a mourning dove, flew from the third-base side of the diamond when Johnson's pitch hit it maybe 25 feet from home plate—the bird "exploded in a flurry of feathers," one account said—and the bird came to rest in foul ground past the first-base line. "I thought it was a practical joke or something, that he threw some tricked-up exploding baseball," Murray told *The Athletic* 20 years later. Mark Gonzales, who covered the Diamondbacks for *The Arizona Republic*, said, "It kind of struck me as one of those old 'Batman' episodes where someone gets punched and—POW!—you see all the feathers fly." The ball sailed to the backstop. And the umpire called it "no pitch."

Curiously, Johnson is not the only Diamondbacks pitcher to fell a bird with a throw. On May 17, 2023, Zac Gallen was warming up in the outfield before a game against the Athletics in Oakland when he threw a curve. The throw hit the bird in midflight; it did not survive.

Even more curiously, only five days later, Cleveland Guardians outfielder Will Brennan slapped a pitch toward the shortstop hole against the Chicago White Sox and hit a bird sitting on the infield grass. That bird, too, died. "I truly am sorry peta and bird enthusiasts," Brennan said in a tweet. "An unfortunate sacrifice." He honored the bird the next day: As he rounded the bases after hitting a homer, he made a bird motion with both hands. The coincidences keep piling up. On June 11, 2009, another Cleveland player battered a bird. This time, Shin-Soo Choo hit a 10th-inning line drive over second base that Royals center fielder Coco Crisp thought he could make a play on. Instead, the ball clipped a seagull and rolled past Crisp, driving in the winning run from second. This lucky seagull, however, survived.

Twenty-Two. August 4

Swarms of bugs had infested Cleveland's Progressive Field for a few weeks, *The Columbus Dispatch*, reported, and gulls then swarmed the ballpark to feed on them. "I guess the bugs brought the birds with that whole nature thing," Crisp said. "I'd rather have the birds, to be honest." (If you are a Yankees fan and remember Joba Chamberlain's misfortune with the bugs in Cleveland at a 2007 playoff game, you would, too.) Choo had been concerned about the birds, but as a defender. "I saw the birds," he said. "I've seen them for weeks and been worried maybe 200 of them would be flying and one would get hit when I was trying to field a ball. Then what would I do?" He found out.

The first time a batted ball hit a bird in a Major League game occurred on April 12, 1987, according to the Elias Sports Bureau. In the third inning at Shea Stadium, Dion James hit a routine fly ball to left field, *The New York Times* reported, but it struck a dove. The ball and the bird both fell in front of left fielder Kevin McReynolds, "who chose to field the ball," *The Times* said. Instead of an F7, James had a double. And some pangs. "The bird died a hero to me," he said. "It's too bad it happened, though." It was part of an all-around bad day for the Mets' Bob Ojeda, the losing pitcher in a 12–4 setback. "I looked around and saw feathers, then a bird falling," he said. "After this, I might go back and lock myself in my room."

That may have been the first batted ball-meets-bird event in the Majors, but not in professional baseball. In 1981, future Cincinnati Reds star Eric Davis, playing for the Eugene Emeralds in a Northwest League game, hit a ball that killed a bird in midflight—but remarkably, Medford A's outfielder Ron Harrison caught the ball to record the out, *The Times* recounted. Harrison, by the way, had an unusually bad season in the outfield—five errors in 40 chances for an .875 fielding percentage.

There *have* been happier moments on the diamond for birds (not even counting Mark "The Bird" Fidrych). None more celebrated than Casey Stengel's stunt. Stengel had been traded to the Pittsburgh Pirates by the Brooklyn Robins (now Los Angeles Dodgers, of course) after the 1918 season, and the teams met in Ebbets Field for the first time the next season in May. Stengel had been popular in Brooklyn, and he was unhappy about having to leave. In the third game of the series, on May 25, Stengel was having a tough game and was hearing razzing from the Brooklyn crowd, Robert Creamer related in *Stengel: His Life and Times*. He was in the midst of going 0 for 4 at bat and had inelegantly missed making the catch on a long fly ball to right-center field. The ball hit the fence, and, *The New York Times* reported, "Rebounding, the sphere hopped through the legs of Casey Stengel, who was trying hysterically to get his hands on it before irretrievable disaster occurred." Instead, disaster did occur: Three runs scored.

The Robins' bullpen was in foul ground along the right-field line, and Creamer wrote that Stengel noticed after the sixth inning that his ex-teammate Leon Cadore, a Brooklyn pitcher, was holding a sparrow. (Yes, a Robin was clutching a sparrow.) Stengel decided he wanted it. He sneaked the bird to the dugout and slipped it under his cap when he went up to bat. Creamer described the scene: "The crowd greeted him with mock applause and a round of good-natured boos. Casey turned toward the stands, bowed and lifted his cap, and there was the sparrow, which immediately fluttered away." Even the umpire laughed, Creamer said. The newspapers couldn't get over it either, *The Times* saying, "He doffed his cap and from out of the darkness of the headpiece there flew an irate but much relieved sparrow." The last word came from Brooklyn's manager, Wilbert Robinson: "Hell, he always did have birds in his garret." But at least this one lived.

Twenty-Three

August 19

The Day in the Life of Eddie Gaedel

The story of Eddie Gaedel is such a part of the story of Bill Veeck that Veeck made it the first chapter of his fascinating autobiography, *Veeck as in Wreck*. Veeck did many things in baseball. He came up with the idea to plant the ivy at Wrigley Field, where his father was an executive with the Chicago Cubs. As owner of the Cleveland Indians, he signed the first Black player in the American League. Later, as owner of the St. Louis Browns, he brought Satchel Paige back into the Major Leagues (and with quite some success, given that Paige was easily the oldest player in the Majors). He had an exploding scoreboard—electronic fireworks—installed at Comiskey Park in Chicago. He owned teams that set attendance records and teams that could not draw any sort of crowd. He won pennants and finished last. He considered moving Major League teams to Milwaukee and Baltimore, but lost out to other franchises. He also bought the White Sox a second time, ensuring that they stayed in Chicago. He lost a leg because of injuries suffered in World War II and had an ashtray fashioned in his wooden leg. He claimed many fantastic exploits (a movable outfield fence for one of his minor league teams and later for the Indians, an idea to buy the Philadelphia Phillies and stock them only with Black players, several years before baseball's segregation ended) that wilt under scrutiny.

And yet even Veeck knew he would be remembered for Gaedel, at 3 feet 7 inches tall the shortest man ever to play Major League Baseball. In *Veeck as in Wreck*, he wrote, "But no one has to tell me that if I returned to baseball tomorrow, won ten straight pennants and left all the old attendance records moldering in the dust, I would still be remembered, in the end, as the man who sent a midget up to bat."

It was on August 19, 1951, that Gaedel stepped onto the field at Sportsman's Park in St. Louis in a Browns uniform: first by bursting out of a large birthday cake, then later as a pinch-hitter. It's a story for which Gaedel and Veeck are remembered, but also others who were drawn into the sideshow—the player Gaedel replaced, the player who replaced Gaedel, the pitcher, the catcher. We'll hear their stories (and it was in the obituaries for all of them). But first we have to know how Eddie Gaedel came to be, for a few fleeting moments, a Major League Baseball player.

Most people who know about Gaedel figure that Veeck got the idea from the short story *You Could Look It Up*, written by James Thurber and published in *The Saturday Evening Post* in 1941. Veeck insisted this was not the case and said the genesis was a team mascot and good-luck charm whom New York Giants Manager John McGraw kept with his team. Veeck said he recalled the man's name as Eddie Morrow and said he was a hunchback. Evidence that McGraw kept an Eddie Morrow around is scant, at best, although he did keep a pitcher who may have had developmental issues, Charlie Faust, around as a good-luck charm. (The Giants were 36–2 when Faust was in uniform in 1912.) And it is well documented that at least a couple of teams, the 1911 Philadelphia Athletics and the New York Yankees of the 1920s, had young men with severe curvature of the spine as batboys and mascots. Demeaning as it sounds, using people with disabilities as mascots or good-luck charms was not unusual in the game for decades.

Whatever the origin of Veeck's ploy, the reason was straightforward: The Browns were terrible and didn't draw crowds. The Browns finished the 1951 season 52–102 (last) and drew, officially, 293,790 fans, an average of 3,815 a game (also last). "Eddie came to us in a moment of desperation," Veeck wrote. "Not his desperation, ours."

Veeck concocted a plan to celebrate the 50th anniversary of the American League, which was true, and the birthday of one of his sponsors, Falstaff beer, which no one knew whether was true. He promoted what he called an explosive idea for a Sunday doubleheader on August 19.

His plan to send a tiny player up to bat started with his calling a booking agent for a suitable act. The booking agent sent 26-year-old, 65-pound Eddie Gaedel of Chicago to St. Louis for an interview. Veeck had Gaedel get in a batting stance, then crouch, and said he measured Gaedel's strike zone at 1½ inches. The deal was arranged—Gaedel (a White Sox fan) would sign an official contract, at $100 a game, the minimum scale for an act like Gaedel's. Veeck conveniently sent the signed contract to the American League office late enough that it could not get there before the Sunday games, but he had the paperwork to prove it was sent. Veeck's biggest fear was that Gaedel would have a burst of inspiration like the character in the Thurber story (so Veeck *did* know the story) and swing at a pitch. Thurber's character hit a 3–0 pitch and was thrown out at first because it took a very short batter a very long time to get down the first-base line.

Veeck's promotion of something extravagantly special worked—the next day *The St. Louis Post-Dispatch*, with a nod to P.T. Barnum, referred to the owner as Phineas T. Veeck—and a crowd of 18,369 was on hand. Among other things, they were treated to acrobats, a band and free beer (Falstaff, of course). Gaedel reluctantly got into an oversize fake cake, which was wheeled onto the field between games of the doubleheader, and burst out, clad in his uniform with the number 1/8 on the back. (The uniform belonged to the son of a team executive. The jersey originally had the number 6 on the back, according to a SABR *Bio Project* profile, but Veeck, ever the showman, had it changed.) The reporters in the press box and the fans were underwhelmed by the between-games show. Veeck, of course, was just getting started.

The seventh-place Detroit Tigers, who had won the first game, went down scoreless in the top of the first in the second game, although, typical of the Browns, they walked two batters and had a passed ball. Frank Saucier was due to lead off for the Browns. Instead, Gaedel was announced as a pinch-hitter for Saucier: "For the Browns, No. 1/8, Eddie Gaedel, batting for Saucier," said the public-address announcer, Bernie Ebert, according to *The Post-Dispatch*. (Veeck wrote that the only regrets he had about the game were for Saucier. "All he had to show for his great promise is that he was the only guy a midget ever batted for.")

Gaedel came out of the dugout swinging three small bats. The umpire, Ed Hurley, yelled, "What the hell?" Browns Manager Zack Taylor showed him a copy of Gaedel's signed contract, and Hurley eventually ordered the game to go on. The Tigers' catcher, Bob Swift, got down on his knees to set up a target—delighting Veeck, who knew it would make a good photo. The Detroit bench yelled, "Get outta that hole!" at the shortest Major Leaguer ever by about 20 inches. The pitcher, Bob Cain, threw four balls—Veeck would write that Cain was laughing as he threw ball three and ball four "about three feet over Eddie's head."

Gaedel had not ruined the plan by swinging (Veeck, presumably joking, had threatened that he would have a sniper on hand), and he trotted to first base, where Veeck had the baseball clown Max Patkin coaching. Jim Delsing, the Browns' usual center fielder, went in to run for Gaedel, who patted Delsing on the butt at first base. "That was the last I saw him," Delsing told *The New York Times* years later. Veeck's fervent hope was that Delsing would score and the Browns would win, 1–0, so that Gaedel would have been instrumental in a Browns victory. Delsing got only to third base, though, and the Browns lost (again), 6–2.

"I never thought I'd live to see the day I'd be a major leaguer," Gaedel said in a postgame interview, but by the next day he was back in Chicago. The shenanigans had limited immediate impact beyond St. Louis, given how slowly news could travel then. *The New York Times*, for example, ran a six-paragraph article from *United Press* on the games that never mentioned Gaedel.

But things blew up quickly. In the August 21 *Times*, the columnist Arthur Daley expressed his umbrage:

> Veeck's madcap antics have never before violated good taste. But this one is positively indecent, an ignoble burlesque of a noble sport. ... Veeck is a great idea man. His promotional schemes even have reached a point where he can attract 18,396 fans into Sportsman's Park to see the Browns, a minor miracle at the very least. But in hiring a midget as a legally signed player of the Brownies, Wild William overreached himself. As far as Major League stature is concerned the Brownies are midgets and they don't need a pint-sized player to make it more obvious.

Gaedel's agent in Chicago, Chuck Lee, told *The Associated Press* that Veeck's plan was to use Gaedel again and "send him to the plate with the bases loaded." He was eyeing the Browns' next series in Chicago, in late September. It wasn't to be. Baseball was between commissioners, but two days after Gaedel's appearance, Will Harridge, the American League president, canceled his contract, citing "the best interests of the game." (Gaedel criticized Harridge for ruining his career.) Two weeks later, Gaedel was in Cincinnati, performing at a rodeo and getting arrested because the police mistook him for a child out very late. Here's the cast of innocent characters.

The Leadoff Hitter

Frank Saucier. A 25-year-old rookie by way of Notre Dame and the Navy, Frank Saucier was making the second start of his Major League career. He was leading off for the Browns and playing right field, where he caught a line drive in the top of the first. But when it came time to bat for Saucier, who had led three minor leagues in hitting, he was replaced by a pinch-hitter: Gaedel. Saucier would make one more start, and play only eight more games (going hitless), before his Major League career was over. Overall, he was 1 for 14 (.071) as a Major Leaguer with a pinch-hit double off Cleveland star Mike Garcia—and also made two errors in seven chances in the outfield. He had raked in three seasons in the minors—.357, .446 and .342—but had injured his shoulder and retired, according to his SABR *Bio Project* biography. He was talked out of retirement, but in trying to get ready quickly to play for the Browns, he took so much batting practice his hands bled and never really healed. Late in the season, he was recalled by the Navy—Veeck had destroyed his first recall notice—and while Saucier played ball in the Navy, he never played professional baseball again.

The Pitcher

Bob Cain. Walking Eddie Gaedel was not out of character for Bob Cain; he walked a lot of batters. That same game, he walked four other Browns, and for his career he averaged an unsightly 4.5 walks per nine innings. In 1951, as in many other seasons, he walked more batters than he struck out. He had mixed feelings about his role in the stunt. "I laughed a little bit, but I was a little angry," he said in *We Played the Game: 65 Players Remember Baseball's Greatest Era, 1947–1964*. "I'd have given my right arm [he pitched left-handed!] just to have gotten one strike on him." In an odd coincidence, he was traded to the Browns the next season. Cain did maintain a relationship with Gaedel—he would send Christmas cards—and was the only person from baseball to attend Gaedel's funeral in 1961. He said he felt obligated.

The Catcher

Bob Swift. His advice to Bob Cain: "Pitch him low." Pitchers tended to listen to Swift, who, despite being a very subpar hitter, lasted 14 seasons in the Major Leagues. He never had 100 hits in a season, scored more than 30 runs once, drove in more than 30 runs twice and hit only 14 home runs. But pitchers liked pitching to him: "I never shook him off once," the longtime Detroit pitcher Fred Hutchinson said. Although he played most of his career with the Tigers, he came up with ... the Browns.

The Umpire

Ed Hurley. He was an American League umpire for 19 years, before he was forced to retire at what had been changed to a mandatory retirement age of 55. Once, when Gino Cimoli of the Kansas City Athletics came to the plate with a green bat—the A's colors were green and gold—Hurley declared it illegal. He also once confiscated a bat of Mickey Mantle.

The Pinch-Runner

Jim Delsing. He went 3 for 4 and scored a run in the first game of the August 19 doubleheader, and Delsing was upset when he was not in the starting lineup for Game 2. "I went up to Zack Taylor, who was manager, and he said: 'Cool it. You'll be all right.'" Delsing didn't understand, as he and the rest of the Browns did not know what was in store. Only when Gaedel walked and Taylor said, "Now go run for Gaedel" did the pieces fall into place. "We never knew what was going on," Delsing told *The New York Times* in 2001. "Something was going on almost every day. This was another of Mr. Veeck's promotions." In another of those oddities, before the '52 season Delsing was traded to the Tigers, for whom he had his best success.

The Pinch-Hitter

Eddie Gaedel. Life as a 43-inch-tall man—that's a mere seven inches longer than bats used by Babe Ruth and Joe DiMaggio—could not have been easy. Eddie Gaedel was 8 pounds at birth, and his brother and sister grew to normal heights. But Gaedel stopped growing early, and he was taunted and bullied the rest of his life, according to a wide array of accounts. Medium, citing a 2001 episode of ESPN's *Outside the Lines,* said his sister, Pearl Rosa, described the effects on him: "He cried a lot because the people used to bother him. And he'd come home swearing." He also drank heavily at times and could become combative (his family said he had "beer muscles").

Gaedel's height factored into much of his employment, especially in the entertainment field, where a very short man could be asked to take on very unusual jobs. His big break, according to Medium, was in 1946, when he dressed up as the Greek god Mercury in a promotional stunt for Mercury Records. His appearance as a ballplayer set him up for some quick money—he pulled in $17,000 within a few weeks of the game, according to his SABR *Bio Project* profile. He did promotional work at stores for Buster Brown shoes (they were for kids) and landed a job with the Ringling Brothers circus. He appeared on numerous television shows. In 1959, Veeck hired Gaedel again, with three other very short employees, to land at Comiskey Park in a helicopter and come out dressed as Martians with "ray guns" who went on to kidnap the White Sox's shortstop and second baseman, Luis Aparicio and Nellie Fox (who were diminutive by baseball standards, listed, no doubt generously, at 5–9 and 160 and 5–10 and 160).

Gaedel turned down numerous job offers outside Chicago because of his uneasiness about traveling, according to his SABR profile, and lived at home with his mother. On June 18, 1961, he went drinking at a bowling alley, and on the walk home he got into an altercation with persons unknown, who severely beat him. His mother found Gaedel, bruised and dead, in his bed the next morning; an autopsy said he had died of a heart attack. He was 36. Veeck wrote that he had promised Eddie Gaedel immortality. He may have gotten that, but only after an unhappy mortal life.

Twenty-Four

September 4
Gill's Boner

When Fred Merkle died in 1956, the headline of his obituary in *The New York Times* noted the base-running mistake that made his name recognizable nearly half a century later: "FRED MERKLE, 67, BALL PLAYER, DIES; Giant 1st Baseman's 'Boner' in Failing to Touch 2d Led to Loss of '08 Pennant / Episode Still in Dispute / Evers Called Play."

"Merkle's boner" lived on. But "Gill's boner" could have easily made Merkle just another name, not the synonym for a dumb play. Had an umpire made the correct call involving Doc Gill, Fred Merkle might never have made the same mistake. Merkle made his gaffe on the bases on September 23, 1908, and it helped cost his New York Giants the pennant. Everybody said so; they still do. Warren (Doc) Gill made the same error 19 days earlier in the heat of that pennant race, and it did not cost his Pittsburgh Pirates a thing—or Gill his reputation.

Here's what happened to Merkle on September 23, an incident that has been widely

Fred Merkle was forever known for his base-running gaffe in the 1908 National League pennant race. Doc Gill made the same mistake in the same pennant race, but no one remembers him (courtesy SABR-Rucker Archive).

chronicled for more than a century: His Giants were tied with the Chicago Cubs for first place, a game ahead of the Pirates, when New York and Chicago met in the Polo Grounds. The game was 1–1 in the bottom of the ninth, but the Giants had Moose McCormick on third and Merkle, a 19-year-old rookie who would become known for aggressive base running, on first with two outs. Al Bridwell hit an apparent single to center field, and McCormick crossed the plate with what would have been the winning run. But Merkle stopped short of second base, as was customary in that era. Cubs second baseman Johnny Evers called for the ball, touched second for what would have been a force out that would have ended the inning while yelling to Umpire Hank O'Day. O'Day called Merkle out, and, with fans streaming on the field in celebration of what they thought was a major victory and with the possibility of darkness encroaching, the game was called a tie. The Giants lost their protest over the play to the National League, which ruled that the game would be made up after the rest of the season's schedule had been played if it was needed to determine the League champion. It was, and the Cubs beat the Giants, 4–2, winning the pennant by a single game over New York (and Pittsburgh).

The Times reported the play this way: "McCormick trots home, the merry villagers trot on the field to worship the hollow where the Mathewson feet have pressed, and all of a sudden there are doings at second base." The doings being inspired by Evers. Whether Evers actually had the baseball that had been hit, however, remains unclear. The throw in from the outfield sailed past Evers into what had become a crowded infield, with fans all over. Many accounts say Giants pitcher Joe McGinnity rushed out, picked up the ball and tried to throw it into the stands, but it wound up in the Cubs' bullpen, where someone—perhaps a fan—picked up a ball. But *the* ball? Impossible to know. There was a bag of balls nearby for relievers to use warming up. Cubs players forcibly retrieved the ball and flipped it to Evers. The out was called.

Merkle's play immediately became the focus. "BLUNDER COSTS GIANTS VICTORY / Merkle Rushes Off Base Line Before Winning Run Is Scored, and Is Declared Out," read the first two of six headlines on the *Times* account of the game. The first sentence of the game story said "Censurable stupidity on the part of player Merkle in yesterday's game at the Polo Grounds between the Giants and the Chicagos placed the New York team's chances of winning the pennant in jeopardy." Charles Dryden called it "the bone-headed finish" in *The Chicago Tribune*.

Merkle never lived it down, even in death. But he could have, had a nearly identical play—also involving second baseman Evers and umpire O'Day—been ruled the same way. It would have saved Merkle a lifetime of ridicule.

Twenty-Four. September 4

Here's what happened to Warren (Doc) Gill on September 4. Gill was a 29-year-old rookie first baseman for the Pirates in his first week in the Major Leagues when he was hit by a pitch from the Cubs' Mordecai (Three Finger) Brown in the bottom of the 10th inning of a scoreless game to load the bases with two out. Another rookie, Owen (Chief) Wilson, plopped a hit into short center field, and Fred Clarke trotted home from third base with the apparent winning run. But Gill did what Merkle would do 19 days later—he peeled off the base path before reaching second base and headed toward the dugout. Evers saw that Gill had not touched second base, so he called for the ball, touched second himself for what would have been an inning-ending force out while yelling to O'Day—the game's only umpire—to insist that Gill was out. O'Day, who went to the bench to get a drink of water as soon as Clarke crossed home plate from third, ruled that Clarke had scored and the game was over. "With his jaw twisted one way, his mouth another and his eyes squinting in the late afternoon sun, Evers repeatedly thrust the ball at O'Day while pressing his case that because Gill had not touched second, he had recorded the third out on a force," Dennis Snelling wrote in *Johnny Evers: A Baseball Life*. "O'Day simply responded, 'Cut it out Johnny, the game is over.'"

The Cubs filed a protest with the National League—I.E. Sanborn wrote in *The Chicago Tribune* that it came "out of Jack Evers' ability to think faster than one bush league player and one veteran major league umpire, to wit: Pirate Gill and Hank O'Day."—but lost.

The protest did benefit the Cubs, however, as the League's president, Harry Pulliam, specified that had there been a force out, "the run could not have scored," David Rapp wrote in *Tinker to Evers to Chance: The Chicago Cubs and the Dawn of Modern America*. That proved to be what happened on September 23: O'Day remembered the earlier play and called it differently when Merkle was the hapless base runner. Rapp wrote that after the September 4 game, O'Day got into an argument with Evers and Cubs shortstop Joe Tinker in a hotel lobby but acknowledged that he might have missed the call. "He signaled that he might rule differently if the circumstance should rise again," Rapp wrote. And he did. So we have Merkle's boner, not Gill's boner.

But the gaffe was rooted in baseball custom and may not have been censurable stupidity. Merkle's *Associated Press* obituary said, "It always had been the custom for runners on base when a winning run was scored to stop their advance and trot off the field." *Baseball Magazine* wrote, "Merkle was careless, to be sure, but withal, he did only what many others had done without suffering criticism." Rapp wrote that Merkle merely followed "in the footsteps of Doc Gill and countless rule-book-oblivious ballplayers before him" and "hightailed it for safety" once thousands of fans crashed the field.

Gill was an unlikely focal point for a key play in a pennant race. He was in his seventh season in the minors and had played most of it with the Grand Rapids Wolverines of the Class B Central League. He hit a team-high .267 (with 38 steals, so he did know his way around the bases). The Pirates needed a first baseman, and had for years. Kitty Bransfield had been Pittsburgh's regular at first base for three years, but in 1904 he hit .223 and was traded away. Brian Martin wrote in *Barney Dreyfuss: Pittsburgh's Baseball Titan* that for Dreyfuss, the team's owner, "the deal to rid himself of Bransfield was dubbed by sportswriter Fred Lieb 'one of Barney's worst moves ... the trade proved one of Pittsburgh's sourest moves.' One player after another was tried at first for more than a decade as the usually shrewd judge of talent Dreyfuss struggled to find a regular and reliable first baseman." Bransfield was a Major League regular elsewhere for another six seasons, even if not a particularly good hitter, while the Pirates had six first basemen play at least 50 games in a season over those six years.

The 1908 season was one of them. Pittsburgh used four first basemen, and none of them hit well. Harry Swacina, who started 48 games at first base, batted .216/.238/.261 in 187 plate appearances for a 59 OPS+. Alan Storke (46 starts) finished at .252/.284/.322 in 222 plate appearances for a 93 OPS+. Jim Kane (36 starts) managed a .241/.299/.303 season in 166 plate appearances with a 93 OPS+. And Gill (25 starts) had the most robust batting line, at .224/.366/.250 in 102 plate appearances for a 97 OPS+. Combined, they hit one home run with 61 runs batted in. At least Gill played errorless ball at first; the other three combined for 31 errors.

The next year, Gill was back in the minors, where he played out his career over five more seasons, mostly in Minneapolis. In a biography of Gill for "Who's Who in Montgomery County," Karen Bazzani Zach quoted a Kansas City newspaper:

> Dr. Warren Darst Gill has been playing great ball for Cantillon's flag winners [the Minneapolis Millers, managed by Mike Cantillon]. Gill has many friends in Kansas City who are glad to know the dentist is setting a hot place for the other first basers of the league. Gill is one of the cleverest fielders in the Association, a speedy base runner and when hitting as he has been this season is invaluable to the club that has his services.

It had been an unusual trip to the Majors. Warren Darst Gill—probably named for a local teacher, Warren Darst—was born in Ladoga, Indiana, then a town of not quite 1,000 and scarcely bigger today. His entry into baseball was delayed by his service in the Spanish-American War and his attending college. (He also served during World War I.) Zach's biography says he was called Doc because he studied dentistry at Washington University in St. Louis. He practiced for 35 years and also taught at the University of Southern California's dental school. After Gill's death in Laguna Beach, California, in 1952 at the age of 73, his 152-word obituary in *The Long Beach (California) Independent* made brief mention of his baseball career and none of his infamous play. No ignominy followed him to the grave.

Not so for Fred Merkle. His *AP* obituary said, "Although Frederick Charles Merkle is dead, it is doubtful the dispute over the failed-to-touch second episode will die down as long as there is a hot-stove league in a baseball-minded country." His baseball career began—and in fact, played out—with much more promise than Doc Gill's did. Merkle had played two seasons in the minors as a teenager before spending the entire 1908 season on the Giants' roster. He played five positions in his 38 games, and on the day of Merkle's boner he was at first base because the regular, Fred Tenney, was out with lumbago. Merkle went to bat only 49 times in 1908, hitting .268/.333/.439 with a 140 OPS+. That was in part because he had four extra-base hits in his limited playing time, more than Gill had (one) in 61 more plate appearances.

Merkle went on to play another 12 seasons, finishing with a .273/.331/.383 line and a 109 OPS+. He played in five World Series and was briefly on the 1926 Yankees, who went on to play in the Series. But the effects of his gaffe lingered; during the 1909 season, he batted .191 in 79 games and, according to his SABR *Bio Project* biography, told Manager John McGraw that he was making a mistake by keeping him on the roster. McGraw replied: "I wish I had more players like you. Don't pay any attention to those weathercocks. They'll be cheering you the next time you make a good play." In fact, Merkle became the cleanup hitter in 1910 and led the Giants in RBIs.

Merkle, however, could not escape controversy. His obituary recounted Merkle's involvement in a World Series misplay in 1912, while playing first base for the Giants against the Boston Red Sox. It was Game 8—there had been a tie—and the game was scoreless until the 10th inning, when Merkle singled in a run for a 1–0 lead. In the bottom of the inning, Boston's Clyde Engle hit a fly ball to center field that the Giants' Fred Snodgrass dropped—an error forever known as "Snodgrass's muff," tainting Snodgrass almost as fully as Merkle was because of its import.

Then it was Merkle's turn, again. With one out and runners on first and second, Tris Speaker singled in the tying run off Christy Mathewson after Merkle was involved in a misplay, and he later scored the Series-winning run. Merkle's *AP* obituary said: "Tris Speaker hit a foul between home and first base. Mathewson, Chief Meyers, the catcher, and Merkle, first baseman, parked under the ball. Each waited for one of the others to make the catch, so the ball dropped and fell through. Speaker then started the Red Sox on their winning rally with a hit off Mathewson." Merkle's SABR *Bio Project* biography says that it was Merkle's ball but that he backed off when Mathewson called for Meyers to make the catch. A headline the next day read: "Bonehead Merkle Does It Again."

Twenty-Five

September 23

The Dominican Pipeline Begins, in New York

In 2023, a little over 10 percent of the 1,457 players in Major League Baseball were born in the Dominican Republic, according to *Baseball Almanac*. What is it about the Dominican Republic, a country smaller than West Virginia with a population equal to North Carolina's, that makes it such a productive nation for baseball players?

No other country outside the United States is even close to matching the Dominican Republic. From 2000 to 2023, 612 Dominican-born players made their Major League debuts—enough players to populate almost 25 full teams—and no other non–U.S. country has produced even 500 players in *all* of baseball history. About 500 Dominican players a year currently sign contracts with Major League teams, fleshing out minor league teams and other professional clubs, a June 2023 *Coral Gables (Florida) Magazine* article said, citing the Major League commissioner's office in the Dominican Republic.

The Dominican Republic's baseball history and passion for the game are strong but not unique, certainly not among Spanish-speaking countries. Baseball was introduced to Cuba in the 1860s, the Dominican Republic by the 1870s (by Cuban émigrés), Puerto Rico in the 1890s and Venezuela in the 1910s. By the middle of the 20th century, all of them had well-developed, competitive winter leagues that drew players from throughout the hemisphere; the Dominican league, in fact, was the last of them to start, in 1951. The Dominican Republic's potential talent pool is not exceptional; Venezuela has a population nearly three times that of the Dominican Republic, and the Dominican population, nearly 11 million, is virtually the same as Cuba's, though more than three times the size of Puerto Rico's. All these places have had troubled governments at some point, and all have been economically distressed to varying degrees.

When Ozzie Virgil became the first Dominican-born player in the Major Leagues, with the New York Giants on September 23, 1956, there was nothing to indicate that he would be the first of hundreds. By the time he made his debut, dozens of Cubans had been playing in the big leagues over half a century. The first players born in Venezuela and Mexico made their Major League debuts in the 1930s; the first Puerto Ricans came along in the 1940s. The first Panamanian ballplayer arrived in the big leagues 17 months before Virgil did. More Dominican players came along, but not in big numbers; through the 1970s, the Dominican Republic was a talent producer no more prolific than many other spots in the Caribbean and Central America, basically an equal with Venezuela, Puerto Rico and pre-revolution Cuba.

Then came the baseball academies. "The academies have been critical to increasing the number of players that get signed, accelerating and improving their development and increasing the percentage who achieve the goal of playing in the majors," Rafael Pérez, then Major League Baseball's director of Dominican operations, told Enrique Rojas of ESPN Deportes in 2015. "In baseball, it's all about numbers, and the academies' numbers are extremely positive."

Alan Klein, the author of *Sugarball: The American Game, the Dominican Dream* and *Dominican Baseball: New Pride, Old Prejudice*, traces the origins of baseball academies in the country to the 1960s, when the United States embargo of Cuba that followed Fidel Castro's Cuban Revolution "choked off what had been the main flow of Latin baseball talent." One scout, Joe Cambria, signed more than 400 Cuban players to professional contracts, mostly for the Washington Senators from the mid–1930s until his death in September 1962, Paul Scimonelli wrote in *Joe Cambria: International Super Scout of the Washington Senators*. By the end of the 1960s, more than 100 Cuban-born players had made it to the Major Leagues, according to figures from *Baseball Reference*; only a dozen Cubans made their MLB debuts in the 1970s and '80s. After the Cuban pipeline was shut down, Klein wrote, several Major League clubs "envisioned the Dominican Republic as picking up the slack and providing significant numbers of players." The Majors, Klein wrote, had been working in the Dominican Republic since the early 1950s, but something new was needed to facilitate the acquisition of Major League–caliber players.

One hurdle was how to train young, amateur ballplayers anywhere to be potential Major Leaguers. The Kansas City Royals embarked on a novel approach in 1970 with a baseball academy in Florida devoted to training athletes who were traditionally overlooked by the Majors. The Royals' failure rate was high, but not total: For example, Frank White, who made five All-Star teams and won eight Gold Gloves as a second baseman in an 18-year career, was a Royals academy graduate. Go back further, and Casey Stengel was having short-term spring "academies" while managing the Yankees, polishing numerous young prospects into regulars or even stars for his New York powerhouse.

So the concept of an academy was not foreign when two baseball men, Epy Guerrero and Ralph Avila, decided independently to build their own academies to train very young players in the Dominican Republic, Klein said. Their plan was to house, feed and train youngsters, as young as 11 or 12, at one site to become professional ballplayers who could legally sign a contract with a team at age 16.

Guerrero was a highly successful scout, mostly for the Houston Astros and the Toronto Blue Jays. He signed 52 Major Leaguers, including César Cedeño, Carlos Delgado, Tony Fernandez and José Mesa. He borrowed money to open an academy, the first in the Dominican Republic, in 1977; the Blue Jays began to use the complex in 1981, according to Guerrero's SABR *Bio Project* profile. In 1982, Klein wrote, Avila, a transplanted Cuban, opened his academy, which in 1987 would become the Los Angeles Dodgers' Dominican facility and "the template for the modern academy system in the DR." Klein calls Avila "the founder of the modern Dominican academy."

Rob Ruck, a University of Pittsburgh professor and author of *The Tropic of Baseball: Baseball in the Dominican Republic,* said in an interview in late 2023 that Guerrero's initial academy, outside Santo Domingo, was a "barebones, ramshackle operation." "Nothing very sophisticated except they have a nice field and Guerrero is training these players," Ruck said. A stark reminder of what failure in baseball could lead to lay just outside the complex, Ruck said: sugar cane fields, where a life cutting cane was an ever-present possibility. The sugar companies had long been the lifeblood of amateur baseball in the Dominican Republic, fielding teams in highly competitive leagues; with the new academies' proximity to the cane fields, the potential for a future in baseball or the fields was starkly juxtaposed.

Avila's academy in Los Palmas, Ruck said, was "head and shoulders above anything that had ever been done": a good dormitory, good meals, great fields, great coaching. Avila had a string of success—brothers Ramon and Pedro Martinez, Adrian Beltre, Raul Mondesi, Jose Offerman, among others—and so, eventually, did the Dodgers.

Teams noticed (the Blue Jays' World Series championships in 1992 and 1993 probably did not hurt; those teams had important Dominican players, although they were not built on academy graduates). Ruck said other teams followed the Blue Jays and the Dodgers, investing millions in academies and building ever-improving facilities. About 5 percent of Major Leaguers were Dominican when he first visited the country to study baseball in 1984, Ruck said, a figure that has doubled in the ensuing four decades.

Teams began clustering their academies in Boca Chica, an area east of Santo Domingo with easy access to the Santo Domingo airport. Eventually, each of the 30 Major League teams had its own Dominican academy for its international signees—players eligible to sign at age 16. (That's a boy the age of an American high school sophomore or junior playing pro ball.) The academies offer intensive baseball instruction, because players who arrive through buscones, or local scouts who often have their own independent academies, have focused less on how to play the game than on how to game the tryouts with Major League teams. Felipe Alou, the longtime Major League player and manager, told Klein, "They are taught to show well at tryouts at the academies—things like pitching and hitting—but we don't know much about how well they can play the game." His brother Jesus Alou, who has a long history in player development, said, "Too many kids prepare for tryouts, and not enough prepare to play the nine-inning game." He cited as an example players who train to run a 60-yard dash—a standard tryout test—rather than to excel at running from home plate to first base.

The most recently opened academy was that of the Miami Marlins, in October 2022. The 35-acre operation, which was double the size of the Marlins' previous academy, resembles a college campus, *Coral Gables Magazine* reported, with dormitories that sleep about 100 (four to a room, unlike the early academy dorms with gang sleeping areas), classrooms with computers, and rec rooms. There are gyms, weight rooms, batting and pitching practice areas and three baseball fields, the magazine said.

The classrooms are one way Major League Baseball has dealt with problems it long neglected. For decades, baseball signed ballplayers who spoke only Spanish and assumed they would assimilate on their own once they were playing in the United States. In his autobiography, *Alou: My Baseball Journey,* Felipe Alou, who broke into the big leagues in 1958 and was the first standout Dominican ballplayer in the Majors, wrote about learning English by watching television and reading newspapers. Many Hispanic players have mentioned not being able to read menus in restaurants and pointing to the items they wanted. Baseball left them on their own to acquire the language skills necessary to succeed in the game.

Classrooms in the teams' academies are a measure to provide Dominican hopefuls with education that includes some English proficiency. A problem, Klein notes, is that many of these teenage players don't take the instruction seriously and, with the high washout rate, leave pro ball uneducated. "Boys usually stop going to school when they begin training with a buscón," Ruck wrote in 2020. In a 2009 paper in the *University of Texas Review of Entertainment and Sports Law,* Adam Wasch wrote: "An estimated ninety-seven percent of these boys [in the baseball academies] get left behind. These boys find themselves without an education and without

Twenty-Five. September 23

hope for a productive future." Wasch has advocated a pledge by Major League Baseball to "maintain certain educational standards for international players," *Columbia Business Law Review* reported in 2021.

The academies also provide instruction on how life may be different in the United States—cultural norms and dealing with authority figures, for example. And the Dominican Summer League gives teenage players who have signed with a Major League team a taste of what it is like to play professionally without having to simultaneously acculturate in a vastly different country. It is the Major League teams' academies that are the pipeline into pro ball for those young amateurs. The academies of buscónes are the pipeline to the MLB academies for even younger aspiring players.

Klein likens buscónes—he likes to call them talent developers—in some ways to the "bird dogs" in the United States before the amateur draft was instituted in 1965; they were freelance scouts who would get a finder's fee for a player they discovered that a Major League team signed. Buscones are everywhere in the Dominican Republic—Ruck wrote in 2020 that there were about 1,000 of them—but they operate, in general, on a larger scale than the old bird dogs. They scour for young players—13, 14 years old—to take to their own academies, which are more basic than those associated with Major League teams. Klein said he had seen buscones' academies, of varying legitimacy, with anywhere from six to 60 players. There, the buscones provide free room, board and baseball instruction. *Cronkite News*, produced by the journalism school at Arizona State University, reported in September 2023 that 58 such academies were affiliated with Major League Baseball.

The payoff for a buscón comes if one of his young players signs with a Major League team, generally at 16. The buscón receives a cut of the player's signing bonus; 35 percent is not unusual. A point of contention is whether such a hefty slice for the several years of gestation at an academy is justified or unconscionable. Klein quotes one buscón, Samuel Herrera, saying that his operation (he had 10 players, six of them boarding at his academy) was an expensive, nerve-racking proposition and "likened it to spending all of one's money to win the lottery." Accounts of mistreatment and financial misconduct by buscónes have been widely published, and baseball has investigated accusations of kickbacks among buscónes. But Klein quotes Astin Jacobo, an influential talent developer in the Dominican Republic, as asking this of an audience: "Which is worse: the major league team that knows a kid is worth $1 million but pays $25,000 for him, or me, who knows [the kid is] worth $1 million, gets it, and the kid goes home with $650,000? Which is better for the kid, for me, and for the game here in the Dominican Republic?"

For many youngsters and their families, the possible financial reward outweighs the sometimes-grim reality of aligning with a buscón. As Ruck has pointed out, some buscónes have substandard housing, falsify players' birth certificates to make them appear younger and more marketable or administer performance-enhancing drugs. If Major League Baseball discovers that, the player, not the buscón, pays the immediate price.

Families in the Dominican Republic weigh the potential tradeoffs all the time, so buscónes are able to find player after player with whom to try to win their baseball lottery. Major League teams' Dominican academies have more than 1,000 players total, but the buscones and their academies have many times that number vying for a professional contract. Ruck said that when he visited the Dominican Republic in 2021, he was told there were about 1,000 such operations training upward of 100,000 boys from age 11 to 17.

Signing with a Major League team is a long shot—of those thousands of players in Dominican academies, 324 signed professional contracts in 2023, many of them for no bonus, according to Spotrac—and the chances of gaining a foothold in pro ball, let alone reaching the Majors has gotten tougher. Major League Baseball has recently reduced the number of minor league players each team can have to 165, down from 180 (which was already down from previous levels), and *Baseball America* noted that the opportunities for long shots will be reduced. But the financial implications of a young Dominican amateur's signing with a Major League can be great. Thirty of the 50 top international signees in 2023 were from the Dominican Republic, *Cronkite News* reported, with signing bonuses ranging from $4.7 million to $900,000. Even with a buscón's cut, that is life-changing money for a Dominican family. Even the cut of a $10,000 signing bonus is meaningful in a country where the income per capita in 2022 was $9,050, according to Statista.

(The explosion of baseball production in the Dominican Republic has also had benefits on the island as well, despite the pitfalls for those who were part of the pipeline. In 2016, Ruck discussed Major League Baseball's economic impact on the island, including spending on baseball academies and bonuses and salaries for players. "It's easy to get to a half-billion dollars that baseball is bringing to the island," Ruck said then—and that was in a country with a gross domestic product in 2014 of about $64 billion. By the time of his interview in late 2023, Ruck had an updated estimate: "It has just become really, I think, a multibillion-dollar business.")

As a result, the youngsters and their families keep dreaming, the buscones keep lining up young ballplayers to train and sell to the Major League academies, and the Major League teams keep funneling hundreds of players a year into the minor leagues hoping to find a Major Leaguer. This is standard practice in the Dominican Republic. It was also once common in Venezuela. In the 1990s, shortly before Hugo Chávez's socialist revolution, 23 of the 30 Major League teams had academies there, and Venezuelans flourished in the Majors: 292 of them made their big league debuts in the 2000s and 2010s. As political and economic upheaval worsened under Chávez and his successor, Nicolás Maduro, Major League teams began shuttering their academies; by November 2022, only four remained. (Major League Baseball in 2018 began a partnership with a few academies in several other countries, including Panama and Colombia.) The number of new Venezuelan Major Leaguers, once growing, has now plateaued. The addition of Dominican ballplayers, however, has continued to mushroom in the 2020s.

One reason is that, relatively speaking, Dominican players still come cheap. There are indeed seven-figure bonuses to the top international signees every year, but their bonuses lag behind those of the top players in the North American amateur draft. Also, as Ruck pointed out, since the 2017 collective bargaining agreement, Major League Baseball has put a cap on teams' spending on international amateur free-agent signings. And as one scout told Klein, it is more cost-effective to sign numerous Dominican players to low five-figure bonuses, hoping a Major Leaguer will emerge, than to pay the much higher bonuses that North American draftees can command. *Time* magazine reported that nine Dominican amateurs signed minor league contracts in 1980, for an average of $1,266 (a total of $11,394); in 2009, 396 Dominican ballplayers signed, for an average of $94,023 (a total of $37.2 million). To compare, in Major League Baseball's 2009 amateur draft, only two of the players who signed after being selected in the first seven rounds received a bonus of less than $100,000; those in the first round got an average of nearly $2.4 million.

By signing international players at a younger age, with less track record, there is a greater chance they won't make it, and yet Major League teams figure they are a worthwhile bet. Here's a look at one recent year and the bonuses that the top 10 draftees and international signees received and the players' age at the time.

2019 Top Bonuses to Amateur Players

Highest Bonuses to U.S. Amateurs		Highest Bonuses to Foreign Amateurs*	
$8.1 million	Adley Rutschman (Orioles)	$5.1 million	Jasson Domínguez (Yankees)
	21 years 4 months		16 years 7 months
$7.8 million	Bobby Witt, Jr. (Royals)	$5.1 million	Robert Puason (Athletics)
	19 years 0 months		16 years 10 months

Highest Bonuses to U.S. Amateurs		Highest Bonuses to Foreign Amateurs*	
$7.2 million	Andrew Vaughn (White Sox)	$3.9 million	Bayron Lora (Rangers)
	21 years 2 months		16 years 3 months
$6.7 million	JJ Bleday (Marlins)	$2.9 million	Ronnier Quintero (Cubs)
	21 years 8 months		16 years 8 months
$6.2 million	Riley Greene (Tigers)	$2.85 million	Roberto Campos (Tigers)
	18 years 9 months		16 years 1 month
$5.4 million	Nick Lodolo (Reds)	$2.8 million	José Salas (Marlins)
	21 years 4 months		16 years 3 months
$5.2 million	C.J. Abrams (Padres)	$2.6 million	Luis Rodríguez (Dodgers)
	18 years 8 months		16 years 9 months
$4.5 million	Alek Manoah (Blue Jays)	$2.5 million	Yolbert Sánchez (White Sox)
	21 years 5 months		22 years 4 months
$4.4 million	Josh Jung (Rangers)	$2.5 million	Emmanuel Rodríguez (Twins)
	21 years 4 months		16 years 4 months
$4.1 million	Hunter Bishop (Giants)	$2.2 million	Ismael Mena (Padres)
	21 years 0 months		16 years 7 months
Average bonus: $5.96 million		Average bonus: $3.24 million	
Average age: 20.6 years		Average age: 17.8 years	

*International players are from the Dominican Republic except Campos and Sánchez (Cuba) and Quintero and Luis Rodríguez (Venezuela).

Twenty-Five. September 23

Seven decades ago, baseball for a Dominican player was nothing like this. Ozzie Virgil was born in the Dominican Republic, but he moved with his family to New York City when he was about 13. He attended DeWitt Clinton High School in the Bronx, but he did not play on his high school team. Instead, he played sandlot ball, in Puerto Rico and in the military after he joined the Marine Reserves in 1950, he said in a 1997 interview with William M. Anderson for *Michigan History Magazine*. After his military service, the Giants signed Virgil out of a tryout.

It was not a simple tryout. Virgil told Enríque Rojas of ESPN *Deportes* in 2006 that he worked out with the Giants for 90 days before he signed, for a $300 bonus, in 1953. "But now things are different," he said. Three years later, he became the first Dominican Major Leaguer, but few took note of it. "It wasn't big in the Dominican Republic at the time," Virgil told Kevin Oklobzija of *The Rochester (New York) Democrat & Chronicle*. "But now, as baseball has grown so much, it's a bigger deal."

David Ortíz, the former Boston Red Sox slugger, said it should be. "Virgil should be for my country as important as [Jackie] Robinson to the African American," he told Rojas and ESPN *Desportes* in 2006. "I'd place his legacy up there with that of those who established our republic." If it weren't for Virgil, Ortíz said, he might not have been able to play professional baseball.

But Ortíz and hundreds of other Dominican ballplayers have made it, in unprecedented numbers. A total of 895 Dominican-born players had appeared in the Major Leagues through the 2023 season, according to *Baseball Reference*, far outpacing anywhere else: There had been 472 Venezuelans, 281 Puerto Ricans and 230 Cubans, for example, through 2023. Since the 1980s, no other Spanish-speaking locale has produced more Major Leaguers in any one decade than the Dominican Republic has, and in recent decades it has not been close, as the table below shows.

Major League Debuts by Country

	Dominican Republic	Venezuela	Puerto Rico	Cuba	Mexico	Panama
1870s	0	0	0	1	0	0
1880s	0	0	0	0	0	0
1890s	0	0	0	0	0	0
1900s	0	0	0	1	0	0
1910s	0	0	0	12	0	0
1920s	0	0	0	5	0	0
1930s	0	1	0	3	2	0

	Dominican Republic	Venezuela	Puerto Rico	Cuba	Mexico	Panama
1940s	0	1	2	22	2	0
1950s	2	4	14	36	12	5
1960s	22	10	23	36	7	13
1970s	38	10	39	4	18	6
1980s	64	28	46	8	12	1
1990s	157	62	59	13	32	17
2000s	213	130	42	20	29	8
2010s	264	162	42	52	19	13
2020s	135	65	14	16	18	7
Total	895	472	281	230	147	70

Source: Baseball Reference

There has been quality as well as quantity in all those Dominican ballplayers, as indicated in this table of Caribbean and Central and South American locales and their players' total Wins Above Replacement (through 2023).

Country (No. of Players)	WAR	Country (No. of Players)	WAR
Dominican Republic (895)	3385.89	Panama (70)	412.17
Venezuela (472)	2003.01	Curaçao (17)	175.95
Puerto Rico (281)	1651.84	Colombia (31)	114.44
Cuba (230)	1358.39	Nicaragua (15)	95.41
Mexico (147)	518.30	Virgin Islands (15)	49.37

Source: Baseball Reference

The influx of Dominican players has certainly benefited Major League Baseball. For example, 12 Dominicans were selected for the 2023 All-Star Game. A list of top Dominican-born players from 2023 reads like an all-star team: Juan Soto, Fernando Tatís, Jr., Vladimir Guerrero, Jr., Manny Machado, José Ramírez, Rafael Devers, Luis Castillo, Emmanuel Clase, Teoscar Hernández. Recent Hall of Fame inductees have included the Dominicans Pedro Martínez, David Ortiz and Vladimir Guerrero, Sr., and Albert Pujols is coming soon. And the *next* Albert Pujols may well be coming soon, too.

Twenty-Six

October 1

Fall Classics, From the Beginning

This was the backdrop for the first modern World Series, which began on this date in 1903.

A week before Game 1, the series between the champions of the long-established National League and the upstart American League was nearly scrapped because of a dispute over money between players and management. (Whether the dispute was real or a ploy by one team's owner was a matter for debate.) The resulting "world's championship series" had to fight for news coverage with numerous interleague series between National League and American League teams. Yet enthusiasm for the series proved so high in the host cities—Pittsburgh (generally rendered "Pittsburg" in news accounts of the day) and Boston—that overflow crowds spilled onto the field, forcing ground rules that affected play. The outcome of the series was also influenced by the sore arm of one pitcher (who may have been injured while trap shooting) and the mental health crisis of another. And the sporting press openly and casually reported about gambling on the games—including by players in the series.

There was not even agreement on what to call the teams. Pittsburgh was sometimes called the Premiers in print, occasionally the Pittsburgs or the Pirates. The Boston team was simply the Americans or the Bostons; they would not be the Red Sox for half a decade. Francis C. Richter wrote in *The Sporting Life*, a national sports publication that called itself "A weekly journal devoted to base ball, trap shooting and general sports," a glowing appraisal of the series. He said that "the public is bound to hail both teams as the very best exemplars of the one great, clean and honest national sport. In all respects has the best world's series been a credit to and good thing for the game of base ball." The gambling, apparently, was not seen as an issue.

Postseason championship series were nothing new in 1903, but they had never been lasting. The National League and the American

Association played a world series of sorts from 1884 to 1890, competing for something called the Dauvray Cup, but the AA folded after the 1891 season. The National League, absorbing some American Association teams, became a 12-team league and played a split season in 1892, with each half's winners meeting for the overall title. But that format fell apart in 1893. The next year, a part-owner of the Pittsburgh team, William C. Temple, devised a best-of-seven-game series between the NL's first- and second-place teams, with the winner receiving a silver cup—modestly called the Temple Cup. It foundered after four years, perhaps because of player apathy involving payouts for the series, Jim Baker wrote in *The Bill James Historical Baseball Abstract*.

In 1901, the American League was deemed a Major League, and a civil war of sorts erupted with the National League for players and attention. A truce emerged in 1903, and so did the world's championship series. The AL, in its third season as a Major League, was eager to assert its stature with a series against the National League champion. Barney Dreyfuss, the Pittsburgh owner, took the challenge.

And yet the series, a best-of-nine affair, almost was not played. Richter wrote in *The Sporting Life* that it looked as if the world's championship series would not materialize because the Boston players and owner, Henry Killilea, could not agree on pay for the series, which was set to begin October 1. Boston's regular season ended September 28 with a doubleheader; Pittsburgh's regular season ended September 26. The Pittsburgh players were under contract through October 15, but the Boston players were under contract only through September 30. On September 25, Richter wrote, Killilea rejected his players' request for their pay for the games and said the series was off, but negotiations resumed and an agreement the next day allowed the series to go forward as scheduled.

But Killilea's posturing may have been a ruse—if so, not the last time management would fudge the truth while negotiating with players. A.R. Cratty, reporting for *The Sporting Life* from Pittsburgh, said that Killilea actually was in touch with the Pittsburgh owners all along, assuring them the series would be played and indicating he was bluffing his players, trying to get a better deal.

Talk of money was everywhere. *The Sporting Life* reported about gambling on the games, including by the players. Cratty wrote: "They say that certain Premiers put on good wads on certain games and got there. [Jimmy] Sebring was the gamest. He posted $500 on the opening game here and landed it. After that Jeems was too wise to bet. [Sam] Leever was so sure that he would get there on Thursday that he is accused of putting up $100." Such open discussion of gambling makes a World Series betting scandal less than two decades later seem almost inevitable.

The 1903 championship series had considerable competition. Richter wrote that after the series looked to be in jeopardy, Giants manager John McGraw challenged the Pirates to a postseason series, but Dreyfuss declined. (He also declined recommendations that the world's series games be played at neutral sites; Cincinnati lobbied for games, for example.) Postseason series like the one McGraw was suggesting were not at all unusual. For example, the Philadelphia Athletics and Phillies met beginning the same day as the 1903 "world's series," as did the Chicago White Sox and Cubs. The Cincinnati Reds and the St. Louis Americans also squared off that day, and later in the month, the St. Louis Nationals and Americans met, while the Reds and the Cleveland Indians hooked up in Ohio. Money was to be made with these postseason ventures, bolstered by interleague matchups of crosstown (or cross-state) teams.

When the world's series play finally began, attention on it outside Boston and Pittsburgh was less than intense. *The New York Times* devoted five sentences and a box score to its coverage of Game 1. The other postseason series—truly just exhibitions—each received a sentence and a line score. *The Times*'s coverage of Game 3 of the world's series was matched by a similar-length news story about the Amateur Baseball League championship between two New Jersey teams. (Montclair beat Englewood.)

But the games merited attention, and they nearly minted a Mr. October long before Reggie Jackson. Charlie Phillippe, who was known as Deacon and whose surname was sometimes written as Phillippi in the papers, was a right-handed pitcher for Pittsburgh who won three of the first four games as his team took a 3-1 lead. Its best pitcher, Sam Leever, was limited to 10 ineffective innings because of a sore arm said to have been caused by cold weather. But, as *The 1902 Pittsburgh Pirates: Treachery and Triumph* noted, it was widely believed that Leever's injury was caused at least in part by a trap shooting incident. More tragically, Pittsburgh's No. 3 pitcher, Ed Doheny, suffered a mental breakdown during the season and, despite hopes that he could return for the postseason, was sent to a mental hospital. He never played again.

Fans were a factor. In the stands, Boston's Royal Rooters were raucous and full-throated singers. ("The Royal Rooters went crazy throughout the game," *Honus Wagner: A Biography* says of Game 6. "Many of the gang were postseason veterans, having followed the Boston Nationals during their 1890s Temple Cup play.") Of greater import were fans on the field. In Game 3—Phillippe pitched a six-hitter, as Pittsburgh took a 2-1 series lead—"Unrestricted fans covered the field prior to the contest, and one urchin made off with second base before being subdued by a policeman," according to *Honus Wagner: A Biography*. It said that during the game, the crowd was within 40 feet of home plate.

They would get even closer in the outfield. At Game 4 in Boston—again won by Phillippe, after rain postponement gave him extra rest—the large crowd of almost 19,000 spilled onto the field, forcing ground rules for balls hit there. "They were massed from just beyond the outfielders' regular positions to the fences and all around the diamond inside the stands," *The New York Times* said. "Fair balls hit into the crowd went as two-baggers." *The Times* reported that "the police had considerable difficulty in clearing the field of play, and later in keeping the people from encroaching on the field." In Game 5, Boston won, 11–2, as balls hit into the crowd standing three or four deep in the outfield were ruled triples. Six triples were hit in the game.

Boston finally defeated Phillippe, 7–3, in Game 7 in Pittsburgh, even though he had an extra day's rest because of another postponement for rain and cold weather. That allowed Boston to take a 4–3 lead in the series. Ground rules to accommodate the outpouring of fans again resulted in triples on balls hit into the crowd, and five of Boston's 11 hits went for three bases. Pittsburgh fans had staged a parade before the game and unveiled a cheer: "Phil, Phil, Phillippe, Phil! He can win, and you bet he will!" The cheers continued at the ballpark, *The Sporting Life* reported:

> The magnificent record made by Phillippe in winning the three games pitched against the Boston pennant winners led the crowd to think he could do so again, but in this they were disappointed. As he walked to the centre of the diamond to begin the game he was given the greatest reception ever given a player on the local grounds and was presented with a diamond pin. He pitched a good, steady game, but Boston's hits came when most needed, while Pittsburg could not bunch theirs.

After another rainout, Boston wrapped up the series, 3–0, in Game 8 as Bill Dinneen pitched a four-hitter to defeat Phillippe. *The Times* put the large crowd in context for its readers: "While the attendance at all the previous games of the series has been larger than to-day, the demonstration which followed Dineen's striking out of 'Hans' Wagner in the ninth equaled any college football game." *The Times* noted the struggles of the Pirates' starter: "Phillippi, who was such an enigma in the first few games, essayed to pitch for the visitors for the sixth time," but he was "batted hard."

Phillippe wound up pitching five of the eight games, with 44 innings of work in which he allowed 38 hits and only three walks. But, relied on so heavily, he weakened as the series progressed, and Pittsburgh's pitching was stretched thin. After Game 7, Jacob C. Morse wrote in *The Sporting Life*: "There is no disguising the fact that Phillippi [sic] has done marvelous work in the box for the Pittsburg champions. He has been made to feel fully the responsibility that has devolved upon him."

Phillippe did receive rewards. He earned the loser's share of $1,316.25

Twenty-Six. October 1

(well over $40,000 in 2024 dollars), a bonus of 10 shares of a dividend-paying stock in a Pittsburgh railway company and a diamond horse scarf pin from a local fan. The checks for Pittsburgh's married players were made out to their wives, which may have made the wives happy but not the players. "There was much growling among some of the Pirates in consequence," *The Sporting Life* reported.

The world's championship series was not repeated in 1904 as John Brush, the president of the NL champion Giants, refused to play the "representative of the inferior American League," *Baseball Almanac* said. The National League even pushed through an expansion of the baseball schedule to make arranging a World Series difficult, Brian Martin wrote in *Barney Dreyfuss: Pittsburgh's Baseball Titan*. Lengthening the season to 154 games from 140, with an April 15 start and October 15 finish, would push a postseason series into inhospitable colder weather, the thinking went. The machinations worked to eliminate a 1904 series, but Brush changed his mind later that year. Rules for play on the field (and finances off it) were set, and in 1905, the World Series returned. For good. (Except for the disaster of 1994, but that's another story.)

October 1 is a landmark date for numerous other highlights. Here are a few:

1919: Eddie Cicotte gave up six earned runs and the Chicago White Sox—soon to be known as the Black Sox—lost the first game of the World Series to the Cincinnati Reds, 9–1. Cicotte had gone 29-7 with a 1.82 earned run average that season. His control was so good that he walked only 49 batters in 306 2/3 innings ... and he hit just two. Why does that matter? Because with his second pitch of Game 1 of the World Series, Cicotte hit the Reds' Morrie Rath. In *Burying the Black Sox,* Gene Carney wrote: "The gamblers and players involved in the fixing of the 1919 Series disagreed on a lot of things, but they all seemed to agree on one detail: the way Eddie Cicotte dealt with the first batter of the Series would be the signal that the fix was in." Carney added, "And so the signal was set up: the first Cincinnati Reds batter would either be walked or hit with a pitch by Cicotte. Anything else, and the fix was *off*." The fix was in, Cicotte later confessed to a grand jury. He and seven other Chicago players were indicted but later acquitted. A week afterward, however, the Black Sox were barred from baseball forever by Commissioner Kenesaw Mountain Landis.

1932: Babe Ruth hit his "Called Shot" home run in Game 3 of the World Series. It was, in fact, the last of his 15 World Series home runs. He singled in his final Series at-bat, in Game 4, and was replaced in the field in the ninth inning by Sam Byrd—known as Babe Ruth's Legs. But no one was Babe Ruth's Bat.

1944: The St. Louis Browns clinched their only American League pennant with a 5–2 victory over the Yankees. Chet Laabs, who played only part time (nights and weekends) that season because he was working in a World War II defense plant, hit two two-run homers. The Browns won only 89 games, but that was second best in franchise history. Of the 53 Browns teams (including a first season as the Milwaukee Brewers in 1901), only 12 had winning records. They never had more than two winning seasons in a row.

1946: The Dodgers and the Cardinals began a best-of-three series in the first playoff to determine a League champion. The National League was founded in 1876, but it took 70 years for a pennant to be won in a playoff. Then playoffs to forge a World Series participant wouldn't stop. Cardinals-Dodgers in 1946. Indians-Red Sox in 1948. Giants-Dodgers in 1951. Dodgers-Braves in 1959. Giants-Dodgers in 1962. That's five tiebreakers in 17 seasons, with the Dodgers playing in all four in the National League.

The move to divisional play, in 1969, also brought tiebreakers, although for lesser stakes, a berth in a league championship series rather than the World Series—Yankees-Red Sox in 1978 and Astros-Dodgers in 1980. Those first four NL playoffs were best-of-three series; after the NL playoff series in 1946, the American League pushed for a one-game playoff in the event a tiebreaker was needed, and that's how Boston and Cleveland came to play a single game in 1948, as Matt Kelly wrote for MLB.com. But the National League clung to the best-of-three format until divisional play.

1951: The Giants and the Dodgers played the first baseball game televised coast to coast, part of their best-of-three playoff series to determine the National League champion. But baseball had been televised, haltingly, for years. The first televised game was actually between two college teams, Princeton and Columbia, on May 17, 1939, in Manhattan, according to a history of baseball on TV by the professors James R. Walker and Robert V. Bellamy, Jr., in 2003. The telecast employed one camera and was not, they said, an artistic success. Later that season, on August 26, the first game of a doubleheader between the Reds and the Dodgers at Ebbets Field was televised, with Brooklyn's radio announcer, Red Barber, handling the TV chores for another flawed effort. Not that many people saw it; History.com says there were only about 400 TV sets in New York at the time. By 1947, there were about 100,000 TVs nationwide when the World Series was televised for the first time.

The All-Star Game was televised in 1950, and then came the nationwide breakthrough in the 1951 NL playoff series, carried by CBS and NBC. Which meant that Bobby Thomson's "Shot Heard 'Round the World" could be seen 'round the country. ABC began televising a Saturday *Game of the Week* in 1953, although Major League Baseball was so hesitant that only three teams signed on initially and telecasts were banned within 50 miles of any Major League ballpark. Eventually, baseball figured out that TV was a fountain of money; in 2022, revenues from national and local/regional television brought in at least $4 billion for MLB, according to figures from Forbes and Cross Screen Media.

1961: Roger Maris hit his 61st home run, breaking Babe Ruth's record. He also struck out once, which was just about as notable. Maris finished the season with barely more strikeouts than home runs, 67 to 61. The last home run champion with more dingers than whiffs? Cincinnati's Ted Kluszewki in 1954, with 49 homers and 35 strikeouts.

1964: The Red Sox drew their smallest crowd at Fenway Park, with paid attendance of 306, for a game against Cleveland. The previous record was 674, set in 1963. These years were part of a dismal near-decade in Boston, a run of eight consecutive losing seasons from 1959 to 1966. Those record-low crowds reflected the hometown disdain; the Red Sox averaged 11,786 in paid attendance in 1963 and 10,904 in 1964. It got worse: In the 100-loss season of 1965, Boston averaged 8,058 fans. What did it take to bring Red Sox fans back to Fenway? The Impossible Dream season of 1967, when attendance more than doubled to 1.7 million—and the pennant was won on the last day of the regular season: October 1.

1973: The Mets clinched the National League East title with a mere 82 wins. This was only the fifth year of divisional play, and baseball nearly realized its big fear: a losing team in the playoffs. The Mets were still below .500 in Game 153, and that was in the midst of a seven-game winning streak. Only one other playoff team has had a worse record than the Mets' 82-79 (.509)—the 2005 Padres at 82-80 (.506). While the Mets shockingly made the World Series—and even led the Series, three games to two—the Padres flamed out as expected in a three-game sweep.

1982: The last Seattle Pilot retired: Fred Stanley. The Houston Astros, who would be in a pennant race late into the season, sold minor league shortstop Fred (Chicken) Stanley to the expansion Pilots on September 8, 1969. The Pilots were 55–84 (.388) at the end of the day's play, and the team was a frightful mess, as Jim Bouton detailed in *Ball Four*. The team was bad on the field and mismanaged off it, played in a dreary, sadly named ballpark (Sick's Stadium) and drew few fans (an average of 8,370 a game). The next year, the team would move to Milwaukee right before the season began, and Stanley would play six late-season games for the Brewers without getting an at-bat. He bounced from one bad team to another (Cleveland, 60–102 and 72–84) to another (San Diego, 58–95), before his luck turned: The Yankees acquired him in 1973. New York was nothing special at that moment (80–82), but Stanley wound up playing in the postseason in three years for the Yankees and one for the Oakland Athletics. Still, his career-best batting average—.279—was as a Seattle Pilot.

1995: The Colorado Rockies and the New York Yankees became the first wild-card teams. The 1994 season was ruined by labor strife that persisted into the 1995 season. The negotiations resulted in the wild-card arrangement; the shortened season resulted in uneven totals of games. The Yankees, for example, finished 79–65 but were a wild-card team, while the Seattle Mariners were 79–66 and a division champion. The Yankees and the Mariners played a divisional series that was as tight as their regular-season records. New York scored 35 runs in the five games, Seattle 33. Both teams hit 11 homers. The Yankees' ERA was 5.79; the Mariners', 5.94. After Randy Johnson gave up the go-ahead run in his third inning of relief in the top of the 11th inning of Game 5, Seattle won the series when Ken Griffey, Jr., slid home just ahead of the throw on Edgar Martínez's two-run double in the bottom of the inning. Only a Rockies fan remembers their series. (For the record, they lost in four games to the Atlanta Braves.)

2004: Ichiro Suzuki broke the Major League record for hits in a season. Would Ford Frick have wanted an unofficial asterisk next to Suzuki's mark? He was chasing George Sisler's record of 257 hits in a season, set in 154 games in 1920. When Roger Maris pursued Babe Ruth's home run record from the 154-game era, Frick declared that if Maris did not reach 61 in the Yankees' first 154 games, he would have to settle for only the 162-game record. Through his first 154 games in 2004, Suzuki had only 250 hits. He got the record by swatting 26 hits in the last 14 games, for a total of 262. That included 225 singles. Ty Cobb held the hits record before Sisler, at 248. Interestingly, Pete Rose, the career hits leader, never came close to the record; he topped out at 230.

2006: Joe Mauer became the first catcher to win the American League batting title. The first catcher in the modern era to win a batting title wouldn't have won it under today's standards. Eugene (Bubbles) Hargrave was a 33-year-old catcher for the Cincinnati Reds in 1926 when he became involved in an unusual race for the National League batting championship. There were no official rules to determine who was eligible, although the unwritten rule was that a player had to appear in at least 100 games. Raymond (Rube) Bressler, a Cincinnati teammate, hit .357 but played in only 86 games. Another Reds player, Walter (Cuckoo) Christensen, batted .350 while playing in 114 games. In between was Hargrave at .353, with 105 games.

Well after the season ended, the National League president, John Heydler, concluded that Hargrave was the champion, even though he had come to bat only 366 times. Heydler tried to codify rules for a batting title but failed, Hargrave's SABR *Bio Project* profile says; no rules were laid down until the 1950s. Under current rules (3.1 plate appearances per game—477 in a pre-expansion season, 502 since), Paul Waner would have won that 1926 title with a .336 average (and 618 plate appearances).

The hazy rules also benefited the only other NL catcher to win a batting title: Ernie Lombardi, who won without question in 1938 (he batted 529 times), but was awarded the 1942 title despite coming to the plate only 347 times. There was no uncertainty about Mauer. He won three batting championships in four years (.347, .328, .365), and the nondescript and shortened end of his career may obscure how good a hitter he was. In his first 10 seasons, Mauer *averaged* .323 with a .405 on-base percentage and an OPS+ of 135. In his final five seasons—none of them as a catcher—Mauer hit .267 with a .353 on-base percentage and an OPS+ of 103.

Twenty-Seven

October 1
That *Close to Batting .400*

It was the last day of the 1939 season, Cardinals catcher Don Padgett was batting .399 and you wouldn't have known it to read the St. Louis newspapers. Not a word about it. Maybe it wasn't that big a deal. Bill Terry of the New York Giants had hit .401 only nine years earlier. A 50-year-old baseball fan would have seen a dozen .400 seasons in the Major Leagues. And to be honest, Padgett wasn't about to win the National League batting title. Even with the relaxed standards of the day—no firm rule, just a generally agreed upon notion that a player had to appear in at least 100 games to qualify—Padgett would not meet the mark. Given injuries, illness, defensive challenges and his use as a platoon player, he had appeared in only 91 games heading into the final game on October 1.

Still, the man was hitting .399 and had gone to bat 253 times. He had been hitting at least .400 every day but one since June 17. Yet even though the Cardinals had spent two months within striking distance of the league-leading Cincinnati Reds, the rookie manager Ray Blades saw no urgency to use Padgett ahead of Mickey Owen, who was hitting about 150 points worse. Of the Cardinals' 35 games in September, Padgett played only 20. Padgett, a left-handed hitter, was batting an even .400 through 151 of the Cardinals' games—92 for 230—before going 1 for 3 in No. 151. His single in his final at-bat left him at .399. He was on the bench for the next two games, a Saturday doubleheader, even though the Chicago Cubs started a right-hander in the nightcap—Bill Lee, against whom Padgett batted .388 in his career. In the final game of the season, the Cubs started another right-hander, Claude Passeau, but still Padgett was anchored on the bench. Until the eighth inning, when Padgett was sent to bat for pitcher Max Lanier with two outs, the score tied and runners on first and second.

This was a spot meant for Padgett. He had already pinch-hit 28 times that year, going 8 for 24 with two homers, two triples, four walks and a remarkable 13 RBIs. And Padgett came through again. "Padgett lined a clean single up the middle, but upon reaching first base learned that the first-base umpire had called time a split second before the pitch because a ball rolled loose in the bullpen," John Snyder wrote in *Cardinals Journal*. The hit that would have given Padgett a .402 average was erased, and back in the batter's box he went. Passeau walked him, and Padgett's batting average remained .39914. *That* close to .400.

Padgett missed a month early in the season after dislocating his left shoulder in spring training, injured an ankle and missed some time during the summer and came down with an undisclosed illness that limited him for a week and a half in late August and early September. But the rest of the year before September? He still did not play regularly, raising questions everywhere except, apparently, in St. Louis. In early August, Harry Grayson, sports editor of the *NEA* news service, wrote: "Rival National League managers cannot understand why the St. Louis Cardinals do not employ Don Wilson Padgett and his .437 batting average steadily in right field, where he belongs, instead of experimenting every once in a while with the North Carolina slugger behind the plate." Grayson called him "the most feared slugger" in the league at the moment. Larry Shropshire, covering the Cincinnati Reds for *The Lexington (Kentucky) Herald-Leader*, wrote of Blades, "But one question that puzzles is how he can keep big Don Padgett, a .400 hitter, out of his regular lineup."

The explanation would have been: defense. Padgett had never played catcher when the Cardinals' general manager, Branch Rickey, sent him a package for Christmas in 1937, as Shropshire related. Inside were four catcher's mitts, a catcher's mask, a chest protector and shin guards, the Baseball Hall of Fame said. The next day, a letter from Rickey came: "We've got more outfielders than we need…. Unless you turn to catching, I'm afraid we'll have to send you back to Columbus. But you're going to be a catcher—a great catcher."

No, he wasn't. Padgett was big (6 feet 2 inches and 190 pounds) and neither fast nor agile. He had proved to be a subpar defensive outfielder, and the 1939 Cardinals had two future Hall of Famers, Joe Medwick and the rookie Enos Slaughter, in the outfield, along with one of the best defensive center fielders in the game, Terry Moore. Padgett was not going to dislodge Johnny Mize at first base, either. He started only 54 games at catcher in 1939. A telling statistic: He finished only 24 of them behind the plate. "Padgett was a shoemaker in shinguards," the Hall of Fame St. Louis sportswriter Bob Broeg wrote years later. In July 1939, *The Associated Press* wrote: "Foul flies are still a bit of a puzzle to him. He still has a hesitating windup when he attempts to nip base runners stealing. He still looks over to the bench for advice at a critical time. But .. Don is hitting the ball at a .400 clip and that's a mighty important asset in the National league race."

You'd think. Padgett started only 38 games between May 26 and August 26, but he batted .454 (69 for 152). That's when he took ill. He returned to the lineup on September 9 and went 3 for 5, and started 16 of 21 games. Until, with a chance to bat .400, he sat. Padgett wasn't truly a .400 hitter, of course. He wasn't even a .300 hitter; his average was .288 over an eight-year career that lost four seasons to World War II. If for anything other than his nearly .400 season, Padgett is remembered for a scouting report that batted .000. In spring training in 1941, he spotted a young outfielder who set up in a crouch in the batter's box, far from home plate. "He'll never hit with that stance," Padgett said, as Broeg wrote. The kid did all right, and became the Man: Stan Musial.

Twenty-Eight

October 2
A Day Off

October 2, 1944, was not a Sunday. It was, in fact, a Monday, but it was a day of rest nonetheless for Ray Mueller of the Cincinnati Reds and Frankie Hayes of the Philadelphia Athletics. It was the day after the end of a season in which they caught every one of their teams' games: 155 in all. No catcher had ever done that in the 20th century, but in that World War II season, Mueller and Hayes both did. Five players in the 1800s also accomplished this feat, but only one of them—Deacon McGuire in 1895—caught as many as 100 games, according to the website Baseball Catchers. (McGuire caught all 133 games for the Washington National League team.)

It was little wonder that catchers played fewer games than other position players. Although pitches and exit velocities were not routinely cracking 100 miles per hour in the early decades of the game, catchers' equipment was rudimentary. So was medical aid; it was an era of "spit on it" or "rub dirt on it," not MRIs and arthroscopic surgery, and athletic trainers called Doc because there often was not a team physician. World War II, however, created unusual conditions. By the start of the 1944 season, about 340 Major Leaguers were serving in the military, according to the website Baseball in Wartime, along with about 3,000 minor leaguers. In *Spartan Seasons: How Baseball Survived the Second World War*, Richard Goldstein wrote that a survey by the National League president, Ford Frick, said the eight NL clubs had 135 players who were classified 4F for the military draft—"physically, mentally, or morally unfit for service"—on their winter rosters. The American League had 125 (including the St. Louis Browns' one-armed outfielder, Pete Gray). If you could play, you played.

Ray Mueller was one of those 4F players—in February 1944, he had been declared unfit for military service because of a stomach ulcer, according to *Spartan Seasons*. Through his first decade as a professional, Mueller had showed few signs of being an ironman catcher. He never caught 100 games in any of his first nine seasons in pro ball (he topped out at 99), six of them at least in part in the Majors.

But in 1942, as a 30-year-old playing for Sacramento in the Pacific Coast League's elongated schedule, Mueller caught 164 of the Solons' 178 games. The next year, he was back in the Majors and caught 140 games for the Reds, including the final 62 of the season. That was a prelude to 1944: He caught all nine innings in a 1–0 loss to the Cubs on Opening Day on April 18 and was never out of the starting lineup, finishing out the season on October 1. He played 155 games in 166 days and played both ends of a doubleheader 35 times. Four times he caught doubleheaders on back-to-back days.

In one ugly stretch in July and August, Mueller caught six complete games in four days—and hit three home runs. In September, he caught eight games in six days—doubleheader, doubleheader, off day, off day, doubleheader, doubleheader—followed the next week by five games in three days. In all, he caught 1,348 of the Reds' 1,386 innings in the field. He even played in the All-Star Game, although he caught only the ninth inning. Maybe we should credit him with 156 games.

Another sign of the times and the team: Cincinnati Manager Bill McKechnie did not rely only on Mueller. Two other Reds, second baseman Woody Williams and shortstop Eddie Miller, also played all 155 games, and first baseman Frank McCormick played in 153. Only one backup infielder had more than 33 plate appearances.

By the end of 1944, Mueller had caught a record 217 consecutive games, but his 1945 season was disrupted by the war. He was re-examined early in the year and wound up in the Army, Goldstein wrote in *Spartan Seasons*. When Mueller returned in 1946, Goldstein said, Frick, the NL president, ruled that his streak was intact, but he added on only 16 more games, for a 233-game streak.

Frankie Hayes wound up breaking Mueller's record for consecutive games catching, although he spent time with three teams—the St. Louis Browns, the Philadelphia Athletics and the Cleveland Indians—to do so. "With no one worth mentioning to come to his rescue, Frank Hayes caught 312 consecutive games for the Browns, Athletics and Indians, starting his streak on the final day of the 1943 season and carrying it into April 1946," Goldstein wrote.

Hayes had more of an ironman pedigree than Mueller, catching 144 games in 1936 for the Athletics and then 124, 136 and 126 from 1939 to 1941 in Philadelphia. Then Hayes, a bat-first catcher, stopped hitting and was traded to the Browns in the middle of the 1942 season. In 1943, Hayes batted his way further into part-timer status, hitting .188 for a sixth-place team. St. Louis sent him back to Philadelphia for the 1944 season for a minor league outfielder, Barney Lutz, and Sam Zoldak, who pitched in 18 games for the Browns. (St. Louis was apparently loading up on Z's, as it already had Al Zarilla and Joe Schultz, but the Browns did get enough W's to win their only pennant.)

Hayes's schedule in '44 was, like Mueller's, harrowing. He caught both games of 34 doubleheaders, including on the final day of the season. He caught doubleheaders on back-to-back days twice. One week he caught 10 games; five times, he caught five games in three days.

After playing every game in 1944, Hayes caught the Athletics' first 32 games in 1945 before being traded to Cleveland, where he played all 119 games he was there for. His streak ended at 312 consecutive games on April 24, 1946, when Manager Lou Boudreau (who was also the shortstop) started 21-year-old Sherman Lollar instead. Lollar and 25-year-old defensive whiz Jim Hegan played the next game before Hayes returned to the lineup. Although he made the All-Star team (and Boudreau did not), it was apparent Cleveland saw no future for Hayes and dealt him to the Chicago White Sox on July 15. He played in only 104 games that season.

As Hayes was catching primarily because of his bat, his defensive numbers were underwhelming. In only three of his 14 seasons did he have positive defensive WAR—and two of them were war years. He led the American League in most stolen bases allowed seven times in 10 years (including 88 in 1944), and in errors by a catcher and passed balls twice each.

The ironman efforts of Mueller and Hayes drew the attention of various sportswriters, including the veteran Fred Lieb, a well-regarded reporter for decades who wrote in *The Sporting News*: "So, while a bow is due to Hayes, an even more sweeping flourish of the fedora is merited by the little Cincinnatian, Mueller with steel springs in his arms, shoulders and legs."

Hayes and Mueller had managed a feat unseen in half a century when they played in every game, but the very next year, another catcher, Mike Tresh, caught every game for his team, the Chicago White Sox. While Hayes was catching a streak-enhancing 151 games in 1945, Tresh caught all 150 games for the White Sox. He had been a part-timer the previous three seasons (catching 72, 85 and 93 games) and resumed a part-time role after 1945, never catching 100 games again in his final four seasons. Perhaps that was because of the 38 doubleheaders he caught (and started) in 1945. Gruesomely, Tresh played both ends of a doubleheader six times in seven days in early September. At least his backup caught a total of 10 innings in a couple of those games. Playing every day didn't seem to hurt Tresh's defense, though; he threw out a league-leading 60 percent of would-be base stealers.

Here's a breakdown of just how much Mueller, Hayes and Tresh caught in the seasons when they did not miss a game behind the plate.

1944 Reds	Games	Innings	1944 Athletics	Games	Innings
Ray Mueller	155	1,348	Frankie Hayes	155	1,333
Joe Just	10	35	Bob Garbark	15	48
Len Rice	5	12	Jon Pruett	2	10
Johnny Riddle	1	1	Tony Parisse	2	5
			Hal Wagner	1	2

1945 A's	Games	Innings	1945 Indians	Games	Innings
Buddy Rosar	85	707	Frankie Hayes	119	989
Charles George	46	344	Jim McDonnell	23	123
Frankie Hayes	32	273	Hank Ruszkowski	14	129
Joe Astroth	8	38	Gene Desautels	10	29
Jim Pruett	4	8	Red Steiner	4	31

1945 White Sox	Games	Innings
Mike Tresh	150	1,236
Vince Castino	25	95

(For Philadelphia in 1945, Rosar, George and Desautels did not play until Hayes was traded on May 29; Pruett relieved Hayes in three games and started one the day after his trade. For Cleveland, the 19-year-old Ruszkowski and Steiner played all of their games for the Indians before Hayes came over. Steiner was later traded; McDonnell played 11 of his games before the Hayes trade.)

Curiously, their play-every-game seasons really did not harm Mueller, Hayes or Tresh in the batter's box. Here's a look at their offensive lines during their everyday seasons compared with their career norms.

Hayes	BA/OBP/SLG	OPS+	Mueller	BA/OBP/SLG	OPS+
1944	.248/.315/367	97	1944	.286/.35/.398	115
Career	.259/.343/.400	101	Career	.252/.314/.368	90

Hayes	BA/OBP/SLG	OPS+	Tresh	BA/OBP/SLG	OPS+
1945	.234/.335/.352	103	1945	.249/.342/.275	82
Career	.259/.343/.400	101	Career	.249/.335/.283	71

They could not go on forever, of course. Trying to hang on to his career, Hayes signed with the Red Sox in 1947 and uttered one of the great understatements: "I've never been a bench warmer." Unfortunately, he was no longer a starter, as Boston released him after five games. After Hayes retired and opened a sporting goods store in Spring Lake, New Jersey, Gordon Cobbledick of *The Plain Dealer* in Cleveland pointed to his 312-game streak and wrote, "He was the hardest working catcher in history, but he is paying for his incredible record of durability by being forced to quit at 32."

That toll should have been obvious, and only one player has caught more games in a season than Mueller and Hayes did in 1944—Randy Hundley, who caught 160 of the Cubs' 162 games in 1968. Hundley caught more than 90 percent of the Cubs' games in each season from 1966 to 1969 (149, 152, 160 and 151 games). At that point he was 27, and, no surprise, injuries bedeviled him the rest of his career. After that four-year run, he caught as many as 100 games only twice in his final eight seasons.

Jim Sundberg also caught 155 games, in the Texas Rangers' 162-game season in 1975 … and batted .199. Think he wore out? In 79 games from July 5 to the end of the season, Sundberg batted .171 with two extra-base hits—a double and a homer—and 11 RBIs. He, like most catchers, could have used a rest.

TWENTY-NINE

November 1

Here Comes Mr. November

For nearly a century, the World Series was an October game. Oh, World War I resulted in a September Series in 1918, but otherwise it was baseball, apple pie and October. The calendar, as well as the home runs, explains why Reggie Jackson came to be known as Mr. October.

Expansion after expansion couldn't force the Series past October. Even in 1962, when it was delayed by a best-of-three National League playoff and slowed by two rain postponements, the Series ended comfortably on October 16. Divisional play, begun in 1969, pushed play later with the addition of the league championship series, but still with a mid–October finish. At that, Commissioner Bowie Kuhn had to pretend mightily that it wasn't too cold for the World Series' new night contests. In 1976, he wore no topcoat and no hat to prove that the weather was just fine—until, in the seventh inning, he gave in and pulled on a topcoat.

The midseason strike of 1981 resulted in some extra one-time-only playoff games, and the Series wasn't completed until October 28. (Baseball got lucky with a mild 52-degree start for Game 7 in New York.) An earthquake created a 10-day delay in 1989 for the World Series between Oakland and San Francisco, but nonetheless, it wrapped up on October 28. In 1995, a divisional series was added to the mix, and the World Series began facing regularly later finishes, though still a few days shy of November.

Then came 2001. The attacks on the World Trade Center ruptured the baseball season, and the divisional series, the first of the three postseason rounds, did not begin until October 9. The World Series opened on October 27—only a day earlier than the latest Series had previously finished. The era of November baseball had arrived.

Since then, baseball has added wild-card rounds and presumably extra coffee and hand warmers, and six of nine World Series from 2015 through 2023 have finished in November. Yes, the summer game now finishes about the same time as the NFL's regular season hits its midway

Twenty-Nine. November 1

point. Through 2023, 18 World Series games had been played in November. Here they are, starting with the first Mr. November.

November 1, 2001, Game 4: One fan went to Yankee Stadium for Game 4 of the World Series on October 31, 2001, with a sign that read "Mr. November" and, apparently, a premonition. No Major League game had been played in November, and it did not look as if this one would either. Then Tino Martinez hit a two-run homer off the Arizona Diamondbacks' Byung-Hyun Kim in the bottom of the ninth inning to tie the score at 3–3, and four minutes after midnight, with two outs and a full count, Derek Jeter became the first Mr. November with a game-ending home run in the 10th.

Jeter said he had never hit a walk-off homer at any level, and you might not have expected it here. Jeter was 1 for 15 in the Series and 0 for 4 that night when he came up. He had never faced Kim, a submarine pitcher who was tough on right-handers: They batted only .221 with a .344 slugging percentage against him in his career. But Jeter sliced a ball into the right-field seats. "Regardless of what you've done, every time you come up to the plate, you have a chance to do something special," Jeter said. Maybe it was the deadline pressure, but newspapers the next day—well, actually the same day—focused a lot on Martinez's tying home run, not Jeter's game-winner. *Newsday* called Martinez's blast the second-biggest moment in Yankees World Series history. But Anthony McCarron of *The New York Daily News* had time to get it right. He opened his game story by writing, "Call him Mr. November." The first one.

November 1, 2001, Game 5: Byung-Hun Kim was proving not to be Mr. November. For the second night in a row, he gave up a two-out, two-run, game-tying home run in the bottom of the ninth, and the Diamondbacks went on to lose to the Yankees in extra innings. Scott Brosius hit this one. Kim had given up only two homers to right-handed batters in the regular season; now he had given up two in 24 hours. With Kim long gone, the Yankees won in the 12th on Alfonso Soriano's RBI single.

November 3, 2001, Game 6: It was win or go home for a long winter for the Diamondbacks in Game 6. What better way to win than to hand the ball to *their* Mr. November, Randy Johnson? Well, and score 15 runs, eight of them in a third inning that Andy Pettitte couldn't get an out in. Johnson allowed six hits and struck out seven in seven innings, six days after pitching a three-hit, 11-strikeout shutout. All the way back in October.

November 4, 2001, Game 7: Yankees fans still curse Luis Gonzalez and the soft single he lofted just into center field off Mariano Rivera to score the winning run with two out in the bottom of the ninth. Often overlooked is the game-tying double Tony Womack rifled to right two batters earlier. And no Diamondbacks fan will forget Randy Johnson, who—one night after throwing 104 pitches—came out of the bullpen to record the final four outs. Johnson picked up one more strikeout, giving him 47 for the postseason (in 41 1/3 innings) and 419 for the year (in 291 innings).

November 1, 2009, Game 4: In the 2008 postseason, Philadelphia Phillies closer Brad Lidge was almost perfect: nine games, nine and a third innings, one run, three saves. Two of them came in the World Series, which the Phillies won for the first time since 1980. A year later, he again breezed through the Division Series and the Championship Series (five games, four innings, three saves). Then he faced the Yankees in the World Series, although not until the ninth inning of Game 4 with the score tied. Lidge recorded the first two outs, then yielded a single, two stolen bases, a hit batter, a run-scoring single and a two-run double. Suddenly, the Yankees led, three games to one.

November 2, 2009, Game 5: Normally, a home run by Chase Utley was no surprise. He had hit 31 in the regular season, and he averaged 29 over the five-year stretch beginning in 2005. But as *The Philadelphia Daily News* pointed out, Utley had lost his home run stroke late in the season. Between August 30 and the beginning of the World Series, he hit only three homers—that's 40 games and 172 plate appearances. Then he hit five homers in the first five games, over 21 plate appearances, in the World Series. That included two in Game 5 as the Phillies stayed alive with an 8–6 victory. He finished the Series with six hits—none of them a single—and his five homers tied the Series record. His big-time power days were behind him, though; Utley never hit more than 16 homers in any of his final nine seasons.

November 4, 2009: Game 6: In the final game Hideki Matsui played for the Yankees, he drove in six runs. The Yankees won the game and their 27th World Series championship. But Matsui would be gone before Christmas, a 36-year-old free agent signed by the Los Angeles Angels. Matt Gagne of *The New York Daily News* captured the moment the next day: "Only after saying goodbye to his teammates did Hideki Matsui realize it might be for good. 'I guess I never looked at it in that way,' he said, speaking through an interpreter at the Stadium following yesterday's victory parade in lower Manhattan. 'Usually we just say goodbye, and just go from there. If we see each other, we see each other.'" They did not see each other again until April 13, 2010, when the Angels played in New York. The Yankees have not returned to the Series since.

November 1, 2010, Game 5: Tim Lincecum pitched a complete-game, two-hit shutout, striking out 14, as the Giants won the NL Division Series opener, 1–0. In the NLCS, he hurled two shutout innings of relief in Game 1 and started Game 4 against the St. Louis Cardinals. On to the World Series. The Giants had pitching—Matt Cain (seven and two-thirds shutout innings) and Madison Bumgarner (eight shutout innings) won Games 2 and 4—but San Francisco really put its faith in Lincecum. He got the win in Game 1 despite a sketchy outing, but when it came to November and Game 5, Lincecum got the nod again. Over eight innings, he allowed only three hits and a run, and struck out 10, and the Giants won, 3–1, to take their first World Series title since 1954. Lincecum reflected on imagining securing Series victory as a youth: "Usually it was being a hitter. But I'll take this."

November 1, 2015, Game 5: For eight innings, Matt Harvey was every bit the Dark Knight. With the New York Mets trailing the Kansas City Royals in the Series, three games to one, he pitched eight shutout innings. The Mets led, 2–0, and Manager Terry Collins told Harvey in the dugout that he was done. Harvey had thrown 104 pitches on this night, and he had thrown 216 innings in his first season after Tommy John surgery. Ready in the bullpen was closer Jeurys Familia, who, although shaky so far in the Series with two blown saves, had saved 43 games in the regular season and five more in the postseason. Harvey, however, was not ready to sit. "No way," he told Collins, as the crowd chanted Harvey's name. "No way." So Collins looked the other way and let Harvey sprint back out to the mound for the ninth inning.

After recording 648 outs in 2015, however, he could not get the final three the Mets needed. He walked Lorenzo Cain, who stole second on the first pitch to Eric Hosmer. Then Hosmer doubled in the Royals' first run. After seven fruitless pitches, Harvey was out of the game, Familia was in and the Mets went from Dark Knight to dark night. Familia allowed the tying run when Hosmer made a nervy dash home on a grounder to third, tying the score, and Kansas City put the Series away with a five-run 12th. "Obviously, I let my heart get in the way of my gut," Collins said. "I love my players. And I trust them. And so I said, 'Go—get 'em out.'" Tim Rohan of *The New York Times* wrote of Collins: "He described it as his responsibility to protect Harvey from himself, as a parent would with a teenager. 'It's my fault. It's not his.'"

November 1, 2016, Game 6: Addison Russell drove in 95 runs in the regular season, but late in the year, he was slumping. He had only five RBIs in the Cubs' final 18 regular-season games and did not drive in a single run in their four-game victory over the San Francisco Giants in the Division Series. After three more fruitless games to open the NLCS against the Los Angeles Dodgers, Russell finally got some runs in with a two-run homer in Game 4. He hit another two-run homer in Game 5. He resumed his scuffles at the plate, but Russell singled in a run in Game 2 of the World Series against the Cleveland Indians and another in Game 5. Then, in November, he rediscovered his groove: six RBIs on a two-run double on a fly ball that dropped between outfielders and a grand slam as the Cubs staved off elimination in Game 6. "Being part of the Cubs, you're put in the limelight," Russell said after the game, "and early on you're forced to deliver whenever the game's on the line."

November 2, 2016, Game 7: This is what the 2016 World Series had come down to. The Chicago Cubs, who had blown a three-run lead in the eighth inning, had come back to lead in the top of the 10th, 8–6. They were three outs from their first World Series title since 1908. The Cleveland Indians, who had blown a three-games-to-one lead, had rallied in the 10th to cut the Cubs' lead to 8–7, and they had the potential winning run coming to the plate. They were one blast from their first World Series title since 1948. Into this historic situation stepped Mike Montgomery, a 27-year-old left-hander who had never saved a game in nine professional seasons, and Michael Martinez, a 34-year-old outfielder who had a .187 career batting average in the Majors. Montgomery had pitched in four of the first six games of the Series, and he had already warmed up four times that night.

"Tired would be an understatement," he said in a 2023 interview, "but at that point, you're just kind of numb to everything." A curveball specialist, he said later he had not thrown a curve for a strike in the bullpen. But a curveball is what he threw on his two pitches to Martinez, who tapped the second one to third baseman Kris Bryant for the Series-clinching out. "I don't got to be the best pitcher to ever live," Montgomery told Tyler Kepner of *The New York Times* in 2022, when he was a minor leaguer trying to make a comeback. "But I've been in the best moment that's arguably ever existed in baseball history."

November 1, 2017, Game 7: What was Charlie Morton doing out on the mound at Dodger Stadium? His Houston Astros led Los Angeles, 5–0, in Game 7 of the World Series, but they had already run through four pitchers, and this was a Dodgers team that had six players who had hit at least 20 home runs. Morton, a 33-year-old right-hander, had not pitched in relief since the final game of his rookie season. He had one winning record in his first nine years in the Majors. But here he was, asked to throttle the Dodgers and help the Astros win their first World Series. It wasn't looking good; four batters into his outing, Morton had allowed two singles, a walk and a run. But the bleeding stopped there: Morton retired the final 11 batters he faced, and Houston had its championship. (Let the trash can talk begin.)

November 2, 2021, Game 6: Had outfielders Ronald Acuña, Jr., and Marcell Ozuna not been injured early in the season, Jorge Soler very likely never would have been in Atlanta. The Braves traded for him on July 30, joining three other outfielders who had only recently been acquired: Joc Pederson, Eddie Rosario and Adam Duvall. Come the World Series, Soler was the DH and, although a home run champ just two years earlier, Atlanta's leadoff hitter in Game 1 against the Houston Astros. He homered off Framber Valdez. He homered twice more in the Series, including a key shot in Game 4 and a three-run blast in Game 6, which Atlanta won, 7–2, to claim the championship—its first since 1995. On November 2, he was the World Series MVP. On November 3, he was a free agent.

November 1, 2022, Game 3: The meeting of the Phillies and the Astros included more full games in November than any other World Series, four. Ranger Suarez pitched five shutout innings, his longest stint in more than a month for the Phillies. Four relievers also pitched shutout ball. Five Phillies homered off Lance McCullers, Jr. As a result, Philadelphia owned a two-games-to-one lead.

November 2, 2022, Game 4: You want a multi-pitcher shutout? How about one with no hits? The Astros constructed the first November no-hitter (and second World Series no-no) with six innings by Christian Javier and single innings by three relievers. The Phillies couldn't get over the movement on Javier's fastball. "Twenty-two inches of vertical drop," center fielder Brandon Marsh said. "Best in the league, probably." The problem wasn't really Javier's nine strikeouts. As David Murphy wrote in *The Philadelphia Daily News*: "The bigger problem was that the non-misses didn't matter. They made plenty of contact against Javier's fastball. It just didn't go anywhere."

November 3, 2022, Game 5: After succumbing to a no-hitter, Phillies Manager Rob Thomson professed not to be worried. "The last time we got no-hit," he said, "we ended up coming back and winning the next day." He was correct; Philadelphia rebounded from a five-pitcher no-hitter by the Mets in April. But this was November. The Phillies managed six hits and cut the Astros' lead to 3–2 in the eighth inning. But Ryan Pressly got the last five outs to preserve Houston's 3–2 victory, and the Astros took a three-games-to-two lead. Pressly entered with one out in the bottom of the eighth with runners on first and third, but got Brandon Marsh to strike out and Kyle Schwarber to ground out. Then in the ninth, he worked around a two-out hit batter, Bryce Harper, to close out the game by inducing Nick Castellanos to ground out to short. Wonderful Series for Pressly: five appearances in six games, five and two-thirds innings, two hits, one run, two saves.

November 5, 2022, Game 6: No one ever needed to think about platooning Yordan Alvarez. He's a left-handed power hitter—more precisely, powerful *and* a hitter—who crushes left-handers. His career line against lefties through 2023 was .301/.382/.565, with 39 home runs in 632 at-bats. That doesn't count the three-run homer he hit off José Alvarado in the sixth inning of Game 6, with Houston trailing, 1–0. It looked as if it could have been launched by NASA. Another save by Pressly, and the Astros had another Series championship. (No trash can talk needed this time.)

November 1, 2023, Game 5: This is how baseball has changed. In the 2023 World Series, the champion Texas Rangers used 14 pitchers; the Arizona Diamondbacks used 12. One of those Rangers relievers was Josh Sborz. He did not save a game all season and rang up a 5.50 ERA in 44 games. He missed 24 days in September with a hamstring strain. In the postseason, however, he was omnipresent and untouchable: 12 innings while pitching in 10 of the Rangers' 17 games, four hits, one run, a 0.75 ERA, a 0.667 WHIP. Because it's Texas: A column in *The Fort Worth Star-Telegram* the next day read, "What can Cowboys learn from World Series champion Rangers?"

Thirty

December 12

Veeck Does (Funny) Business at the Winter Meetings

Bill Veeck never did things small (except for Eddie Gaedel), and everyone in baseball knew it. Veeck was angling to repurchase the Chicago White Sox in the spring of 1975 when, *The Chicago Tribune*'s David Condon wrote, Phil Seghi, the general manager in Cleveland, made this prediction: "The first thing he'll do is put up a sign a block long and 50 feet high across the front of the stadium. It'll say: 'Under new management ... open for business.'"

Bill Veeck made baseball lively. Even the winter meetings (National Baseball Hall of Fame, Cooperstown, NY).

Veeck didn't wait that long. Shortly after his purchase was approved at baseball's winter meetings that December in Hollywood, Florida, Veeck and his general manager, Roland Hemond, set up shop in the lobby of the Diplomat Hotel, the meetings' host, with a sign that read, in all capitals: "OPEN FOR BUSINESS." Eventually, Veeck added, "Anytime."

It was one of the most memorable moments in winter meetings history, which goes back to 1857—before professional baseball existed—when representatives of 14 clubs met in early winter, according to Richard Hershberger in *Base Ball's 19th Century Winter Meetings, 1857–1900*. Among the important results of that first convention was the codification of baseball's rules: the dimensions of the field, the size of the ball, the length of the game (nine innings replaced the first team to 21 runs).

Winter conventions continued, through wars (Civil, Spanish-American, World Wars I and II, Korea, Vietnam); the advent of professional baseball; the addition and subtraction of leagues; expansion. There were rules changes, trades, administrative maneuverings—mostly to help the owners pad their bank accounts, if you believe the *New York Daily News* columnist Jimmy Powers. "They meet each December to decide on methods of making more money the next Summer," he wrote in the heart of the Depression.

And then came 1975, when Veeck created an image for the ages. He almost did not have a chance. Veeck had sold the White Sox in 1961, but in 1975 the team was struggling financially. Suitors emerged, including Veeck, who—undercapitalized, as usual—had a raft of investors that eventually reached about 40. A sale to keep the White Sox in Chicago was not assured, and there were widely reported fears that the team might be headed to Seattle, which had lost the Pilots after one season, in 1969, and had been strongarming Major League Baseball, even filing a lawsuit, to get a new franchise.

Veeck made his proposal to American League owners, who told him a week before the winter meetings that it did not have enough cash, *The Chicago Tribune* reported. The owners gave him a week to improve his offer, and Veeck just squeaked in, as the winter meetings started in Florida on December. 10. It wasn't good enough: Veeck's offer fell one vote short of the three-quarters needed, Gregory H. Wolf wrote in *Baseball's Business: The Winter Meetings: 1958–2016*.

Veeck could have been sidelined right then, with the Sox having a good chance of moving to Seattle, but he received an unexpected boost from John Fetzer, the Detroit Tigers' owner and "no great fan of Veeck's," *United Press International* said. Fetzer urged the owners to look again at Veeck's group. "We have to be men about this," he said. "I don't like the idea of letting a guy back in here who's called me a son of a bitch over and over again, but gentlemen, we've got to take another vote." Fetzer's appeal apparently worked: Despite the earlier vote, the AL owners took a second one even though it was not required, and Veeck's deal was approved, 10–2.

This wasn't a highly desirable team. The White Sox had finished 75–86 in 1975, fifth in a six-team division. They had had one winning record in the last eight years, hadn't won a pennant since 1959 or a World Series since 1917. Chicago's official paid attendance was 750,802, although Veeck insisted it was actually 675,609. (If true, that would have made the White Sox last in the league.) The 1975 White Sox were 10th in a 12-team league in runs, eighth in earned run average.

But Veeck wanted back in the game. And he knew he needed to sell his team to fans, however he could. So as soon as he won approval to buy back the White Sox, he very publicly opened for business. Hemond, the general manager, told Bill Nowlin for Hemond's SABR *Bio Project* profile that the idea for the sign was his, after Veeck told him to "let your imagination run rampant." Hemond concluded that the Diplomat's lobby "was the perfect place to set up shop," Gordon Edes wrote in *The Boston Globe*, for a very public announcement that the White Sox were about to shake things up. "No whispering behind a potted palm for the White Sox," Edes said. Hemond suggested an "Open for Business" sign, and Veeck responded, "What are you waiting for?" Hemond got the OK from hotel management and put up the sign; Veeck supplied coffee, three packs of Salem cigarettes and his typical unflagging energy, Phil Pepe of *The New York Daily News* wrote.

Veeck and Hemond also supplied some subterfuge. Hemond told Nowlin that they engaged the team's public relations man, Buck Peden, to call every half-hour. "Bill would answer as if another GM was on the line and say, 'Hey Buzzie,' how you doing?' to make other clubs think we were doing business."

Trickery aside, they were. The White Sox made six trades involving 22 players at the meetings. One deal had already been in the works—20-game winner Jim Kaat to the Philadelphia Phillies, but Hemond said he held off until after the team's sale because Kaat was the favorite player of the outgoing owner, John Allyn. Kaat became a Hall of Famer, but don't look for any others on the list of players in those deals:

- Kaat and minor league shortstop Mike Buskey to Philadelphia for pitchers Dick Ruthven and Roy Thomas and outfielder Alan Bannister.
- Third baseman Bill Melton and pitcher Steve Dunning to California for first baseman Jim Spencer and outfielder Morris Nettles.
- Outfielder Ken Henderson and pitchers Ruthven and Dan Osborn to Atlanta for outfielder Ralph Garr and shortstop Larvell Blanks.
- Blanks to Cleveland for second baseman Jack Brohamer.
- Pitcher Rich Hinton and catcher Jeff Sovern to Cincinnati for reliever Clay Carroll.
- Infielder BeeBee Richards to St. Louis for outfielder Buddy Bradford and pitcher Steve Terlecky.

Veeck and Hemond were shuffling deck chairs until the last minute. Nowlin wrote that Hemond said Veeck told him at 10:15 p.m. on the final night of the meetings, "We're going to make four deals by midnight." That was the deadline. And they made it, with seconds to spare.

Not everyone was impressed. Whitey Herzog, the Kansas City Royals' manager, told *The Kansas City Star*: "I can't believe what the White Sox did. They did a lot of swapping, but I can't see how they helped themselves." From Herzog's perspective, the White Sox wound up with too many left-handed hitters and no one, really, to play center field. Herzog wasn't wrong. The retooled White Sox were worse in 1976 than they were in 1975, finishing 64–97 and in last place. Veeck had predicted that the White Sox would draw between 1.2 million and 1.3 million fans—Chicago had not reached that level since 1965—but official attendance was instead 914,945.

The crazy trading was not a total loss, however. Although the 1977 White Sox became known as the South Side Hit Men after rental sluggers Richie Zisk and Oscar Gamble and newly acquired Eric Soderholm provided unheard-of power in Comiskey Park, some of the previous season's trade acquisitions also helped Chicago surge to a 90–72 record. Bannister moved from the outfield to shortstop (although he did make 40 errors). Garr hit .300. Spencer won a Gold Glove at first base and added an unexpected 18 home runs. Brohamer was a useful infield backup.

"Undoubtedly, they will say I'm making a travesty of trading," Veeck said of his peers in baseball. "But the game is fun." It's not as if the rest of Major League Baseball was standing pat; 17 other deals involving 42 players were concluded at the 1975 winter meetings. And there was precedent for such maneuvering at the winter meetings. Including by the White Sox.

On the opening day of the winter meetings in 1954, Chicago's general manager, Frank Lane, sharply criticized the 17-player swap between the Baltimore Orioles and the New York Yankees that had taken place in mid–November, as Bill Felber recounted in *Baseball's Business: The Winter Meetings: 1901–1957*. That megadeal sent Bob Turley and Don Larsen, among many others, to New York. "I would have asked as much for Jack Harshman [a White Sox starting pitcher who could also hit] as Richards received for Bob Turley, Don Larsen and Billy Hunter combined," Lane said. He contended that the Orioles, who had just finished next to last in their first year in Baltimore, had "traded away the only worthwhile things they had." But before the day was over, Lane had consummated a seven-player trade himself … with the Orioles. Lane sent pitchers Don Ferrarese and Don Johnson, catcher Matt Batts and second baseman Fred Marsh to Baltimore for catcher Clint Courtney, shortstop Jim Brideweser and pitcher Bob Chakales. Not an All-Star in the bunch. And the same day, Lane brokered a five-player deal with the Tigers.

Thirty. December 12

This was, of course, Lane's M.O., one sliver of evidence for his earning the nicknames Trader Lane and Frantic Frank. He was the general manager for five teams and made 414 transactions involving at least 690 players over a decade and a half. In his seven seasons with the White Sox, Lane made 241 deals involving 353 players, *Sports Illustrated* said in 1968.

Making news at the winter meetings was a staple for Veeck, too, even when he wasn't trading player after player. In fact, Veeck, then the owner of the Cleveland Indians, made news by *blocking* trades at the 1948 winter meetings, just months after his team had won the World Series. The Yankees, the White Sox, the Athletics, the Browns and the Tigers were all trying to make deals, and New York Giants Manager Leo Durocher was open to trading many of his players, Gary Levy related in *Baseball's Business: The Winter Meetings: 1901–1957*. None materialized as Veeck maneuvered to prevent his American League rivals from improving. According to Levy, "Every time one of the better clubs in his circuit steps out to make a deal, the dynamic Cleveland owner throws a block with a better offer," one sportswriter wrote. But Cleveland never made a trade itself; it merely got in the way.

Veeck was a player at the winter meetings even when trades were not the focus. In 1952, he was owner of the Browns. (Yes, he kept buying and selling teams; Veeck was an owner of teams four times, on and off from 1946 to 1980, but never for more than five seasons at a time.) He wrote in *Veeck as in Wreck* that he had announced his acquisition in July 1951 by having installed a canvas streamer at the Browns' ballpark, Sportsman's Park, that read: "OPEN FOR BUSINESS UNDER NEW OWNERSHIP." By mid-month, he had signed Satchel Paige. At the winter meetings in 1952, he cemented his gadfly status by making two proposals. The first would have prohibited Major League teams from signing amateur players in that pre-draft era, so only minor league teams would have been able to, and a Major League team would then have had to draft minor league players, Gregory H. Wolf wrote in *Baseball's Business: The Winter Meetings: 1901–1957*. The second proposal would have shrunk Major League rosters in midseason to 23 players from 25. These ideas were so unpopular that the first was voted down without any discussion and the second never came to a vote; Commissioner Ford Frick did not permit one.

Until the end of his career in baseball, Veeck continued to make headlines at the winter meetings. In 1980, he tried to sell the White Sox to Edward DeBartolo, Sr., who had previously bought the NFL's San Francisco 49ers and the NHL's Pittsburgh Penguins and had tried in vain to buy a Major League team. He failed again in October 1980, when the owners rejected his bid for the White Sox. Critics, who included Commissioner Bowie Kuhn, were wary of DeBartolo's ties to gambling; he owned horse racing tracks. (David Condon of *The Chicago Tribune* pointed out the inconsistency of that stance: The Pittsburgh Pirates owner John W. Galbreath was the owner of two Kentucky Derby winners and was said to have offered Pete Rose some thoroughbreds while trying to lure Rose to the Pirates. DeBartolo addressed the issue himself, telling *The Tribune*: "Kuhn is worried so much about the association with a sport in which there is gambling. Well, why doesn't he do a study of how much is bet on baseball? I'll tell him right now that it's far more than is bet on horse racing.") There were also whispers that DeBartolo—an Italian American from Youngstown, Ohio, which *The Saturday Evening Post* once called "Crimetown U.S.A."—had mob ties.

The October veto and the behind-the-scenes sniping aside, Veeck was anxious to sell his team, so he asked his fellow owners at the winter meetings to reconsider a sale to DeBartolo. There was no John Fetzer in Veeck's corner this time: Only three of the 14 AL owners voted to approve DeBartolo; 10 votes were needed, and the $20 million sale was off. "I suppose my Italian heritage may have been a factor in losing," DeBartolo said, which Kuhn stiffly disputed. "There is no question about his decency," Kuhn said. "There is nothing in his background that haunts us."

New suitors quickly emerged. And that's how Jerry Reinsdorf became a co-owner of the Chicago White Sox. It was 25 years before the White Sox won a World Series. They have had a winning record in only 20 of Reinsdorf's first 44 seasons.

As for DeBartolo? In his 23 years owning the 49ers, San Francisco won five Super Bowls. And his Penguins won the Stanley Cup in 1991.

Thirty-One

December 21

The Seldom-Seen Winter of Baseball

Baseball winter is longer than calendar winter. Baseball winter begins with November, after the World Series ends, and persists until mid–February, when teams report to spring training. That is about 15 weeks, an excruciating wait that exceeds the 12-week march toward spring for calendar winter. The Hot Stove League may be appropriately named for winter baseball contemplation, but it can't do enough to warm the souls of baseball fans.

Maybe this overlong winter explains why baseball has turned its back on Winter. Or more precisely, players named Winter. Or Winters. A single player named Winter has graced a Major League roster; only four players named Winters have, according to *Baseball Reference*. There has been the occasional Snow (J.T.) or Frost (Dave) or even, to stretch a point, Freese (Dave, Gene and George), but they are not the dreaded Winter. Who were those Winter outliers? Mostly players who weren't *born* in winter. And whose careers turned cold pretty quickly.

George Winter, pitcher, 1901–1908. Winter and the future Hall of Famer Eddie Plank were teammates on the Gettysburg College baseball team in 1901, sharing pitching and outfield duties even though they were not actually attending Gettysburg College. They were enrolled in the Preparatory Department of Gettysburg College, Winter's SABR *Bio Project* biography says, which, under the arcane rules of the day, was good enough to play college ball. Winter was a 23-year-old right-hander and Plank a 25-year-old left-hander that season, but neither finished it on the college team. Plank was signed by the Philadelphia Athletics' Connie Mack, who declined to add Winter, his SABR biography says, because of his size—5 feet 8½ inches and 133 pounds. A mistrust of small pitchers has apparently always been a part of the game. The Boston Americans overlooked Winter's size, however, and on June 15, the little guy known as Sassafrass—sassafras was a flavoring in root beer, and a lively player had sassafras—made his Major League debut.

Over three weeks' time, Winter won his first six starts, with a 2.00 ERA. In his seventh start, Winters squared off against Plank—and picked up the victory in a rain-shortened game. Four days later, however, Winter lost to Plank when he gave up six runs and 14 hits in seven innings. The rest of the season was similarly up and down, with Winter allowing at least six runs nine times in his next 21 starts. (Given the state of defense, there *were* plenty of unearned runs in there—30 of the 66 runs Winter allowed in those nine starts. Another reason ERAs of the Deadball Era look so good to us now.) His success having deteriorated, Winter was acquired on waivers in 1908 by the Tigers, who just happened to have a pitcher named Ed Summers. "Spring and Fall have yet to come to terms," *The Sporting Life* reported.

Nip Winters, pitcher, 1923–29, 1932

Shades of Glory: The Negro Leagues and the Story of African-American Baseball says that Winters "is considered by many the best pitcher of the Eastern Colored League," an early Black Major League. In *Voices from the Great Black Baseball Leagues,* the veteran Negro leaguer Newt Allen said of Winters that "oh, he was a tough man"—praise for a pitcher who beat Allen's Kansas City Monarchs three times in the first Black baseball World Series in 1924. *Baseball Reference* shows Winters leading the ECL in wins four consecutive seasons, 1923 to 1926, with records of 10–3, 20–5, 17–8 and 17–4. His four-year totals: 64–20 (a .762 winning percentage) with a 2.81 ERA. But that may understate Winters's accomplishments. *Shades of Glory* reports Winters's records in his first three seasons at 32–6, 19–5 and 21–10, including two no-hitters. "With numbers like these," according to *Shades of Glory,* "it is no surprise that he led his club to pennants all three years." His career ended at the age of 32, hastened, his *Baseball Reference Bullpen* page suggests, by struggles with alcoholism.

Matt Winters, first baseman-outfielder, 1989. Winters was one of the Yankees' three first-round draft picks in 1978, ahead of a guy the Orioles tapped in the second round: Cal Ripken, Jr. First-round selection notwithstanding, his hopes were never too high. "My first big-league spring training, you're sitting there with Dave Winfield, Steve Kemp, Ken Griffey, Sr., and Lou Piniella in the outfield," Winters told *The Athletic* in 2021. "OK, I got no chance." He was a solid minor league hitter—pretty good average (.275), pretty good power (190 homers), pretty good eye (more than 100 walks in two seasons)—but he was right, and he was never a Yankee. His one Major League season came with the Royals, and it had taken 1,255 minor league games to get there. "I wouldn't say I was intimidated, but watching George Brett and Bo Jackson take BP, I'm going: 'Holy mackerel. This is a different league,'" Winters said.

So he wound up trying a really different league: Japan's Pacific League. He became a star as a Nippon Ham Fighter in five seasons in Japan, bashing 160 homers. And he became a beloved figure, entertaining the fans during rain delays. He also improved his lot financially. "My first purchase after I got drafted to the big leagues was a color TV," Winters told *The Athletic*. "My first purchase after going to Japan was a house." In 2023, he was still working for Nippon Ham, scouting American players who might be the next Matt Winters.

Jesse Winters, pitcher, 1919–23. Jesse Winters was, at least, born in the winter. Though barely: on December 22, 1893. He earned the nickname T-Bone, according to *The Flash Today*, a news site in Stephenville, Texas, his hometown, because of his appreciation for a T-bone steak. *The Flash Today* said that when Winters was on a road trip with the baseball team for what is now Tarleton State University, he ordered a T-bone—and was sorely disappointed when the steak he was served came without a bone. He raised a fuss and earned a nickname that stuck with him for life. As a Major Leaguer, he had the dubious distinction of being the best pitcher for the 1921 Phillies, who finished 51–103. Winters had the best ERA (3.63) and ERA+ (116) of any Philadelphia pitcher with at least 60 innings, but all it earned him was a 5–10 record. It was a soft-tossing era, but he apparently could not strike out a tackling dummy; he whiffed 22 of the 509 batters he faced, a paltry 4.3 percent.

Clarence Winters, pitcher, 1924. One of his nicknames was Chilly. It would have made for great headlines if only Major League hitters had not heated up against him. The 1924 Red Sox were not very good (67–87), and Winters, a late-season call-up, fit right in. Boston was playing five doubleheaders in six days, and in the second of those twin bills, he gave the Athletics one hit and no runs in the first three innings while being staked to a 7–0 lead. And then before he could record another out, Winters gave up four runs and was out of the game. Two days later, he started again and was worse: Winters allowed six runs in an inning and a third. Two days later, another doubleheader, another disaster: three runs in two-thirds of an inning of relief. He had an additional day to recover before his next appearance, but it didn't help: He gave up seven hits and three runs in two more innings of relief. His total for the four games: seven innings, 16 runs, a 20.57 ERA, an ERA+ of 22. Of the 48 Major League batters he faced, Winters retired only 22 of them. Opponents' batting average: .512. Subsequent Major League games: zero.

Bibliography

Alou, Felipe, with Peter Kerasotis. *Alou: My Baseball Journey*. Lincoln: University of Nebraska Press, 2018.
Bevis, Charlie. *Baseball Under the Lights: The Rise of the Night Game*. Jefferson, NC: McFarland, 2021.
_____. *Red Sox vs. Braves in Boston: The Battle for Fans' Hearts, 1901–1952*. Jefferson, NC: McFarland, 2017.
Boswell, Thomas. *Why Time Begins on Opening Day*. New York: Doubleday, 1984.
Bouton, Jim. *Ball Four*. New York: Dell, 1970.
Boxerman, Burton A., and Benita W. Boxerman. *George Weiss: Architect of the Golden Age Yankees*. Jefferson, NC: McFarland, 2016.
Bryant, Howard. *Shut Out: A Story of Race and Baseball in Boston*. Boston: Beacon Press, 2002.
Carney, Gene. *Burying the Black Sox: How Baseball's Cover-Up of the 1919 World Series Fix Almost Succeeded*. Dulles, VA: Potomac Books, 2006.
Cramer, Richard Ben. *Joe DiMaggio: The Hero's Life*. New York: Simon & Schuster, 2000.
Creamer, Robert W. *Babe: The Legend Comes to Life*. New York: Simon & Schuster, 1974.
_____. *Stengel: His Life and Times*. New York: Simon & Schuster, 1984.
Crissey, Harrington E., Jr. *Teenagers, Graybeards, and 4-Fs*. Sharon Hill, PA: Archway Press, 1981.
DeValeria, Dennis, and Jeanne Burke DeValeria. *Honus Wagner: A Biography*. Pittsburgh: University of Pittsburgh Press, 1995.
Dickson, Paul. *The Dickson Baseball Dictionary*, 3d ed. New York: W.W. Norton, 2011.
Faber, Charles F., and Richard B. Faber. *Spitballers: The Last Legal Hurlers of the Wet One*. Jefferson, NC: McFarland, 2006.
Fountain, Charles. *Under the March Sun: The Story of Spring Training*. New York: Oxford University Press, 2009.
Fuchs, Robert S., and Wayne Soini. *Judge Fuchs and the Boston Braves, 1923–35*. Jefferson, NC: McFarland, 1998.
Gietschier, Steven P. *Baseball: The Turbulent Midcentury Years*. Lincoln: University of Nebraska Press, 2023.
Goldstein, Richard. *Spartan Seasons: How Baseball Survived the Second World War*. New York: Macmillan, 1980.
Green, G. Michael, and Roger D. Launius. *Charlie Finley: The Outrageous Story of Baseball's Super Showman*. New York: Walker, 2010.
Heffron, Joe, and Jack Heffron. *The Local Boys: Hometown Players for the Cincinnati Reds*. Birmingham, AL: Clerisy Press, 2014.
Hodges, Jeremy K., and Bill Nowlin, editors. *Base Ball's 19th Century Winter Meetings, 1857–1900*. Phoenix: Society for American Baseball Research, 2018.
Hogan, Lawrence D. *Shades of Glory: The Negro Leagues and the Story of African American Baseball*. Washington, D.C.: National Geographic, 2006.
Holway, John. *Voices from the Great Black Baseball Leagues*, Revised Edition. Mineola, NY: Dover, 2010.

Hopkins, Lyman. *The Real Book About Baseball*. Garden City, NY: Garden City, 1951.
James, Bill. *The Bill James Historical Baseball Abstract*. New York: Villard, 1986.
_____. *The New Bill James Historical Baseball Abstract*. New York: Free Press, 2001.
_____. *The Politics of Glory: How Baseball's Hall of Fame Really Works*. New York: Macmillan, 1994.
Kelley, Brent. *Baseball's Bonus Babies*. Jefferson, NC: McFarland, 2006.
Kepner, Tyler. *K: A History of Baseball in Ten Pitches*. New York: Anchor Books, 2019.
Kinsella, W.P. *Shoeless Joe*. New York: Ballantine Books, 1982.
Klein, Alan. *Dominican Baseball: New Pride, Old Prejudice*. Philadelphia: Temple University Press, 2014.
Kuhn, Bowie. *Hardball: The Education of a Baseball Commissioner*. Lincoln: Bison Books, 1997.
Leerhsen, Charles. *Ty Cobb: A Terrible Beauty*. New York: Simon & Schuster, 2015.
Lester, Larry. *Black Baseball's National Showcase: The East-West All-Star Game 1933–1962*, Expanded Version. Kansas City: NoirTech Research, 2020.
Levitt, Daniel R. *The Outlaw League and the Battle That Forged Modern Baseball*. Chicago: Ivan R. Dee, 2012.
Martin, Brian. *Barney Dreyfuss: Pittsburgh's Baseball Titan*. Jefferson, NC: McFarland, 2021.
McGregor, Robert Kuhn. *A Calculus of Color: The Integration of Baseball's American League*. Jefferson, NC: McFarland, 2015.
Moffi, Roger, and Jonathan Kronstadt. *Crossing the Line: Black Major Leaguers, 1947–1959*. Iowa City: University of Iowa Press, 1994.
Moore, Jack B. *Joe DiMaggio: Baseball's Yankee Clipper*. Westport, CT: Praeger, 1986.
Neyer, Rob, and Bill James. *The Neyer/James Guide to Pitching*. New York: Touchstone, 2004.
Nowlin, Bill. *Tom Yawkey: Patriarch of the Boston Red Sox*. Lincoln: University of Nebraska Press, 2018.
Okrent, Daniel. *Nine Innings*. New York: Ticknor & Fields, 1985.
Peary, Danny. *We Played the Game: 65 Players Remember Baseball's Greatest Era, 1947–65*. New York: Hyperion, 1994.
Perry, Gaylord, with Bob Sudyk. *Me and the Spitter*. New York: Berkley, 1974.
Posnanski, Joe. *The Baseball 100*. New York: Avid Reader, 2021.
Rapp, David. *Tinker to Evers to Chance: The Chicago Cubs and the Dawn of Modern America*. Chicago: University of Chicago Press, 2018.
Ritter, Lawrence S. *The Glory of Their Times: The Story of the Early Days of Baseball Told by the Men Who Played It*. New York: Collier Books, 1966.
Ruck, Rob. *The Tropic of Baseball: Baseball in the Dominican Republic*. Lincoln: Bison Books, 1999.
Scimonelli, Paul. *Joe Cambria: International Super Scout of the Washington Senators*. Jefferson, NC: McFarland, 2023.
Seidel, Michael. *Streak: Joe DiMaggio and the Summer of '41*. New York: Penguin Books, 1988.
Snelling, Dennis. *Johnny Evers: A Baseball Life*. Jefferson, NC: McFarland, 2014.
Spatz, Lyle. *Dixie Walker: A Life in Baseball*. Jefferson, NC: McFarland, 2011.
_____. *Hugh Casey: The Triumphs and Tragedies of a Brooklyn Dodger*. Lanham, MD: Rowman & Littlefield, 2017.
Stevens, Ed. *The Other Side of the Jackie Robinson Story*. Mustang, OK: Tate, 2010.
Stockton, J. Roy. *The Gashouse Gang and a Couple of Other Guys*. New York: A.S. Barnes, 1949.
Thorn, John, and John Holway. *The Pitcher*. Hoboken, NJ: Prentice Hall, 1988.
Tygiel, Jules. *Baseball's Great Experiment: Jackie Robinson and His Legacy*. New York: Oxford University Press, 1983.
Veeck, Bill, with Ed Linn. *Veeck as in Wreck*. New York: Simon & Schuster, 1962.
Waldo, Ronald T. *The 1902 Pittsburgh Pirates: Treachery and Triumph*. Jefferson, NC: McFarland, 2015.

Bibliography

Weingarden, Steve, and Bill Nowlin, editors. *Baseball's Business: The Winter Meetings: 1901–1957.* Phoenix: Society for American Baseball Research, 2016.

_____, and _____. *Baseball's Business: The Winter Meetings: 1958–2016.* Phoenix: Society for American Baseball Research, 2017.

Wulff, Rick, editorial director. *The Baseball Encyclopedia,* Ninth Edition. New York: Macmillan, 1993.

Periodicals

Akron Beacon Journal, Associated Press, Baseball America, Baseball Digest, Baseball Magazine, Baseball Research Journal, Boston Globe, Boston Herald, Brooklyn Eagle, Cape (Delaware) Gazette, Chicago Sun-Times, Chicago Tribune, Cincinnati Daily Star, Cincinnati Enquirer, Cincinnati Evening Star, Cleveland Leader, Cleveland News, Cleveland Press, Columbia Business Law Review, Columbus (Ohio) Dispatch, Coral Gables Magazine, Dayton (Ohio) Daily News, Dayton (Ohio) Herald, Detroit Free Press, Elmira (New York) Star-Gazette, Enid (Oklahoma) News & Eagle, Forbes, Fort Worth Star-Telegram, Guardian, Hartford Courant, Hattiesburg (Mississippi) American, Indianapolis Star, Ironton (Ohio) Tribune, Kansas City Star, Kenosha (Wisconsin) News, Lafayette (Indiana) Journal and Courier, Lexington (Kentucky) Herald-Leader, Long Beach (California) Independent, Los Angeles Times, Louisville (Kentucky) Courier-Journal, Lubbock (Texas) Avalanche-Journal, Marquette Sports Law Review, Michigan History Magazine, Milwaukee Journal, Muncie (Indiana) Star-Press, Nashville Banner, NEA, New York Clipper, New York Daily News, New York Evening World, New York Journal-American, New York Times, Newsday, North American Review, Northeast Popular Culture Association, Oakland Tribune, Philadelphia Daily News, Philadelphia Inquirer, Philadelphia Record, (Cleveland) Plain Dealer, Rochester (New York) Democrat & Chronicle, St. Louis Post-Dispatch, St. Petersburg Times, Saturday Evening Post, Seattle Post-Intelligencer, Seattle Times, Sporting Life, Sports Illustrated, (Newark) Star-Ledger, Time, Tacoma (Washington) News-Tribune, Tampa Bay Times, (Nashville) Tennessean, United Press, University of Texas Review of Entertainment and Sports Law, USA Today, Washington Evening Star, Washington Herald, Washington Post.

Websites

Arkansas Baseball Encyclopedia, Armory Power Pitching Academy, The Athletic, Baseball Almanac, Baseball Catchers, BaseballGuru, Baseball Hall of Fame, The Baseball Impurist, Baseball in Wartime, Baseball Prospectus, Baseball Reference, BatDigest.com, Cardinals Journal, CBS.com, Cronkite News, Cross Screen Media, Diamonds in the Dusk, ESPN.com, ESPN Deportes, Fangraphs, Fenway Fanatics, The Flash Today, The Great Game, Hardball Times, History.com, Medium, Milb.com, MLB.com, The (Mostly) Complete List of Knuckleball Pitchers, Newspapers.com, 19th Century Base Ball, The Pecan Park Eagle, Pittsburgh Baseball History, Retrosheet, RetroSimba, RIPBaseball, SB Nation, Society for American Baseball Research, Society for American Baseball Research Bio Project, Spotrac, Statista, STLRedbirds.com, StudioGaryC.com, Twins Almanac, USA Baseball, Who's Who in Montgomery County (Indiana), YouTube.

Index

Aaron, Henry 53, 58, 127, 160
Abrams, C.J. 184
Acuña, Ronald Jr. 208
Akron Acorns 98
Alexander, Grover Cleveland 106
Alexander, Matt 9–10
All-American Girls Professional Baseball League 30, 141
All-Star Baseball board game 71
All-Star Game 130–141, 192, 200–201
Allegheny City 45
Allen, Dick 127
Allen, Ethan 71–72
Allen, Newt 218
Allyn, John 213
Alomar, Roberto 132
Alou, Felipe 160, 180
Alou, Jesus 180
Alou, Matty 57
Alston, Tom 160
Alston, Walter 114
Altman, George 160
Alvarado, José 209
Alvarez, Yordan 209
Amaro, Ruben 160
Amateur Baseball League 189
Amateur draft 88, 117, 183
American Association (major league) 45, 85, 98, 188
American Association (minor league) 21, 32, 92, 104, 154, 174
American League 32, 33, 34, 35, 36, 39, 45, 47, 62, 66, 86, 102, 108, 122, 130–132, 149, 154, 157–159, 165–166, 168, 187–188, 191–192, 194, 201, 212
Amoros, Sandy 159
Anderson, Sparky 43, 46, 94, 125
Anderson, William M. 185
Anderson Packers 55
Angell, Roger 1
Angelos, Peter 125

Aparicio, Luis 12, 170
Appling, Luke 51
Aragón, Angel 112
Aragón, Jack 112
Archer, Jimmy 106
Arizona Diamondbacks 162, 205, 210
Armbrister, Ed 125–126
Arnovich, Morrie 112
artificial turf 12
Asbury Park, New Jersey 25–26
Astroth, Joe 202
Atlanta Braves 11, 17, 94, 194, 208–209, 213; *see also* Boston Bees; Boston Braves; Milwaukee Braves
Atlanta Crackers 60
Atlantic City, New Jersey 26
August, Don 94
Aurora Indians 124
Averill, Earl (father) 53, 140
Averill, Earl (son) 140
Avery, Steve 11
Avila, Ralph 179
Ayers, Doc 20

The Babe Ruth Story 76, 83
Babe: The Legend Comes to Life 14
Baer, Arthur (Bugs) 102
Bagby, Charles 144–145
Bagby, Jim, Jr. 142, 144–145
Bagby, Jim, Sr. 142
Baker, Gene 160
Baker, Home Run 47–48, 90
Baker, Jesse 107
Baker, Jim 188
Baker Bowl 71, 132
Ball Four 53, 61, 193
Ball State Teachers College 25
Baltimore Orioles (American Association, major league) 45, 98
Baltimore Orioles (early American League) 66

Baltimore Orioles (later American League) 40, 86, 87, 117, 128, 146, 160, 183, 214, 218; *see also* Milwaukee Brewers (early American League); St. Louis Browns
Baltimore Orioles (minor league) 32, 39
Baltimore Terrapins 33
Bancroft, Dave 89
Bando, Sal 9
Bankhead, Dan 159
Banks, Ernie 116, 160
Bannister, Alan 213–214
Barber, Red 59, 192
Barkley, Charles 61
Barnes, Donald 34
Barnes, Frank 160
Barnett, Larry 125
Barnum, P.T. 167
Bartell, Dick 73, 134
Baseball (book) 110
baseball academies 177–191
Baseball Almanac 177, 191
Baseball America 182
baseball antitrust status 33, 35
Baseball Digest 19, 108
Baseball Encyclopedia 2, 4, 97, 100, 114, 122
baseball expansion 38, 212
Baseball Hall of Fame 12, 15, 71, 73, 86, 130, 132, 134, 143, 186, 197
baseball integration 2, 37, 38, 50, 60, 146–160
Baseball Magazine 19, 130, 173
baseball on TV 192–193
The Baseball 100 1
Baseball Reference 4
Battey, Earl 160
Battle of Marathon 65
Battle of Menotomy 65
Batts, Matt 214
Baumholtz, Frank 50
Beamon, Charlie 160
Bear Mountain, New York 24
Beattie, Jim 128–129
Becquer, Julio 160
Bedford, Indiana 25
Bellamy, Robert V. Jr. 192
Beltre, Adrian 179
Bendix, William 76
Bendy and the Ink Machine 99
Bennett, Joe 108
Benswanger, William 36
Berg, Moe 111
Berger, Wally 134
Bergman, Ron 9
Berle, Milton 38
Bernier, Carlos 160

Berra, Yogi 75, 141
Best Interests of Baseball Clause 2, 13, 15, 17, 168
Bethel College 63
Bi-State League 105
Biancalana, Buddy 119
Biggio, Craig 75
Bigler, Ivan (Pete) 106–107
Bilko, Steve 115
The Bill James Historical Baseball Abstract 1
Birmingham Barons 149
Birmingham Black Barons 149
Bishop, Hunter 184
Bivin, Jim 74
Black, Joe 159
Black ballplayers 2, 12, 130, 146–160
Blades, Ray 196–197
Blanks, Larvell 213
Bleday, JJ 184
Bloomington, Indiana 24, 25
Blue, Vida 14–16
Blue Ridge League 93
Blues Stadium 40
Boggs, Wade 129
Bohl, Hap 110
Bonds, Barry 21
Bonura, Zeke 73
bonus baby players and rules 88, 90
Booth, Clark 158
Bosse Field 27
Bostic, Joe 148
Boston Beaneaters 66
Boston Bees 36, 134; *see also* Atlanta Braves; Boston Braves; Milwaukee Braves
Boston Braves 4, 18, 20–21, 24, 27, 31, 35–36, 40, 50–54, 63, 66, 71–72, 78, 79, 80, 82, 89, 109, 113, 121–122, 134, 150, 160; *see also* Atlanta Braves; Boston Bees; Milwaukee Braves; Miracle Braves
Boston Bruins 150
Boston Celtics 150, 154
Boston Marathon 65–67
Boston Red Sox 2–3, 11, 13–16, 21, 29, 31, 35–37, 43, 54, 65–67, 69, 80, 89, 93, 110–111, 114–115, 119, 125, 128, 140–141, 146–160, 175, 185, 187–190, 192, 203, 217, 219; integration 37, 146–160; Royal Rooters 189
Boswell, Thomas 1, 43
Bouchee, Ed 41
Boudreau, Lou 139, 144, 201
Bouton, Jim 193
Bowman, Joe 74
Boyd, Bob 160

Index

Boyle, Jim 109
The Boys of Summer (book) 92, 137
The Boys of Summer (song) 92
Bradford, Buddy 213
Bradley, Bill 122
Bradley, George 123
Bragan, Bobby 57
Branca, Ralph 56
Brandt, Bill 26
Bransfield, Kitty 174
Braves Field 36, 38, 52, 81
Breadon, Sam 34, 82
Brenegan, Sam 104–105
Brennan, Will 162
Bresnahan, Roger 107
Bressler, Raymond (Rube) 194
Bressoud, Eddie 155
Brett, George 119, 219
Brideweser, Jim 214
Bridges, Marshall 160
Bridwell, Al 172
Briggs, Walter O. 152
Briggs Stadium 27
Britt, Jim 37
Britton, Helene 28
Brock, Lou 41
Broeg, Bob 197–198
Broglio, Ernie 41
Brohamer, Jack 213–214
The Bronx Home News 135
Brooklyn Dodgers 18, 21, 24–25, 31–32, 40, 50, 54–59, 60–62, 69, 72, 75, 112–114, 134, 148–151, 153, 159, 192; *see also* Brooklyn Grooms; Brooklyn Robins; Brooklyn Superbas; Los Angeles Dodgers
Brooklyn Grooms 46
Brooklyn Robins 20, 163–164
Brooklyn Superbas 66, 100
Brooklyn Ward's Wonders 85
Brosius, Scott 205
Brouthers, Dan 126
Brown, Gates 8
Brown, Larry 118
Brown, Mordecai (Three Finger) 173
Brown, Willard 160
Brush, John 88, 191
Bruton, Billy 127, 160
Bryant, Bear 62
Bryant, Howard 148–150, 154, 158–159
Bryant, Kris 208
Bumgarner, Madison 207
Bunning, Jim 117
Burdette, Lew 21, 72
Burgess, Smoky 8, 83
Burnett, A.J. 121
Burr, Tom 105

Burton, Ellis 160
Busby, Steve 124
Busch, Gussie 153
Busch Brewery Company 35
Buschhorn, Don 118
Buscones 180–182
Bush, Bullet Joe 16, 89
Bush, George H.W. 71
Bush, Guy 79–80, 82–83
Buskey, Mike 213
Buster Brown shoes 170
Byrd, Samuel (Babe Ruth's Legs) 76, 191

Cactus League 3
Cadore, Leon 164
Cain, Bob 167, 169
Cain, Lorenzo 207
Cain, Matt 206
Caldwell, Ray 20
California Angels 86, 213; *see also* Los Angeles Angels
Callison, Johnny 117
Cambria, Joe 178
Camilli, Dolph 72
Campanella, Roy 56, 91, 159
Campbell, Gilly 76
Campbell, Mike 92
Campos, Roberto 184
Cape Girardeau, Missouri 24
Capone, Al 28
Carney, Gene 191
Carpenter, Hick 45
Carroll, Clay 213
Carroll, Dorsey (Dixie) 63
Casey, Hugh 58–59, 114
Castellanos, Nick 209
Castilla, Vinny 126–127
Castillo, Luis 186
Castino, Vince 202
Castro, Fidel 178
Cedeño, César 179
Central League 174
Central Park Zoo 161
Cepeda, Orlando 160
Chakales, Bob 214
Chamberlain, Joba 163
Chance, Frank 105
Chandler, A.B. (Happy) 150, 159
Chapman, Ben 55, 137–138, 151
Chapman, Ray 2, 106
Chapman College 95
Chávez, Hugo 182–183
Chesbro, Jack 19, 59
Chicago Black Sox 89, 108; *see also* Chicago White Sox
Chicago Cubs 19, 21, 24, 28–29, 33, 41, 47,

54, 64, 69, 77, 82–83, 87, 93, 96, 106, 108, 113, 116, 131, 133, 136–137, 139, 160, 165, 172–173, 184, 189, 196, 200, 203, 207–208
Chicago Green Sox 33
Chicago Orphans 45
The Chicago Tribune 130–131
Chicago White Sox 4, 18–21, 24, 26, 29, 61, 63–64, 70, 92, 94, 105–106, 108, 127, 131, 135, 138–139, 147–148, 160, 162, 165–166, 184, 189, 191, 201, 211–216; *see also* Chicago Black Sox
Chiozza, Dino 71
Chiozza, Lou 71
The Choate School 24
Choo, Shin-Soo 162
Christensen, Walter (Cuckoo) 194
Christopher, Joe 156, 160
Cicotte, Eddie 92–93, 107, 191
Cieradkowski, Gary 107
Cimoli, Gino 169
Cincinnati Reds 15, 18, 20, 23–27, 36, 43, 45–46, 51, 53, 61, 68–71, 74–75, 77, 81–83, 94–95, 100, 110, 113, 116, 119–121, 124–125, 133, 135, 146, 153, 160, 163, 184, 189, 191–194, 196–197, 199–200, 202, 213
Citi Field 161
Civil War 212
Clark, Will 95
Clarke, Fred 82, 101, 104, 173
Clarkson, Buzz 160
Clarkson, John (Dad) 95
Clase, Emmanuel 186
Clear, Mark 119
Clemens, Doug 41
Clemente, Roberto 160
Cleveland, Grover 106
Cleveland Bears 95
Cleveland Blues 122
Cleveland Browns 95
Cleveland Buckeyes 95
Cleveland Cubs 95
Cleveland Elites 95
Cleveland Giants 95
Cleveland Guardians 162–163; *see also* Cleveland Blues; Cleveland Indians; Cleveland Naps
Cleveland Hornets 95
Cleveland Indians 10, 20, 25–26, 37, 61, 87, 106, 110–111, 118, 139, 140–145, 159–160, 165, 189, 192–193, 200–202, 207–208, 211, 213, 215; *see also* Cleveland Blues; Cleveland Guardians; Cleveland Naps
Cleveland Naps 64
Cleveland Red Sox 95
Cleveland Spiders 32, 99
Cleveland Stars 95
Cleveland Tate Grays 95
Cleveland Tigers 95
Cobb, Ty 102, 107, 130, 194
Cobbledick, Gordon 203
Coffey, John Joseph 101–103
Cohen, Andy 72
Colavito, Rocky 56
Coleman, Vince 12
College of the Holy Cross 101, 111
Collins, Eddie 103, 147–148, 158
Collins, Ray 54
Collins, Terry 207
Colombia 183, 186
Colorado Rockies 127, 194
Columbia University 192
Columbian League 33
Columbus Buckeyes 45, 98
Columbus Red Birds 69
Combs, Earle 55
Comiskey Park 70, 131, 165, 170, 214
Concord Hymn 65
Condon, David 211, 216
Conroy, Wid 122
Cooper, Chuck 150
Cooper, Mort 53–54
Cooper, Walker 53, 111–112
Corriden, John 113–114
Corriden, John (Red) 113–114
Corridon, Frank 19
Cotton States League 106, 108
County Stadium (Milwaukee) 35
Courtney, Clint 115, 214
Coveleski, Stan 20
Covington, Wes 117, 160
Cox, Billy 91
Craft, Harry 75
Cramer, Richard Ben 142, 144
Crandall, Del 72
Cratty, A.R. 188
Creamer, Robert 14, 16, 163–164
Crisp, Coco 162–163
Cronin, Joe 139–140, 148, 150, 158
Crosley Field 68
Crowder, Gen. Enoch 140
Crowe, George 127, 160
Cruz, Deivi 120
Cruz, Julio 12
Cuba 177–178, 184–186
Cuccinello, Tony 134
Culler, Dick 51
Curaçao 186

Daley, Arthur 25, 50, 168
Dallas Eagles 116
Daniels, Bennie 160
Dark, Al 9, 37

Index

Darst, Warren 174
Dartmouth College 128
Daughters, Bob (Red) 110-111
Daughters, Don 111
Dauvray Cup 188
Davis, Al 125
Davis, Eric 163
Davis, Frank Talmadge (Dixie) 62
Davis, George (Iron) 121-122
Davis, Kiddo 73
Davis, Lorenzo (Piper) 150-151
Davis, Otis 114
Davis, Tommy 159
Dayton Veterans 105
Deadball Era 6, 12, 19, 122, 129, 218
Dean, Dizzy 72-74, 77
Deane, Bill 123
DeBartolo, Edward, Sr. 215-216
Deese, Paul 95
Delgado, Carlos 75, 179
Delsing, Jim 2, 167, 169-170
Demaree, Al 89
Demeter, Don 117
Derringer, Paul 75-77
Desautels, Gene 202
designated hitters 7-8
designated runners 7-10
Des Jardien, Shorty 106
Detmer, Reid 121
Detroit Tigers 20-21, 24, 27, 30, 60, 62, 69, 93-94, 100-103, 107, 114, 117-121, 137-139, 151-152, 160, 167-169, 184, 212, 214-215, 218
Devers, Rafael 186
DeWitt, Bill 139
DeWitt Clinton High School 185
Dickey, Bill 140-141
Dickey, R.A. 93
The Dickson Baseball Dictionary 104
Diddley, Bo 87
Digby, George 149
Diloné, Miguel 10
DiMaggio, Joe 2, 51, 142-145, 170; hitting streak 2, 142-145
Dinneen, Bill 190
Dioso, Lino 160
Doak, Bill 20
Doby, Larry 159
Dodger Stadium 208
Dodgertown 153
Doheny, Ed 189
Domínguez, Jasson 183
Dominican Republic 126, 177-191
Dominican Summer League 181
Douglas, Phil 20
Dowling, Pete 122

Downing, Al 58
Drake, Solly 160
Dreyfuss, Barney 19, 21, 82, 90, 104, 174, 188
Dropo, Walt 114
Druery, Charles 92
Dryden, Charles 172
Drysdale, Don 21
Dubuque Packers 118
Dugan, Jimmy 141
Dugan, Joe 16, 89
Duke University 117
Dunning, Steve 213
Durham, Joe 160
Durocher, Leo 50, 56-57, 215
Duvall, Adam 208
Dykes, Jimmy 26, 29-30, 139

Eaddy, Don 160
Easley, Damion 120
East-West All-Star Game 131
Easter, Luke 159
Eastern Colored League 218
Eastern League 152
Eastman, Joseph 24
Ebbets Field 50, 52, 163, 192
Ebert, Bernie 167
Edes, Gordon 67, 213
Edison, Thomas 70
Edwards, Bruce 56
Eisenhower, Dwight 48
Eldred, Cal 141
Elias Sports Bureau 163
Elliott, Bob 51-52
Elliott, Rowdy 106
Emerson, Ralph Waldo 65
Empire State Building 25
Engle, Clyde 175
English, Woody 137
Ennis, Russ (Hack) 109
Erskine, Carl 91
Erstad, Darrin 117
Escalera, Nino 160
Eugene Emeralds 163
Evansville, Indiana 24, 27, 30
Everett, Carl 121
Evers, Joe 103
Evers, Johnny 103, 172-173
Exhibition Stadium 161

Faber, Charles F. 19-20, 22
Faber, Red 18, 20
Faber, Richard B. 20, 22
Fallon, Charlie 101
Falstaff beer 166-167
Familia, Jeurys 207

Faust, Charlie 166
Federal League 16, 33, 103
Federal Reserve Board 130
Felber, Bill 214
Feller, Bob 53, 117, 121, 142, 145
Feller, Jack 117, 140
Fenway Park 14, 27, 35, 65–67, 128, 147, 154, 157
Fernandez, Chico 159
Fernandez, Nanny 51
Fernandez, Tony 179
Ferrarese, Don 214
Ferrell, Rick 140
Ferrell, Wes 140–141
Fetzer, John 212, 216
Fidrych, Mark (The Bird) 163
Field of Dreams 3, 97, 100, 104
Fielder, Cecil 8
Fillingim, Dana 20
Fillmore, Millard 62
Findlay Market 46
Fingers, Rollie 14, 16
Finley, Charlie 8, 12–14, 127
Fisher, Ray 20
Fisk, Carlton 54, 125
Fitzsimmons, Freddie 72
Flood, Curt 17, 33, 160
Florence, Paul 109
Florida 28–29
Florida Marlins 121
Forbes Field 52, 79–80, 104–105, 133
Ford, Whitey 21
Fort Wayne Daisies 141
Fort Wayne Kekiongas 3
Fort Wayne Pistons 55
42 137
Fox, Nellie 170
Foxx, Jimmie 17, 141
Foy, Joe 156
Fraley, Oscar 50
franchise moves 3–4, 31–40
Frazee, Harry 14–15, 35, 80, 89
free agency 14
Freese, Dave 217
Freese, Gene 217
Freese, George 217
French Lick, Indiana 24, 26–29
French Lick Springs Hotel 26, 28–30
Frey, Lonny 73
Frick, Ford 22, 151, 194, 199–200, 215
Frisch, Frankie 26, 132, 139
Frost, Dave 217
Fuchs, Emil 36, 79, 80, 81
Fullerton Union High School 124
Furillo, Carl 56, 91

Gaedel, Eddie, 2–3, 165–170, 211
Gagliano, Phil 118
Gagliano, Ralph 118
Gagne, Matt 206
Galarraga, Armando 121
Galbreath, John W. 36, 216
Gallen, Zac 162
Gamble, Oscar 214
gambling on baseball 3, 44, 187–188, 191, 216
Gandil, Chick 106
Ganter, Jimmy 23
Ganter, Leo 23
Garbark, Bob 202
Garcia, Mike 168
Garr, Ralph 213–214
Gedeon, Elmer 111
Gehrig, Eleanor 138
Gehrig, Lou 80, 85, 89, 137–138, 141
Gehringer, Charlie 138
George, Charles 202
Gessler, Doc 47–48
Gettysburg College 111, 217
Gibson, Bob 160
Giles, Warren 22, 82
Gill, Warren (Doc) 3, 171, 173–174
Gilliam, Jim 159
Gillick, Pat 162
Glavine, Tom 11
Gleason, Bill 160
Gleason, Kid 95
Godfrey, Arthur 38
Goldstein, Richard 24, 199–200
Gomez, Lefty 131, 138, 140
Gomez, Ruben 160
Gonzales, Mark 162
Gonzalez, Luis 205
Gonzalez, Tony 117
Goodman, Billy 115
Goodman, Ival 75–76
Goodwin, Marv 21
Gordon, Joe 139
Gowdy, Curt 37
Graham, Archibald (Moonlight) 2–3, 97, 100–101, 104–105, 109, 114, 119–120
Graham, Gordon 26
Graham, Peaches 100
Graham, Skinny 100
Graham, Tiny 100
Grand Rapids Chicks 30
Grand Rapids Wolverines 174
Grant, Jim (Mudcat) 160
Grapefruit League 3
Gray, Glen 29
Gray, Pete 199
Grayson, Harry 197

Green, Dick 9
Green, Lenny 155–156, 160
Green, Pumpsie 2, *146*–147, 150–155, 158–159
Greene, June 94
Greene, Riley 184
Greenlee, Gus 131
Gregg, Hal 58
Griffey, Ken, Jr. 194
Griffey, Ken, Sr. 218
Griffith, Clark 19, 21, 47, 107, 139, 157
Griffith, Tommy 109
Grimes, Burleigh 18, 20–24
Grimes, Oscar 144
Grimm, Charlie 83, 139
Grove, Lefty 17, 110, 131, 134–135, 140
Guerrero, Epy 179
Guerrero, Vladimir, Jr. 186
Guerrero, Vladimir, Sr. 186
Gwynn, Chris 95
Gwynn, Tony 12

Hafey, Chick 133
Hairston, Sam 160
Halas, George 135
Hale, Bob 8
Hallahan, Bill 131, 136, 138
Hamby, Jim 109
Hamilton, Billy 10
Hancken, Buddy 111
Hargis, Gary 118–119
Hargrave, Eugene (Bubbles) 194
Harmon, Chuck 160
Harper, Bryce 209
Harper, Tommy 156–157
Harrell, Billy 155
Harridge, Will 168
Harrington, Mickey 117
Harris, Bucky 139, 158
Harrison, Ron 163
Harshman, Jack 214
Hartford Dark Blues 123
Hartnett, Gabby 112, 136
Hartung, Clint 50
Harvey, Matt 207
Haslin, Mickey 73–74
Hatten, Joe 57–58
Hayes, Frankie 111, 199–203
Heard, Jay 160
Hearst Sandlot Classic 116
Hebner, Richie 94
Hegan, Jim 201
Hegman, Bob 119
Hemingway, Ernest 59
Hemond, Roland 211, 213
Henderson, Ken 213

Henley, Don 92
Henrich, Tommy 58–59
Herman, Billy 113
Hern, Gerald 53
Hernández, Teoscar 186
Herrera, Pancho 160
Herrera, Samuel 181
Hershberger, Richard 211, 213–214
Hershiser, Orel 141
Herzog, Whitey 128–129, 214
Heydler, John 194
Hietpas, Joe 120
Higgins, Mike (Pinky) *146*, 153–155, 158–159
High, Andy 133
Hildebrand, George 19
Hildebrand, Oral 141
Hinton, Rich 213
Hodges, Gil 87
Hogan, Ben 76
Holloman, Bobo 122
Holmes, Oliver Wendell 33
Holmes, Tommy (ballplayer) 51, 53
Holmes, Tommy (columnist) 50
Holtzman, Ken 14
Holway, John 19, 92
Honeycutt, Rick 22
Honig, Donald 139
Hooper, Harry 108
Hooton, Burt 93
Hopkins, Don 9–10
Hopp, Harry 51
Hopp, Johnny 51
Hopper, Clay 77
Horner, Bob 94
Hornsby, Rogers 137, 139
Hoskins, Dave 160
Hosmer, Eric 207
Houk, Ralph 129
House of David 70
Houston Astros 8, 17, 93, 111, 129, 178, 192–193, 208–209
Howard, Elston 147, 151, 156, 160
Howell, Homer (Dixie) 61–62
Howell, Jay 22
Howell, Millard (Dixie) (major leaguer) 61–62
Howell, Millard (Dixie) (minor leaguer) 62
Hoyt, Waite 16, 89
Hubbell, Carl 131, 134
Hudlin, Willie 110
Hundley, Randy 203
Hunter, Billy 214
Hunter, Eddie 110
Hunter, Jim (Catfish) 118

Index

Hunter, Torii 157
Huntington Avenue Baseball Grounds 66
Hurley, Ed 167, 169
Hurst, Don 109
Huston, Tillinghast L'Hommedieu 88
Hutchinson, Fred 169

Idaho-Washington League 108
Illinois-Iowa League 124
Independence Producers 70
Indiana 23–30
Indiana University *23*, 25–27, 113
Indianapolis Indians 61, 92
Irvin, Monte 160

Jackson, Al 160
Jackson, Bo 219
Jackson, Reggie 14, 189, 204
Jacobo, Astin 181
James, Bill 56, 81–82, 132–135, 137–138
James, Dion 163
Javier, Christian 209
Jennings, Hughie 102
Jensen, Jackie 149
Jersey Shore 24, 26
Jessee, Dan 110
Jeter, Derek 138, 205
Jethroe, Sam 37, 147–148, 150, 160
Johnson, Arthur 39, 40
Johnson, Ban 90, 102
Johnson, Connie 160
Johnson, Don 214
Johnson, Randy 162, 194, 205–206
Johnson, Walter 47, 61, 124, 130, 136, 140
Joiner, Roy 83
Joliet Convicts 124
Jones, Bumpus 124
Jones, K.C. 150, 154
Jones, Sad Sam 16, 89
Jones, Sam 150, 159
Jorgensen, Spider *49*, 57
Joyce, Jim 121
Jung, Josh 184
Junior World Series 75, 148
Jurges, Billy 137, 154–155, 159
Just, Joe 202

Kaat, Jim 213
Kahn, Roger 91
Kalamazoo Kazoos 98
Kampouris, Alex 76
Kane, Jim 174
Kansas City Athletics 17, 39, 40, 87, 117, 169; *see also* Oakland Athletics; Philadelphia Athletics
Kansas City Monarchs 70, 218
Kansas City Royals 119, 178, 183, 207, 214, 219
Keane, Clif 148–149, 158
Keefe, Tim 126
Kelleher, Duke 106
Keller, Charlie 51, 75
Kelly, Matt 192
Keltner, Ken 142–145
Kemp, Matt 218
Kennedy, John 160
Kennedy, John F. 25
Kenosha Comets 30
Kepner, Tyler 92, 208
Kerr, Mel 108–109
Kill the Umpire 76
Killilea, Henry 188
Kim, Byung-Hyun 205
Kinsella, W.P. (Bill) 2, 97–98, 100
Kirkland, Willie 160
Kison, Bruce 86
Kitsos, Chris 116
Kitty League 63
Klein, Alan 178–181, 183
Klein, Chuck 132–133, 141
Kluszewski, Ted 26–27, 116, 193
knuckleball 2, 91–93
Koenig, Mark 137
Korean War 97, 212
Kosman, Mike 113
Koufax, Sandy 121
Krah, Steve 24, 26–27, 29
Kruger, Jack 120
Kuhn, Bowie 13, 15–16, 215–216

Laabs, Chet 192
Labine, Clem 91
Laboy, Coco 126
Lachemann, Rene 118
Lafayette, Indiana 26
Lakeland, Florida 30
Lancaster, Burt 100
Landis, Kenesaw Mountain 13, 15, 17, 24, 29, 33, 68, 90, 137, 150, 191
Landis-Eastman Line 24
Lane, F.C. 130
Lane, Frank 57, 139, 214–215
Lanfranconi, Walt 54
Lanier, Hal 129
Lanier, Max 196
Lansky, Meyer 125
Larkin, Barry 95
Larsen, Don 87, 124, 214
Lasorda, Tommy 41
Latino ballplayers 12, 155, 177–191
Lawrence, Brooks 160
Lazzeri, Tony 141

Index

A League of Their Own 141
Lee, Bill 196
Lee, Chuck 168
Leever, Sam 188–189
Lefferts, Craig 94
Leonard, Dutch 21
Lester, Larry 131
Leverett, Gorham (Dixie) 62–63
Levy, Gary 215
Lewis, Allan 9
Lewis, Duffy 80
Lickert, John 119
Lidge, Brad 206
Lieb, Fred 174, 201
Limestone League 3, 24–25, 30
Lincecum, Tim 206–207
Lincoln Memorial 25
Lintz, Larry 10
Litwhiler, Danny 52
Lockwood, Skip 118
Lodolo, Nick 184
Lollar, Sherman 201
Lombardi, Ernie 74, 195
Longworth, Alice Roosevelt 46
Lopez, Hector 160
Lora, Bayron 184
Lorenzen, Michael 121, 124
Los Angeles Angels (major league) 117, 120–121, 206; *see also* California Angels
Los Angeles Angels (minor league) 31, 34, 63
Los Angeles Dodgers 9, 11, 179, 184, 207–208; *see also* Brooklyn Dodgers; Brooklyn Grooms; Brooklyn Robins; Brooklyn Superbas
Louisville Colonels 32, 92, 99, 112, 115, 148–149
Lowdermilk, Grover Cleveland 106
Lucas, Red 79, 83–84
Lucker, Claude 102
Lyons, Terry 109–110

Machado, Manny 186
Mack, Connie 13–14, 16, 19, 21, 39, 102–103, 131, 139, 217
Mack, Earle 39
Mack, Katherine 39
Mack, Ray 144
Mack, Roy 39
MacPhail, Larry 68–70, 76, 159
MacPherson, Harry 113
Madden, Michael 157
Maduro, Nicolás 183
Mahady, Jim 108
Mahar, Frank 99
Mahoney, Dan 101

Mahoney, Danny 101
Malamud, Bernard 52
Malkmus, Bobby 129
Maloney, Jim 121
Mancuso, Gus 111–112
Mann, Garth (Red) 113
Manoah, Alek 184
Mantilla, Felix 155, 160
Mantle, Mickey 169
Maris, Roger 87, 193–194
Marolewski, Fred 115–116
Marquez, Luis 160
Marr, Lefty 45
Marsh, Brandon 209
Marsh, Fred 214
Marshall, Chip 111–112
Marshall, Mike 9
Marshall College 107
Martin, Billy 115
Martin, Brian 174, 191
Martin, Pepper 132, 137
Martinez, Edgar 126, 194
Martinez, Michael 208
Martinez, Pedro 179, 186
Martinez, Ramon 179
Martinez, Tino 205
Masi, Phil 53
Massachusetts Commission Against Discrimination 147, 153, 156–157
Mathews, Bobby 19
Mathews, Eddie 72
Mathewson, Christy 105, 123, 172, 175–176
Matsui, Hideki 206
Mauer, Joe 194–195
Mavis, Bob 114
Maye, Lee 160
Mays, Carl 2, 16, 89
Mays, Willie 149, 160
McArthur, Oland (Dixie) 63–64
McAuley, Ed 26
McCarron, Anthony 205
McCarthy, Joe 78
McCormick, Frank 200
McCormick, Mike 51
McCormick, Moose 172
McCormick, Robert 130
McCovey, Willie 116, 160
McCullers, Lance, Jr. 209
McCulloch Park 25
McDermott, Sandy 98
McDonnell, Jim 202
McDuffie, Terris 148
McGinnity, Joe 172
McGraw, John 88, 100, 104, 109, 131, 133, 166, 175, 189
McGrew, Ted 58, 151

McGuire, Deacon 101, 103, 199
McGwire, Mark 21, 95
McKechnie, Bill 36, 79, 81–83, 200
McKinley, William 46
McLish, Cal 113
McMillan, Roy 116
McNally, Mike 90
McQuillan, Hugh 90
McReynolds, Kevin 163
Meche, Gil 141
Medeiros, Ray 113
Medford A's 163
Medwick, Joe 197
Mejias, Roman 155, 160
Mele, Sam 50
Mellor, Sammy 66
Melton, Bill 213
Memorial Stadium (Cleveland) 142
Mena, Ismael 184
Merkle, Fred 3, *171*–173, 175–76
Merritt, John 103–104
Merullo, Len 29
Mesa, José 179
Metropolitan Basketball League 103
Meusel, Irish 89
Mexico 185–186
Meyers, Chief 175–176
Miami Marlins 180, 184
Miksis, Eddie 116
Miller, Eddie 200
Miller, Gus 80
Milwaukee Braves 127, 129, 192; *see also* Atlanta Braves; Boston Bees; Boston Braves
Milwaukee Brewers (early major leagues) 122, 192; *see also* Baltimore Orioles (later American League); St. Louis Browns
Milwaukee Brewers (later major leagues) 8, 193; *see also* Seattle Pilots
Milwaukee Brewers (minor league) 31, 32, 35
Minneapolis Lakers 55, 117
Minneapolis Millers 149, 153–154, 174
Minnesota Twins 11, 184; *see also* Washington Senators (original)
Minoso, Minnie 159–160
Mississippi Southern College 117
Mississippi Valley League 110
Mitchell, Clarence 18, 20–21
Mize, Johnny 85–86, 197
Mondesi, Raul 179
Montgomery, Mike 208
Montgomery Rebels 151
Montreal Expos 10, 48, 119–120, 126; *see also* Washington Nationals

Montreal Royals 55–56, 58, 75, 128, 148
Moore, Jo-Jo 72
Moore, Johnny 72
Moore, Terry 197
Moreland, Nate 148
Moren, Lew (Hicks) 92
Moreno, Omar 11
Morgan, Joe 125
Morrow, Eddie 166
Morton, Charlie 208
Mowry, Joe 83–84
Muchnick, Isadore 147
Mueller, Ray 199–203
Mumphrey, Jerry 12
Muncie, Indiana 23–26
Muncie Fruit Jars 25
The Muncie (Indiana) Star-Press 23
Murphy, Dale 75
Murphy, David 209
Murphy, Johnny 144
Murray, Calvin 162
Murray, Ed 106
Musial, Stan 198
Muskogee Chiefs 70
Mussina, Mike 121
Myers, Billy 73–75

National Association 32
National Basketball Association 55
National Football League 204, 215
National Hockey League 150, 215
National League 32–37, 43–46, 51, 68, 86, 96, 99, 101, 119, 123, 130–134, 136, 149, 172–173, 187–188, 191–192, 194–195, 199, 204
The Natural 52
Navin, Frank 102
Neal, Charlie 159
Negro leagues 70, 94–95, 126, 131, 147–150, 218
Nehf, Art 89
Neighbors, Cecil (Cy) 101
Neill, Tommy 54
Nettles, Morris 213
Neu, Otto 106–107
New Orleans Pelicans 149
New York Giants 2, 18, 20, 24, 32, 40, 55, 61, 72–73, 75, 85, 88–90, 97, 99–100, 103–104, 108–110, 112, 124, 126, 131–135, 137–138, 160, 166, 171–172, 177, 185, 189, 191–192, 196, 215; *see also* San Francisco Giants
New York Highlanders 19, 32, 101–103; *see also* New York Yankees
The New York Journal-American 116
New York Metropolitans 45, 85

Index

New York Mets 12, 86, 93, 120, 127, 129, 155, 193, 207, 209
New York State League 103
New York Yankees 2, 10, 13–16, 21, 24–26, 34, 37, 39–40, 51, 53, 55, 59, 67, 70, 78, 82, 85–90, 105, 108, 111, 114–115, 118–119, 124, 128, 131, 133, 135, 137–138, 140–144, 146, 149, 151, 156–157, 160–161, 166, 175, 179, 183, 192–194, 205–206, 214–215, 218; *see also* New York Highlanders
Newcombe, Don 159
Newport Reds 107
Newsom, Bobo 75
Neyer, Rob 19, 21, 92
The Neyer/James Guide to Pitchers 19, 92
Nicaragua 186
Niekro, Joe 22
Niekro, Phil 57
night baseball 2, 8, 36, 37, 68–77
Nine Innings 1
Nippon Ham Fighters 219
Nixon, Otis 10–11
no-hitters 2, 121–124, 209, 218
Noble, Ray 160
Northern League 73
Northwest League 163
Northwestern University 120
Nowlin, Bill 147, 151, 154–159, 213–214
Nunn, Bill 131

Oakland Oaks 72, 150–151
Oakland, Athletics 8, 14, 17, 40, 127, 162, 183, 193, 204; *see also* Kansas City Athletics; Philadelphia Athletics
O'Connell, Dick 154–155
O'Connor, Johnny 106
O'Day, Hank 172–173
O'Doul, Lefty 135–136
Offerman, Jose 179
Ohio State League 98, 105
Ohtani, Shohei 135
Ojeda, Bob 163
Oklahoma City Indians 152
Oklobzija, Kevin 185
Okrent, Daniel 1
Oldham, John 116
Olympics 65, 95, 109
O'Malley, Walter 31, 61
O'Neal, Skinny 87
O'Neill, Harry 111
O'Neill, Paul 52, 133
O'Neill, Steve 30, 75
Opening Day 43–48, 58, 75, 86–87, 109, 126–127, 200
Oquendo, José 127–128
O'Ree, Willie 150

Orr, Dave 85
Ortíz, David 185
Osborn, Dan 213
Ouachita Baptist College 62
Owen, Mickey 59, 112, 196
Ozuna, Marcell 208

Pacific Coast League 21, 34, 38, 63, 72, 76, 116, 118, 135–136, 141, 149–151, 200
Pacific League (Japan) 219
Padgett, Don 3, 112, 196–198
Pafko, Andy 127
Pagan, Jose 160
Pagliaroni, Jim 151
Paige, Satchel 41, 159–160, 165, 215
Palace of the Fans 70
Palmer, Dean 120
Panama 183, 185–186
Parisse, Tony 202
Parker, Dave 127
Parker, Douglas Wooley (Dixie) 63
Parsons, Edward (Dixie) 62
Passeau, Claude 196–197
Patkin, Max 167
Patriots' Day 43, 65–67
Patton, Gene 113
Paula, Carlos 160
Pauley, Edwin 34
Pawtucket Red Sox 119
Peckinpaugh, Roger 89
Peden, Buck 213
Pederson, Joc 208
Peete, Charley 160
Pegler, Westbrook 133
Pena, Orlando 160
Pence, Elmer 108
Pendleton, Jim 160
Pennington, George (Kewpie) 106–107
Pennock, Herb 151, 158
Pennsylvania State Basketball League 103
Pentagon 25
Pepe, Phil 213
Perez, Pascual 94
Pérez, Rafael 178
Perini, Lou 31, 35–39
Perry, Gaylord 21
Perry, Gerald June 96
Pettis, Gary 12
Pettitte, Andy 205
Pezzullo, Pretzel 71
Pheidippides 65
Philadelphia Athletics 13, 16, 19, 21, 32, 34, 39–40, 47, 69, 87, 89, 93, 102–103, 108, 110–111, 122, 131, 139–141, 160, 166, 189, 199–202, 215, 217, 219; *see also* Kansas City Athletics; Oakland Athletics

Index

Philadelphia Phillies 32, 44, 47, 53, 55, 63, 71, 73, 89, 99, 106, 109, 117, 121, 129, 132, 134–135, 137, 151, 153, 158, 160, 165, 189, 206, 209, 213, 219
Philley, Dave 8
Phillippe, Charlie (Deacon) 189–191
Phillips University 70
Piedmont League 87
Piersall, Jimmy 115
pinch-hitters 6–7, 83, 101, 106, 110, 127, 134, 167–168
pinch-runners 8–10, 98, 101, 103, 105–110, 112–114, 116–118, 167, 170
Piniella, Lou 218
Pinson, Vada 160
The Pitcher 19
The Pittsburgh Courier 131, 147
Pittsburgh Crawfords 131
Pittsburgh Penguins 215–216
Pittsburgh Pirates 3, 10–11, 18–19, 21, 23, 25, 28, 36, 45, 58, 60, 63–64, 74, 79, 81–83, 86–88, 90, 101, 104–105, 107, 109, 118, 124, 127, 133–134, 148, 160, 163, 171–174, 187–190, 216; *see also* Pittsburgh Premiers
Pittsburgh Premiers 187–188; *see also* Pittsburgh Pirates
The Pittsburgh Sun-Telegraph 131
Pizarro, Juan 160
Plank, Eddie 106–107, 217–218
Players League 85
Point Loma High School 124
Polo Grounds 72, 132, 172
Pompez, Alex 126
Ponikvar, Veda 101
Pool, Harlin 76
Pope, Dave 159–160
Portland Beavers 118
Posnanski, Joe 1, 56
Powell, Jake 138
Power, Vic 160
Powers, Jimmy 212
Pressly, Ryan 209–210
Priddy, Jerry 114
The Pride of the Yankees 76, 138
Princeton University 192
Proctor, Jim 160
Progressive Field 163
Pruett, Jim 202
Pruett, Jon 202
Puason, Robert 183
Pucetas, Kevin 93
Puerto Rico 177, 185–186
Pujols, Albert 186
Pulliam, Harry 173
Purdue University 26

Qualls, Jimmy 121
Queen, Mel 56
Quinn, Bob 36
Quinn, Jack 18, 21
Quintero, Ronnier 184

Racine Belles 30, 105
Rackley, Marv 57
Raines, Larry 160
Ramírez, José 186
Ramsey, Toad 92
Rapp, David 173
Rath, Morrie 191
The Real Book About Baseball 1
Redford, Robert 52
Reese, Jimmie 69
Reese, Pee Wee **49**, 57, 91
Reichler, Joe 50
Reilly, Arch 107
Reinsdorf, Jerry 216
Reiser, Pete 55
Renfroe, Chico 94
Revering, Dave 15
Revolutionary War 65
Reynolds, Allie 26
Rhodes, Greg 43–44, 46
Rice, Len 202
Richards, BeeBee 213
Richards, Gene 11–12
Richardson, Tom 106
Richmond Colts 107
Richter, Francis C. 187–189
Rickey, Branch 57–58, 60, 61, 69, 148, 151, 197
Rickwood Field 149
Riddle, Johnny 202
Riggs, Lew 75
Righetti, Dave 116
Rigney, Bill 72
Ringling Brothers circus 170
Ripken, Cal, Jr. 218
Rittwage, Jim 118
Rivera, Mariano 205
Robello, Tony 110
Roberts, Curt 160
Robinson, Frank 160
Robinson, Humberto 160
Robinson, Jackie 2, **49**, 55, 57, 58, 60, 75, 77, 87, 91, 137, 147–148, 150, 156, 158–159, 185
Robinson, Wilbert 164
Rochester Red Wings 74
Rocker, John 17
Rodgers, Andre 160
Rodgers, Buck 11
Rodríguez, Emmanuel 184

Index 237

Rodriguez, Hector 160
Rodríguez, Luis 184
Roe, Preacher 21, 91
Rohan, Tim 207
Rojas, Enrique 178, 185
Rommel, Eddie 93
Roosevelt, Franklin D. 48, 68, 147
Roosevelt, Theodore 46
Root, Charlie 82
Rosa, Pearl 170
Rosar, Buddy 115, 202
Rosario, Eddie 208
Rose, Pete 51, 139, 194, 216
Roseboro, John 159
Roth, Braggo 106
Round Rock Express 120
Rowell, Bama 52
Ruck, Rob 179–183
Rucker, Nap 92
Rudi, Joe 14, 16, 117
Rudolph, Dick 21
Ruel, Muddy 29
Ruppert, Jacob 14, 79, 88
Rushin, Steve 109
Russell, Addison 207–208
Russell, Allan 21
Russell, Bill 150, 154
Russell, Kurt 42
Ruszkowski, Hank 202
Ruth, Babe 2–3, 13–16, 19, 36, 55, 58, 72, 74, 76, 78–84, 89, 108, 132–133, 135, 137–138, 141, 170, 191, 193–194; called shot 34, 72, 79, 191
Ruthven, Dick 213
Rutschman, Adley 183
Ryan, Connie 51, 53
Ryan, Nolan 58, 121

SABR Bio Project 5
Sacramento Solons 112, 200
Sain, Johnny 37, 53
St. Cloud State University 119
St. Joseph (Pennsylvania) College 103
St. Louis Brown Stockings 123
St. Louis Browns 4, 21, 24, 32–35, 38, 40, 44, 50, 62, 64, 90, 95, 99, 103, 106–108, 112, 115, 122, 138, 140, 146, 160, 165–170, 189, 191–192, 199–201, 215; see also Baltimore Orioles (later American League); Milwaukee Brewers (early American League)
St. Louis Cardinals 12, 20–21, 24, 28, 34, 35, 41, 69, 73–74, 81, 85, 99, 108, 110–111, 115, 118, 128, 132, 136, 139, 146, 153, 160, 189, 192, 196–198, 206, 213; see also St. Louis Perfectos

St. Louis Perfectos 99; see also St. Louis Cardinals
St. Louis Terriers 103
St. Paul Saints 69
Salas, José 184
Salazar, Angel 128
Salt Lake City Bees 141
San Diego Padres 11, 94, 184, 193
San Francisco 49ers 215, 216
San Francisco Giants 15, 116–117, 126, 152, 162, 184, 204, 206–207; see also New York Giants
San Francisco Seals 72, 108, 135, 149, 192
Sanborn, I.E. 173
Sánchez, Yolbert 184
Sanders, John 117–118
Sandusky Maroons/Sands/Suds 98
Sanguillen, Manny 127
Santana, Pedro 119–120
Santiago, Jose 156, 160
Santos Baseball Academy 120
The Saturday Evening Post 166, 216
Saucier, Frank 167–168
Sauer, Hank 81
Savage, Larry 161
Scantlebury, Pat 160
Schang, Wally 16
Schelle, Jim 111
Scherbarth, Bob 114–115
Scherzer, Max 22
Schilling, Chuck 155
Schmelz, Gus 46
Schmulbach, Hank 112
Schultz, Howie 54–55, 58, 113
Schultz, Joe 201
Schumacher, Hal 132, 137
Schwarber, Kyle 209
Scimonelli, Paul 178
Scott, Everett 16, 89
Scott, George 156
Scranton Miners 100, 148, 150
Scully, Vin 9
Seattle Mariners 12, 128, 194
Seattle Pilots 193, 212; see also Milwaukee Brewers (later major leagues)
Seaver, Tom 121
Sebring, Jimmy 188
Seghi, Phil 211
Segovia, Andrés 87
Shafer, Ralph 105
Shantz, Bobby 41
Shea Stadium 163
Sheets, Larry 129
Shellenback, Frank 21
Sherman, James 48
Sherman Antitrust Act 33

Index

Shibe Park 102
Shocker, Urban 21
Shoeless Joe 2, 97, 100
Shook, Ray 105–106
Short, Ed 22
Shorz, Josh 210
Shropshire, Larry 197
Shuba, George 56, 91
Sick's Stadium 193
Sievers, Roy 117
Siewert, Ralph 27
Simmons, Al 17, 139
Simmons, Ted 118
Simpson, Harry 159
Sisler, George 62, 106, 194
Sisti, Sibby 51
Slaughter, Enos 197
Smalley, Roy, Jr. 162
Smith, Al (outfielder) 155, 160
Smith, Al (pitcher) 142, 144
Smith, George 156
Smith, Jack 101–103
Smith, Milt 160
Smith, Ozzie 12, 128
Smith, Pop-boy 106
Smith, Red 22
Smith, Reggie 156
Smith, Wendell 147
Smoltz, John 11
Snelling, Dennis 173
Snider, Duke 91
Snodgrass, Fred 175
Snow, J.T. 217
Snyder, John 197
Society for American Baseball Research 5
Society of Jesuits 29
Soderholm, Eric 214
Soler, Jorge 208–209
Sommers, Jesus 94
Soriano, Alfonso 205
Sosa, Sammy 21
Sothoron, Allen 21
Soto, Juan 186
South Atlantic League 92, 117
South Avenue Grounds 66
South Portland High School 128
Southern Association 64, 95, 101, 113
Southworth, Billy 82
Sovern, Jeff 213
Spahn, Warren 37, 53
Spanish-American War 174, 212
Sparrow, Roy 131
Speaker, Tris 106, 130, 175–176
Spencer, Darryl 117
Spencer, Jim 213–214
spitball 2, 18–22

Spokane Indians 105
Sportsman's Park 165, 168, 215
Spring, Jack 41–42
spring training 3, 23–30, 152–153, 157, 162, 217
Springer, Brad 42
Springer, Dennis 42
Springer, Ed 42
Springer, George 42
Springer, Russ 42
Springer, Steve 42
Springs, Jeffrey 42
Stallings, George 122
Stanky, Eddie 37, **49**, 54, 114
Stanley, Bob 58
Stanley, Fred 193
Stargell, Willie 127
Steele, Bob 89
Stein, Henry (ballplayer) 99
Stein, Henry (video game character) 99
Steinbrenner, George 125, 128
Steiner, Red 202
Stengel, Casey 86, 89, 115, 163–164, 178
Steubenville Stubs 98
Stevens, Ed 58
Stevens, RC 64, 160
Stieb, Dave 116
Stirnweiss, Snuffy 135
Stockton, J. Roy 136–137
Stockton, John 42
Stockton Ports 151
Storke, Alan 174
Street, Gabby 47, 136
Streeter, Kurt 120
Stricklett, Elmer 19
Stripp, Joe 18
Sturm, Johnny 142
Suarez, Ranger 209
Sullivan, Billy 75
Summers, Champ 94
Summers, Ed **91**–94, 219
Summers, Kid 94
Summers, Lonnie 94
Summers, Tack 94
Sundberg, Jim 203
Surhoff, B.J. 75
Suzuki, Ichiro 194
Swacina, Harry 174
Swift, Bob 167

Tacoma Yankees 128
Taft, Charles 47
Taft, William Howard 46–48
Tampa Bay Devil Rays 127
Tampa Bay Rays 120
Tanner, Chuck 127

Index

Tarleton State University 219
Tartabull, Jose 156
Tasby, Willie 155, 160
Tatis, Fernando, Jr. 186
Tatum, Tommy 55, 56
Taveras, Frank 12
Taylor, Joe 160
Taylor, Leo 108
Taylor, Tony 116, 160
Taylor, Zack 167, 169–170
Tebbetts, Birdie 115, 137
Temple, William C. 188
Temple Cup 188–189
Tenney, Fred 175
Terlecky, Steve 213
Terre Haute, Indiana 29–30
Terry, Bill 73, 132–133, 196
Testa, Nick 116
Texas League 72, 116, 152, 184
Texas Rangers 11, 203, 210; *see also* Washington Senators (expansion)
Theriot, Ryan 72
Thomas, Dave (Showboat) 148
Thomas, Dylan 91
Thomas, Frosty 92
Thomas, Roy 213
Thomas, Valmy 160
Thompson, Carl 103
Thompson, Hank 160
Thompson, Homer 103
Thomson, Bobby 127, 192
Thomson, Rob 209
Thorn, John 19, 92, 123
Three-I League 74, 106
Thurber, James 166
Thurman, Bob 160
The Times, Streator, Illinois 131
Tinker, Joe 173
Todd, Al 72–73
Toledo Mud Hens 35, 107
Tom Petty and the Heartbreakers 92
Tommy John surgery 207
Toney, Fred 89
Topps baseball cards 9, 129
Torgeson, Earl 52–53, 140
Toronto Blue Jays 11, 161–162, 178, 184
Torre, Joe 75, 118
Toth, Paul 41
trade deadline 88–90
Travers, Al 103
Traynor, Pie 132, 134
Tresh, Mike 201–202
Trice, Bob 160
Trinity College (Connecticut) 110
Tristate Semipro League 110
Troy Haymakers 32

Trucks, Virgil 121
Truman, Harry 48
Tunney, Gene 113
Turley, Bob 214
Turner, Ted 17, 36
Twain, Mark 99
Tygiel, Jules 147

Union Association 32
United States League 33
University of Alabama 62
University of Arkansas 62
University of Cincinnati 105
University of Georgia 103
University of Kentucky 117
University of Maryland 100
University of Nebraska 117
University of Notre Dame 101, 168
University of South Alabama 54
University of Southern California 175
Upright, R T (Dixie) 64
Urbanski, Billy 73
Utley, Chase 206

Valdes, Rene 159
Valdez, Framber 209
Valo, Elmer 8
Vander Meer, Johnny 69, 124
Van Slyke, Andy 11
Vargas, Roberto 160
Vaughan, Arky 56, 73
Vaughn, Andrew 184
Veeck, Bill 3, 35, 38–39, 165, **211**–216
Veeck, William, Sr. 19, 21, 165
Veeck as in Wreck 165, 215
Venezuela 177, 182–186
Verdi, Frank 115
Vergez, Johnny 72
Vietnam War 212
Villanova University 111
Virgil, Ozzie 2, 152, 160, 177, 185
Virgin Islands 186
Virginia League 107

Wagner, Billy 136
Wagner, Hal 202
Wagner, Honus 28, 56, 190
Wagner, Leon 160
Walden, Fred 103
Walker, Ernie 61
Walker, Ewart Gladstone (Dixie) 61
Walker, Fleet 50
Walker, Fred (Dixie) 2, 55, 60–61
Walker, Harry 61
Walker, James R. 192
Walker, Roy (Dixie) 64

Walsh, Davis J. 132
Walsh, Ed 19
Walters, Bucky 77, 135
Wambsganss, Bill 106
Waner, Paul 79, 133, 195
Ward, Arch 130–131
Ward, Preston 87
Warneke, Lon 136–137
Warren, Mike 124
Wasch, Adam 180–181
Washington, Herb 7–10
Washington Nationals 48; *see also* Montreal Expos
Washington Senators (expansion) 86, 155; *see also* Texas Rangers
Washington Senators (original) 19, 21, 32, 46, 47, 48, 98–99, 103, 107–109, 138–141, 146, 157, 160, 178; *see also* Minnesota Twins
Washington University 112, 174
Watkins, George 73
Watson, Bob 94
Weiss, George 157
Welch, Mickey 126
Welf, Ollie 106
Wells, David 124
Wenatchee AppleSox 151
Werber, Billy 75
Wertz, Vic 50
West, Sam 132, 138
West Baden, Indiana 24, 27–29
West Baden Springs Hotel 28
Western Association 63, 70, 95
Western International League 151
White, Bill 160
White, Charlie 160
White, Frank 178
Whitehead, Burgess 72
Whitson, Ed 94
Wiggins, Alan 12, 94
Wilkinson, J.L. 70
Williams, Billy 160
Williams, Dick 9
Williams, Joe 133
Williams, Marvin 147–148, 150
Williams, Ted 36, 115, 136, 149
Williams, Woody 200
Wills, Maury 12, 57, 159
Wilson, Art 106
Wilson, Artie 151, 160
Wilson, Earl 150–152, 154–156, 160
Wilson, Hack 141
Wilson, Jimmie 74, 135
Wilson, Owen (Chief) 173

Wilson, Woodrow 48
Winfield, Dave 161–162, 218
Winter, George 217–218
winter meetings 4, 15, 29, 34, 211–216
Winters, Clarence 219
Winters, Jesse 219
Winters, Matt 218–219
Winters, Nip 218
Wisner, Phil 98–99
Witt, Bobby Jr. 183
Wolf, Gregory H. 212, 215
Womack, Tony 205
Wood, Wilbur 127
Woodall, Larry 149
Woodling, Gene 86
World Series 2–3, 9, 13–14, 16–17, 20, 26, 34–35, 46, 48, 53, 58, 62, 72, 74–75, 77, 81–82, 86, 88–89, 93–94, 106, 108, 110, 119, 122, 125–129, 133, 135–137, 142, 147, 175, 179, 187–191, 193, 204–210, 212, 217
World War I 16, 103, 105, 109, 123, 140, 174, 204, 212
World War II 3, 24, 31, 34, 38, 48, 51, 55, 62, 69, 86–87, 93, 97, 109, 111–112, 148, 165, 192, 197, 199, 212
World's Fair: A Century of Progress Exposition 130
Wright, Steven 93
Wright, Teresa 138
Wrightstone, Russ 108
Wrigley, Phil 34
Wrigley Field 3, 27, 72, 82, 165
Wulf, Steve 138
Wyatt, John 156

Xavier University (Ohio) 109

Yale University 71
Yankee Stadium 13, 40, 75, 85, 114, 161, 205–206
Yawkey, Jean 159
Yawkey, Tom 16–17, 35, 36–37, 80, 147–150, 153, 156–159
You Could Look It Up 166
Young, Cy 124

Zach, Karen Bazzani 174
Zachary, Tom 58
Zanesville Kickapoos 98
Zarilla, Al 201
Zeile, Todd 75
Zeller, Bart 118
Zeller, Jack 30
Zisk, Richie 214

www.ingramcontent.com/pod-product-compliance
Ingram Content Group UK Ltd.
Pitfield, Milton Keynes, MK11 3LW, UK
UKHW041938140426
5217IPUK00014B/552